# GEOMETRY

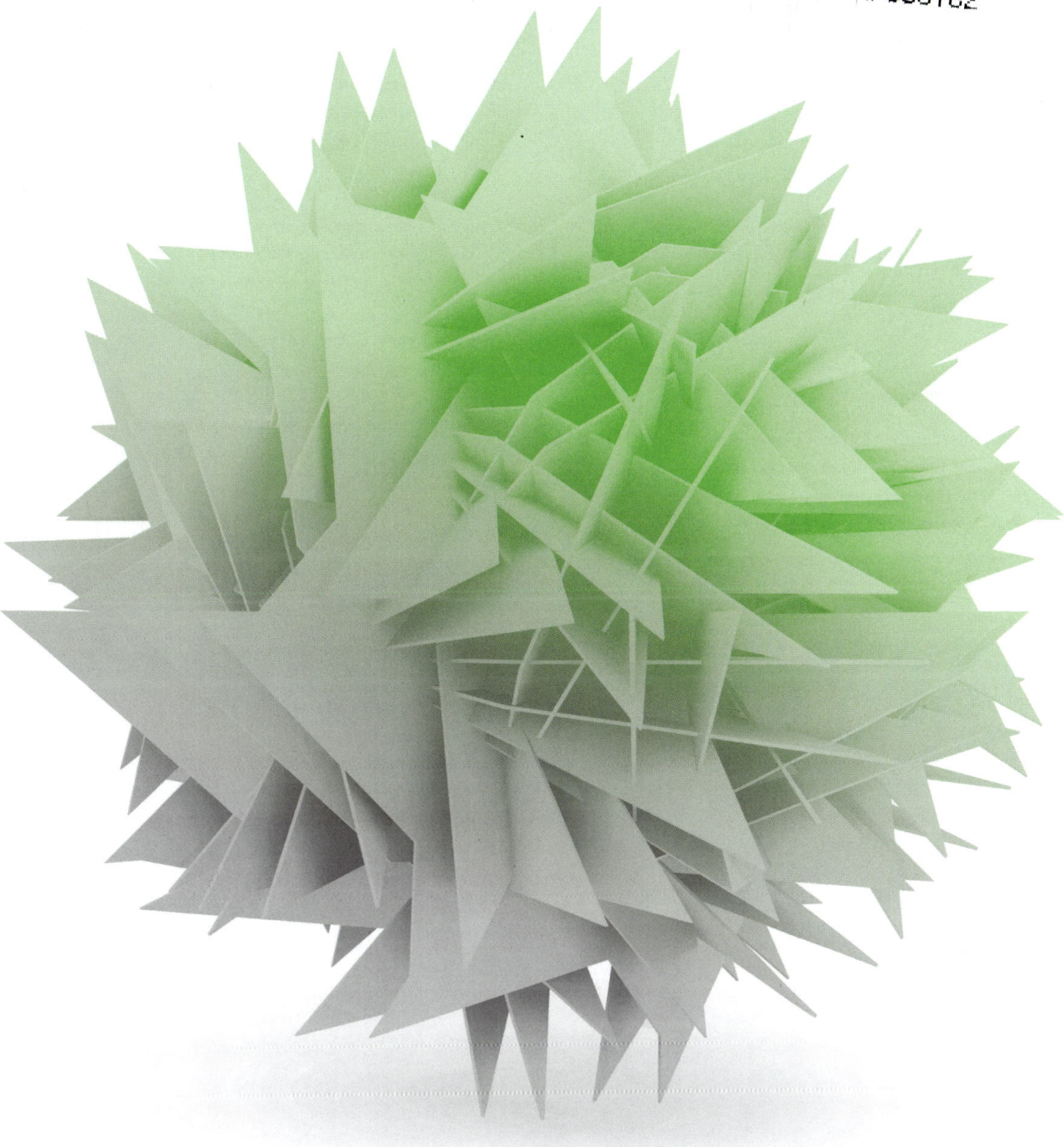

**Walker Maths Essentials: Geometry 5**
**1st Edition**
**Charlotte Walker**
**Victoria Walker**

Cover design: Cheryl Rowe, Macarn Design
Text designer: Cheryl Rowe, Macarn Design
Production controller: Siew Han Ong



**Acknowledgements**
Cover photo courtesy of Shutterstock.

We wish to thank the Boards of Trustees of Darfield and Riccarton High Schools for allowing us to use materials and ideas developed while teaching. Our thanks also go to all past and present colleagues, especially Kath Wilson, who have generously shared their experience and ideas.

For product information and technology assistance,
in Australia call **1300 790 853**;
in New Zealand call **0800 449 725**

For permission to use material from this text or product, please email
**aust.permissions@cengage.com**

**National Library of New Zealand Cataloguing-in-Publication Data**
A catalogue record for this book is available from the National Library of New Zealand

978 0 17 045154 3

**Cengage Learning Australia**
Level 7, 80 Dorcas Street
South Melbourne, Victoria Australia 3205

**Cengage Learning New Zealand**
Unit 4B Rosedale Office Park
331 Rosedale Road, Albany, North Shore 0632, NZ

For learning solutions, visit **cengage.co.nz**

Printed in China by 1010 Printing International Limited.
1 2 3 4 5 6 7 26 25 24 23 22

# CONTENTS

**Glossary** .......... 4

**Language of geometry** .......... 6

**Angles** .......... 7
Angle revision .......... 7
Angles in a triangle .......... 10
Angles in a quadrilateral .......... 12
Polygons .......... 14
Parallel lines .......... 18
Mixing it up .......... 21

**Isometrics** .......... 23
Challenge 1 .......... 25

**Position and orientation** .......... 26
Direction: bearings .......... 26
Using a protractor to find bearings .......... 28
Location: loci .......... 30
Distances: scales on maps and diagrams .......... 35
Mixing it up .......... 40

**Transformation geometry** .......... 42
Revision of translation, reflection and rotation .......... 44
Enlargement .......... 46

**The theorem of Pythagoras** .......... 52
Finding the length of the hypotenuse .......... 53
Finding the lengths of short sides .......... 56
Mixing it up .......... 58
Mixing the theorem of Pythagoras with geometry .......... 59

**Trigonometry** .......... 61
What is trigonometry? .......... 61
SOHCAHTOA .......... 63
Finding sides using sine .......... 63
Finding sides using cosine and tangent .......... 67
Mixing it up .......... 70
Finding sides using trigonometry and geometry .......... 72
Finding angles using sine .......... 74
Finding angles using cosine and tangent .......... 76
Mixing it up .......... 79
Finding angles using trigonometry and geometry .......... 80
Challenge 2 .......... 82

**Revision 1** .......... 83
**Revision 2** .......... 86

**Answers** .......... 89

# Glossary

Make your own glossary of key terms:

| Term | Definition | Picture/Example |
|---|---|---|
| Degrees | | |
| Equilateral triangle | | |
| Isosceles triangle | | |
| Scalene triangle | | |
| Quadrilateral | | |
| Acute angle | | |
| Right angle | | |
| Obtuse angle | | |
| Reflex angle | | |
| Polygon | | |



ISBN: 9780170451543

| Term | Definition | Picture/Example |
|---|---|---|
| Regular | | |
| Irregular | | |
| Symmetrical | | |
| Two-dimensional (2D) | | |
| Three-dimensional (3D) | | |
| Complementary angles | | |
| Supplementary angles | | |
| Translation | | |
| Reflection | | |
| Rotation | | |
| Enlargement | | |
| Locus (plural: loci) | | |

ISBN: 9780170451543 

# Language of geometry

Use the terms in the box and match them to the most appropriate image below. The terms are used once only.

| Obtuse angle | Regular | Trapezium | Right angle |
|---|---|---|---|
| Quadrilateral | Supplementary angles | Irregular | Acute angle |
| Parallel lines | Hexagon | Reflex angle | Complementary angles |

**1**

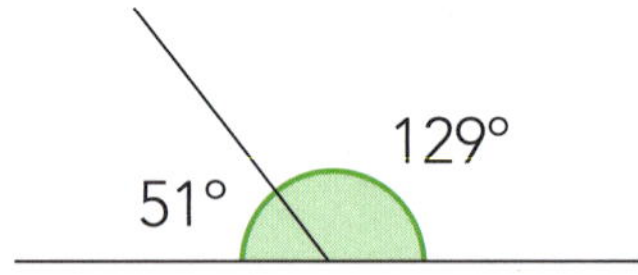


______________________

**2**

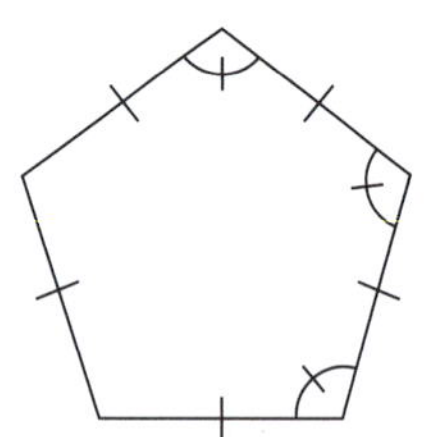

______________________

**3**

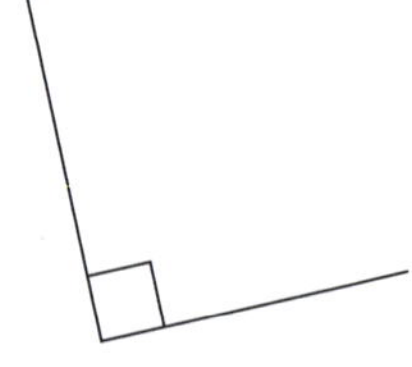

______________________

**4**

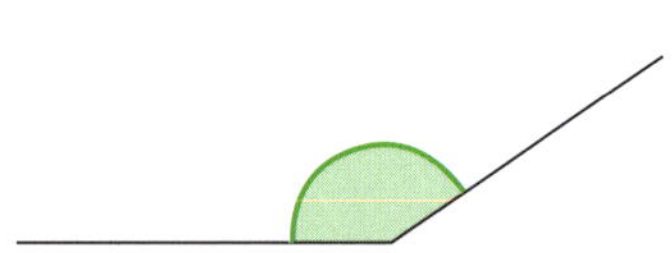

______________________

**5**

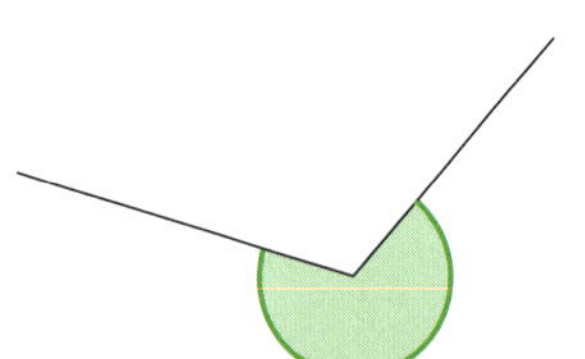

______________________

**6**

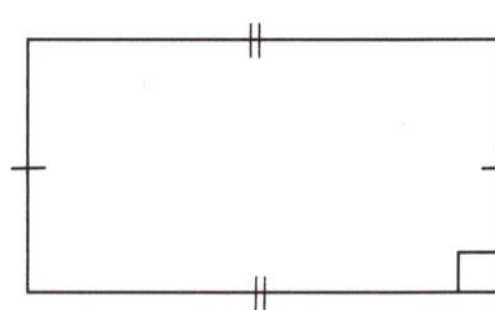

______________________

**7**

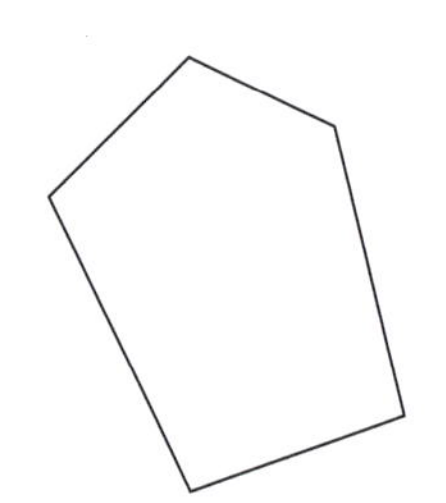

______________________

**8**

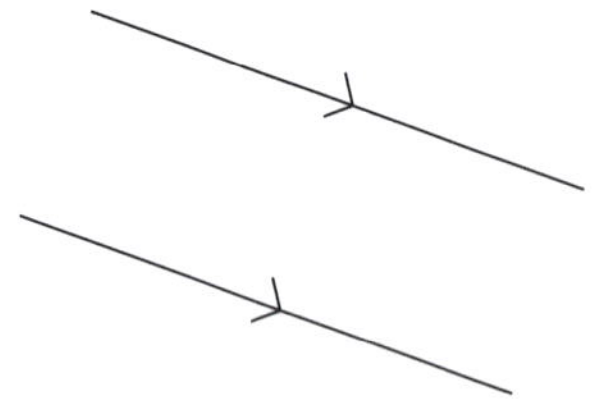

______________________

**9**

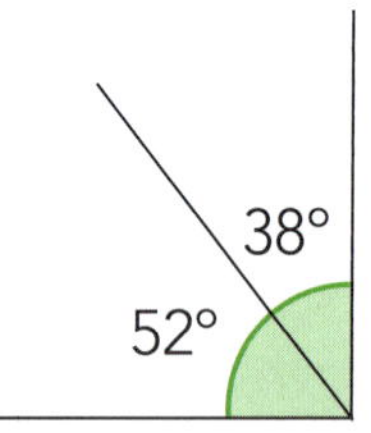


______________________

**10**

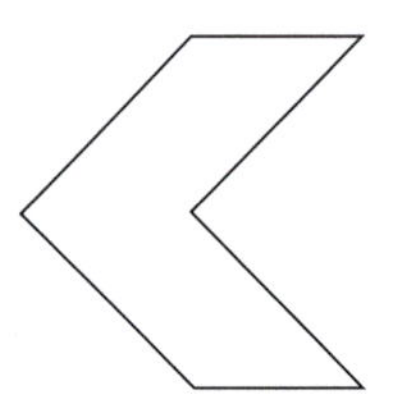

______________________

**11**

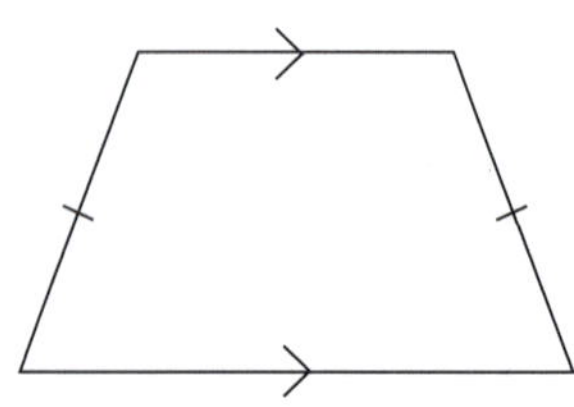

______________________

**12**

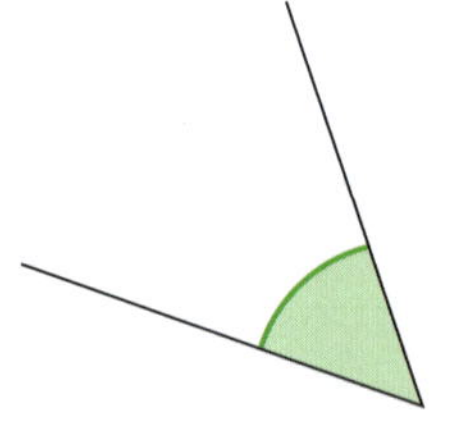

______________________




ISBN: 9780170451543

# Angles

## Angle revision

### Angles on a line

- Angles on a line **add to 180°**.
- These are also known as **supplementary** angles.

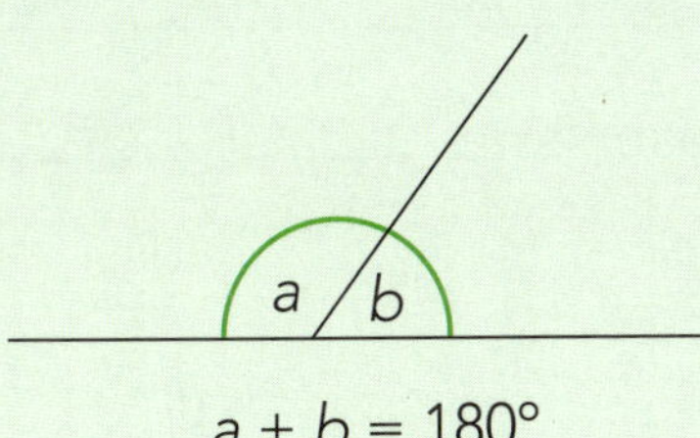


$a + b = 180°$

**Example:**

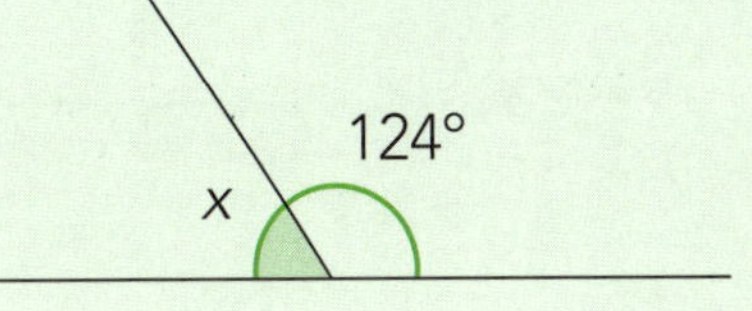


$x = 180° - 124°$
$x = 56°$

You are allowed to shorten 'angles on a line add to 180°' to this:

**Reason:** ∠s on a line = 180°.

### Angles at a point

- Angles at a point, or angles in a full rotation, **add to 360°**.

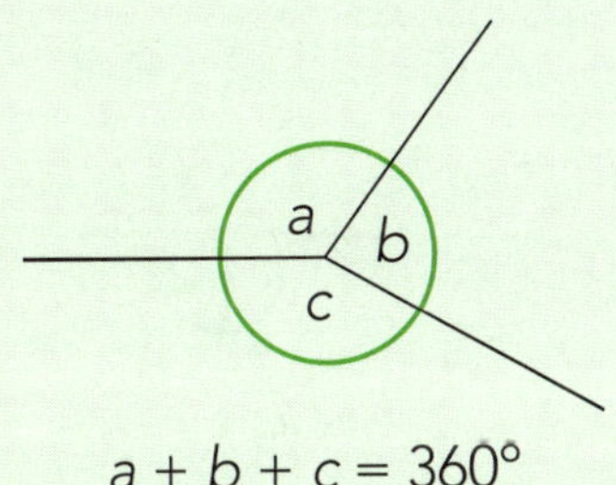


$a + b + c = 360°$

**Example:**

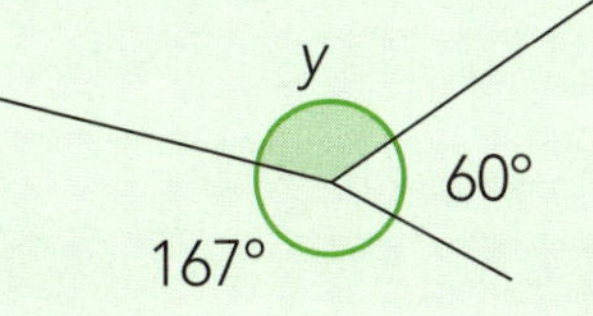


$y = 360° - 167° - 60°$
$y = 133°$

Angles at a point add to 360°.

**Reason:** ∠s at a point = 360°.

### Vertically opposite angles

- Vertically opposite angles **are equal**.

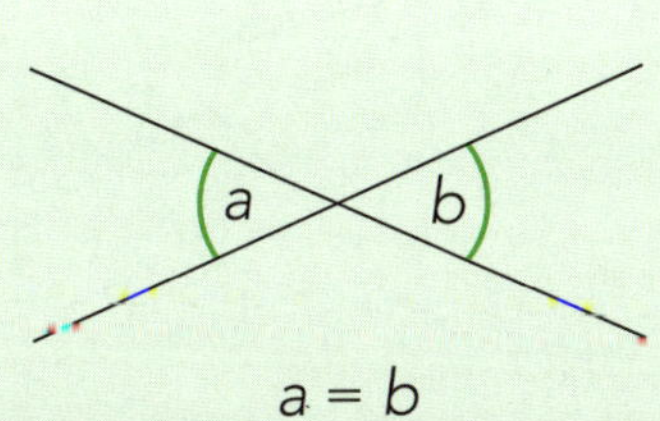


$a = b$

**Example:**

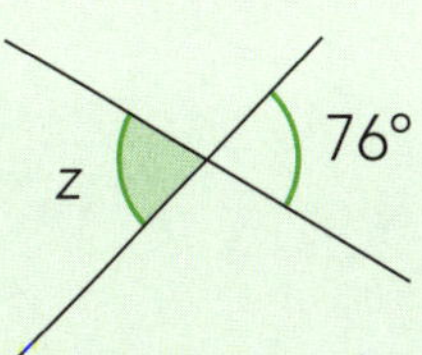


$z = 76°$

Vertically opposite angles are equal.

**Reason:** Vert opp ∠s =.

ISBN: 9780170451543 

Calculate the missing angles and write the reason(s) used. If your reasons are different from those in the answers, check with your teacher.

**1**

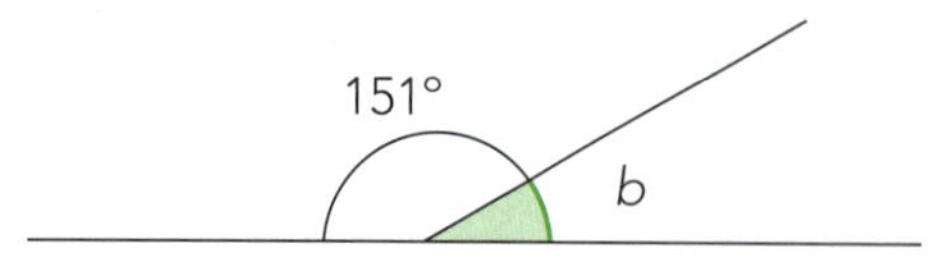


Reason(s):

**2**

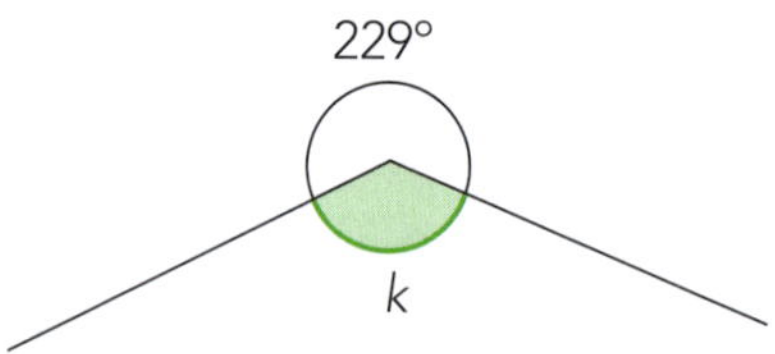


Reason(s):

**3**

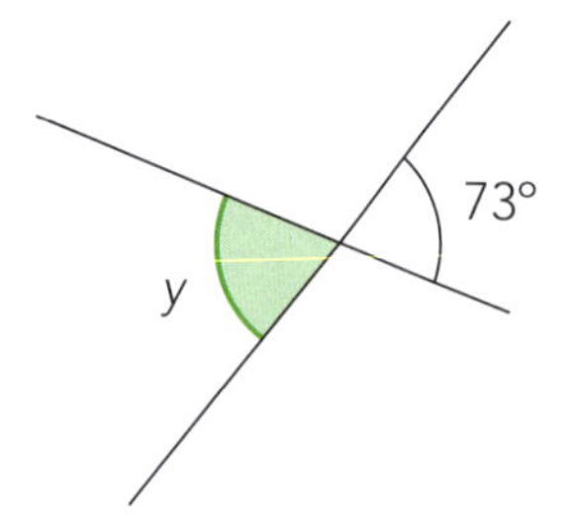


Reason(s):

**4**

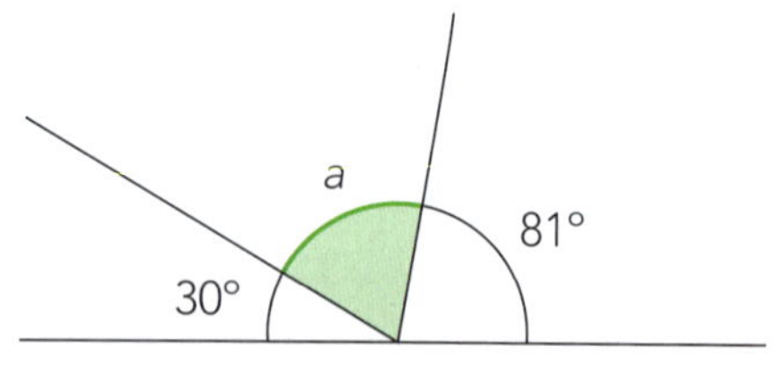


Reason(s):

**5**

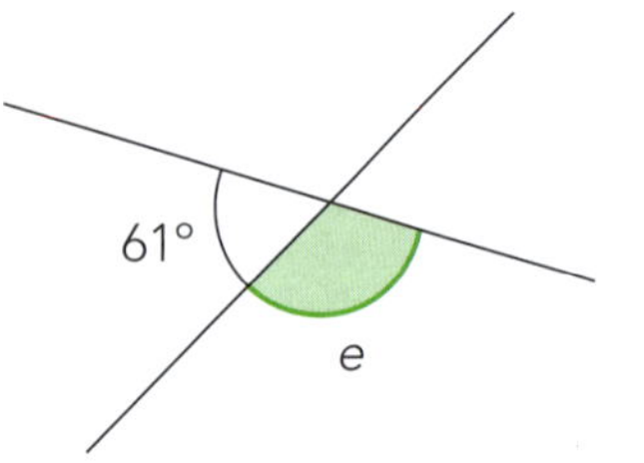


Reason(s):

**6**

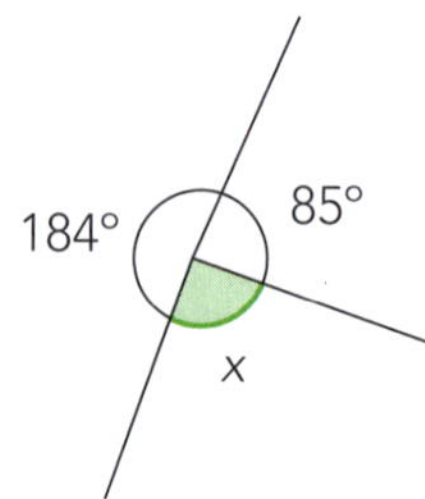


Reason(s):

**7**

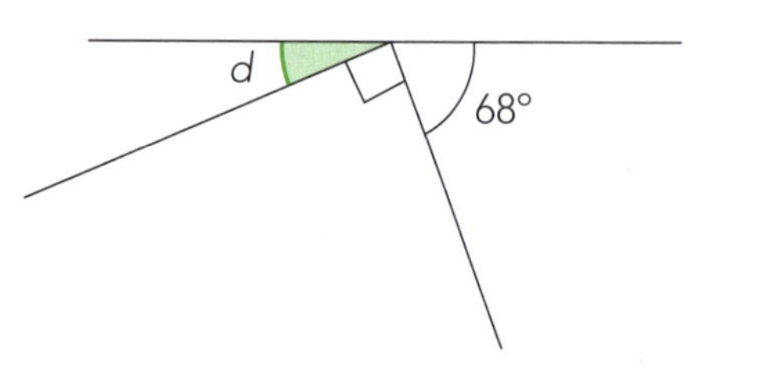


Reason(s):

**8**

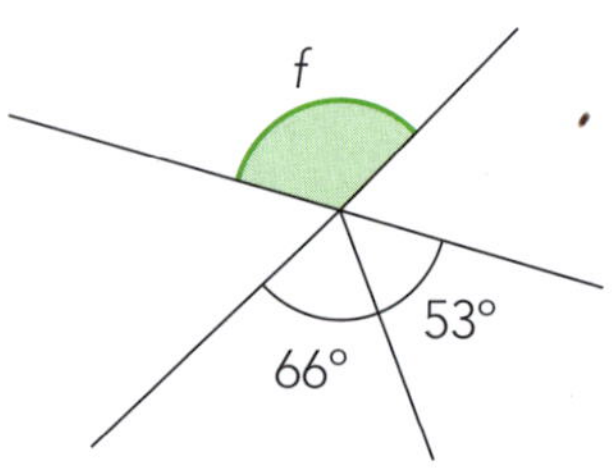


Reason(s):



 ISBN: 9780170451543

**9**

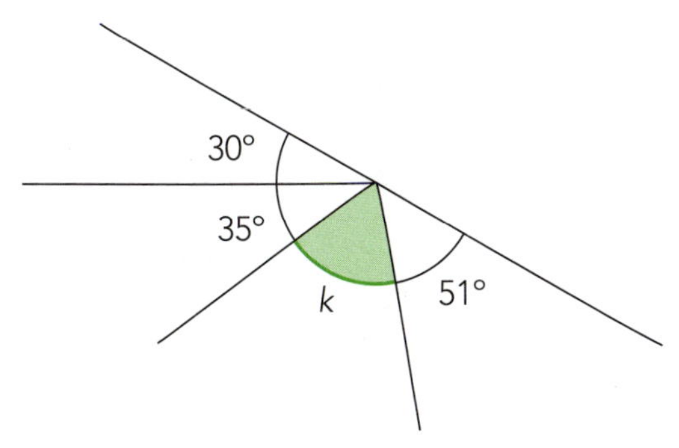


Reason(s):

**10**

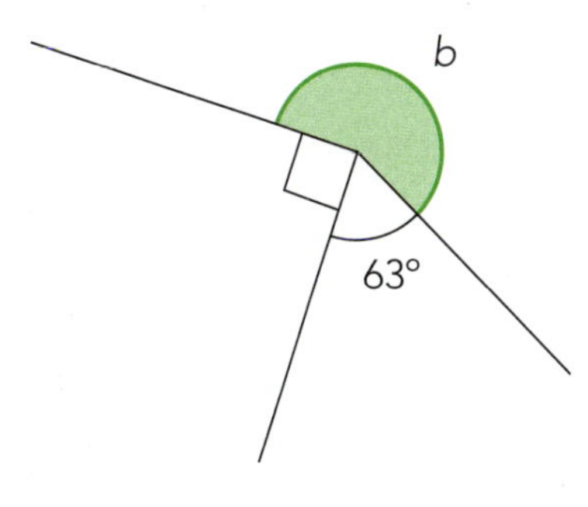


Reason(s):

**11**

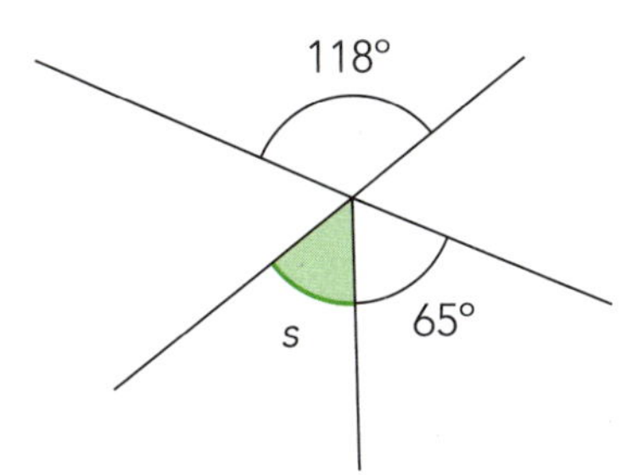


Reason(s):

**12**

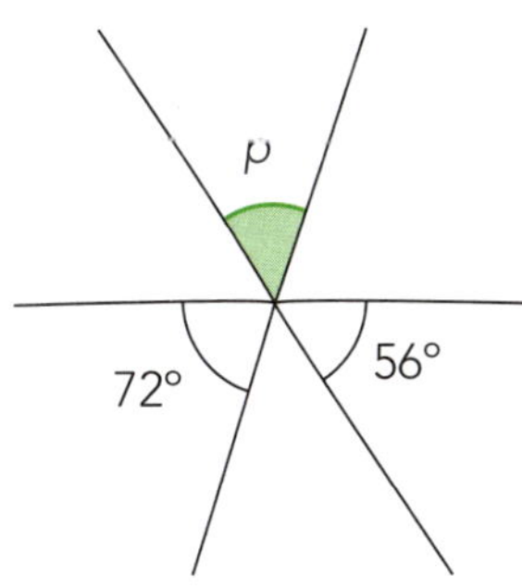


Reason(s):

**13**

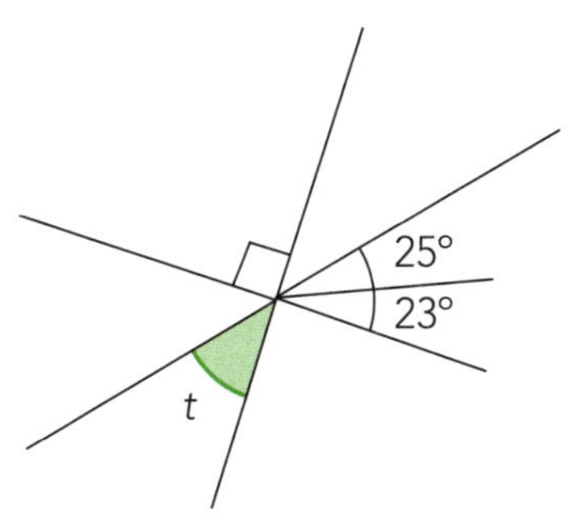


Reason(s):

**14**

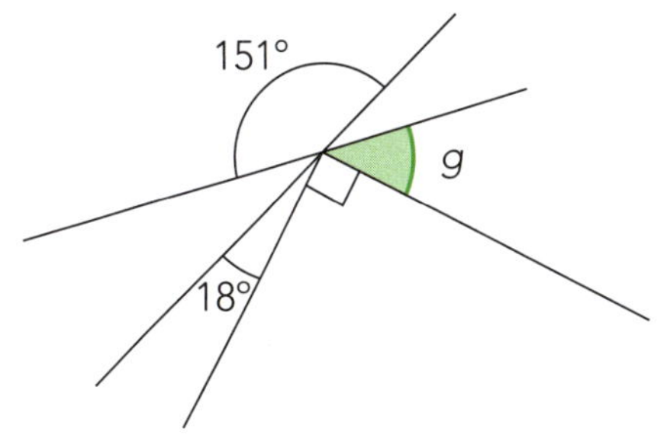


Reason(s):

# Angles in a triangle

## Interior angles

- The angles in a triangle **add to 180°**.

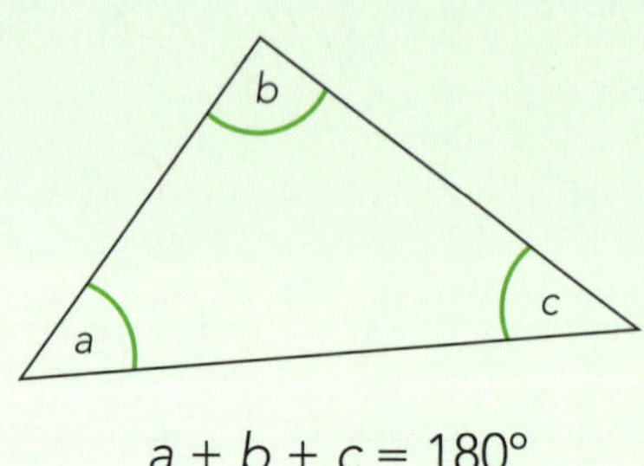


$a + b + c = 180°$

**Example:**

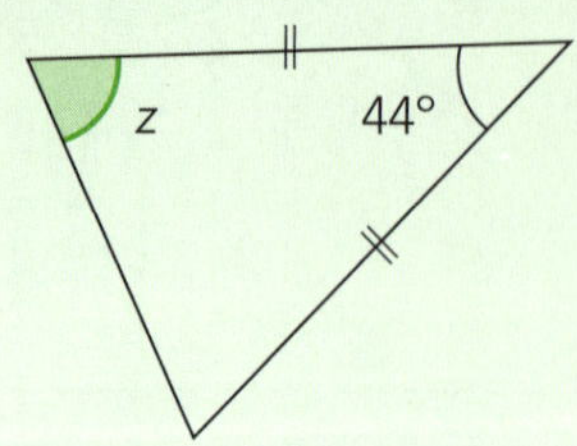


$2z + 44 = 180°$

$z = (180° - 44°) \div 2$

$z = 68°$

**Reason:** ∠s in a △ = 180°.

## Exterior angles

- The exterior angle of a triangle = sum of the interior opposite angles.

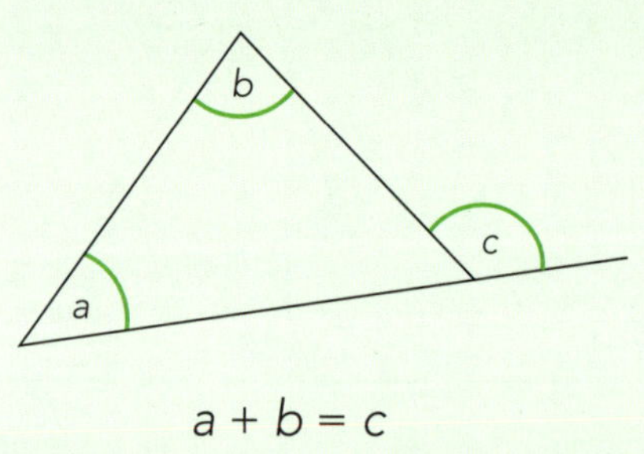


$a + b = c$

**Example:**

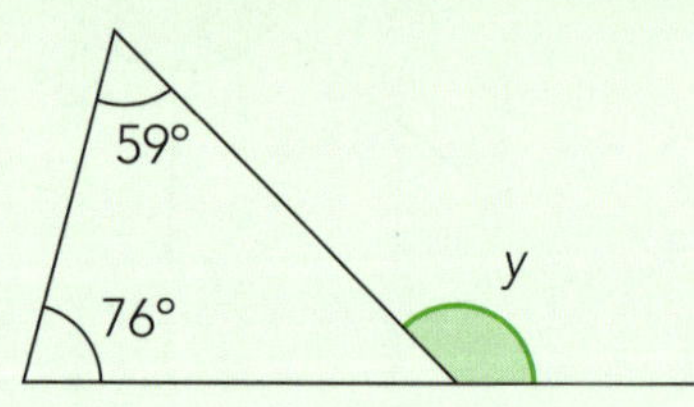


$y = 59° + 76°$

$y = 135°$

**Reason:** ext ∠ of △ = sum of int opp ∠s.

Calculate the missing angles and write the reason(s) used. If your reasons are different from those in the answers, check with your teacher.

**1**

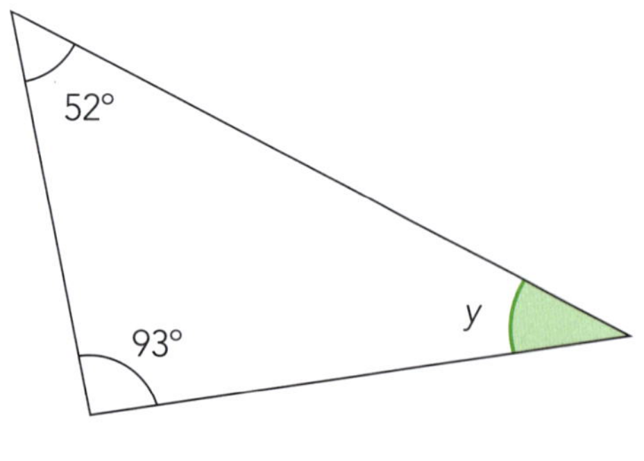


Reason(s): ______

**2**

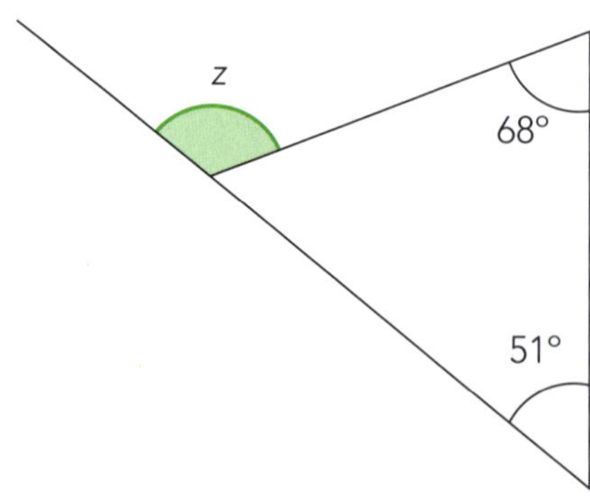


Reason(s): ______



 ISBN: 9780170451543

**3**

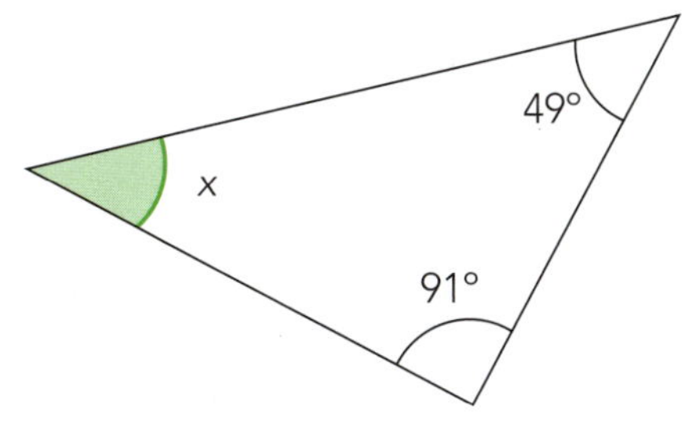


Reason(s):

**4**

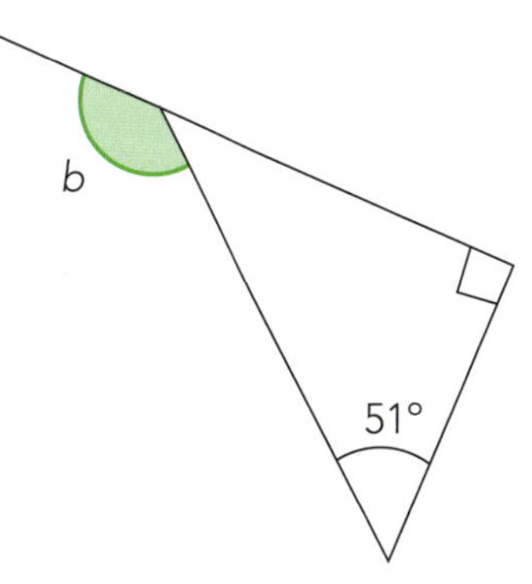


Reason(s):

**5**

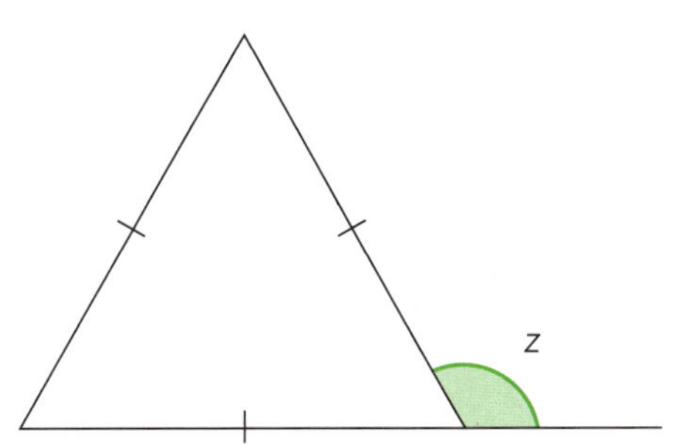


Reason(s):

**6**

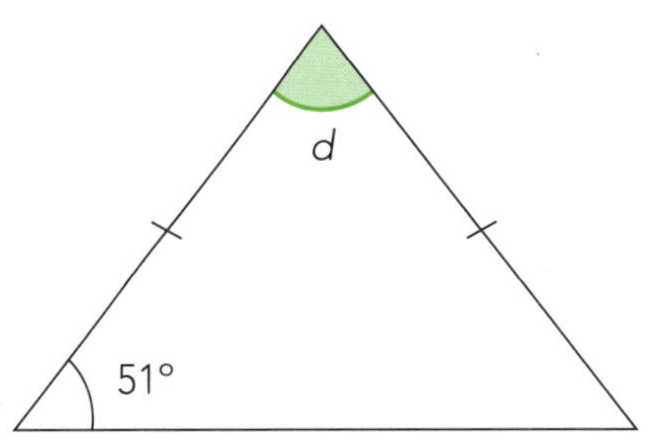


Reason(s):

**7**

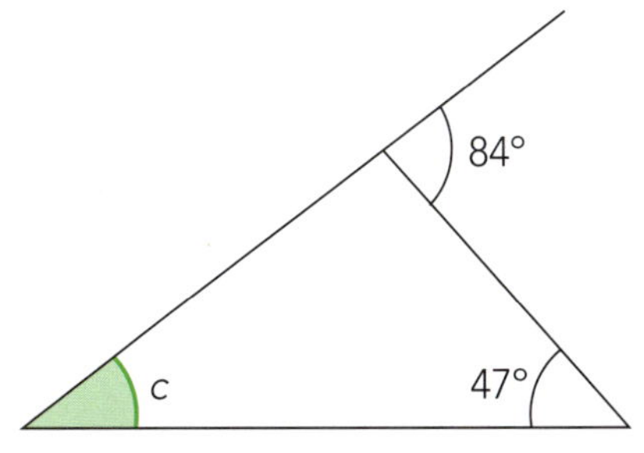


Reason(s):

**8**

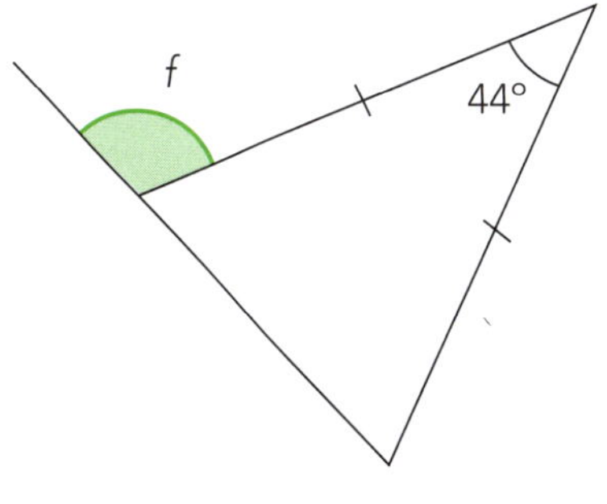


Reason(s):

ISBN: 9780170451543 

# Angles in a quadrilateral

- A quadrilateral is any closed shape (no gaps) with exactly **four straight sides**.
- The four angles in a quadrilateral **add to 360°**.

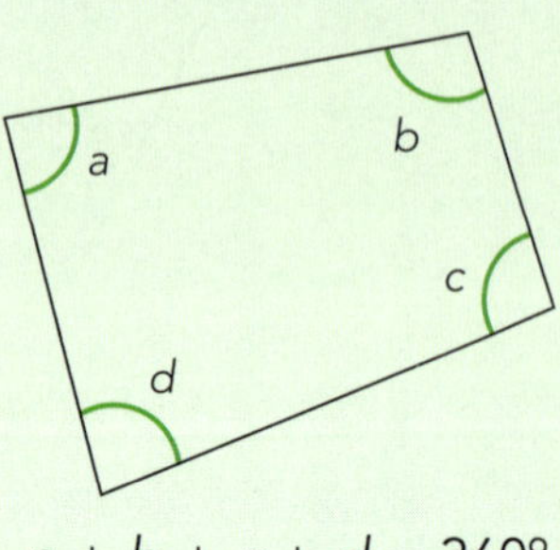


$a + b + c + d = 360°$

**Examples:**

**1** Find the value of $a$.

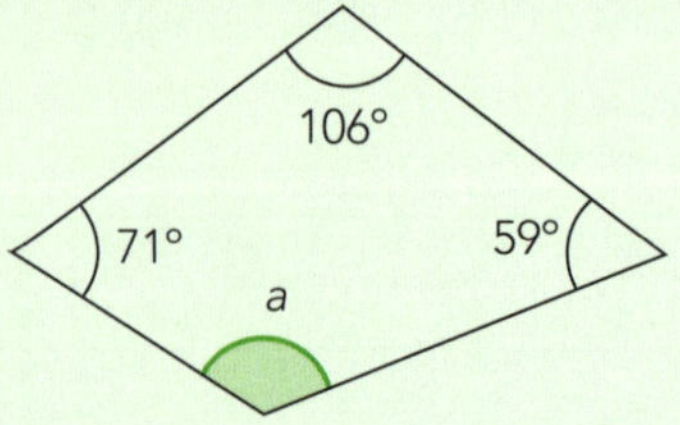


$71° + 106° + 59° + a = 360°$

$a = 360° - 71° - 106° - 59°$

$a = 124°$

**Reason:** ∠s in quad = 360°.

**2** Find the value of x.

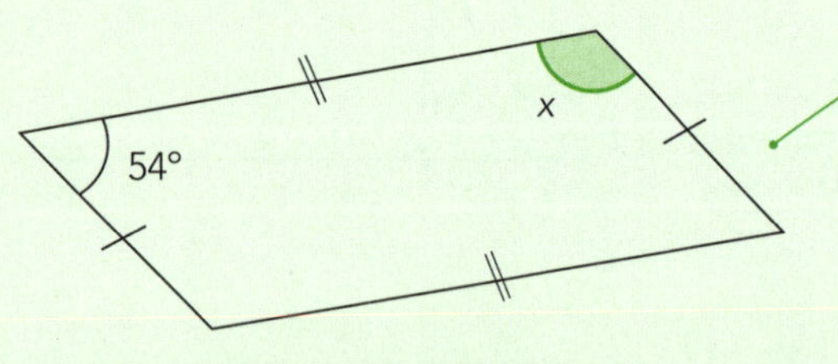


Remember that parallelograms and rhombuses have two pairs of equal angles.

$(54° \times 2) + 2x = 360°$

$x = (360° - (54° \times 2)) \div 2$

$x = 126°$

**Reason:** ∠s in quad = 360°.

Calculate the missing angles and write the reason(s) used. If your reasons are different from those in the answers, check with your teacher.

**1**

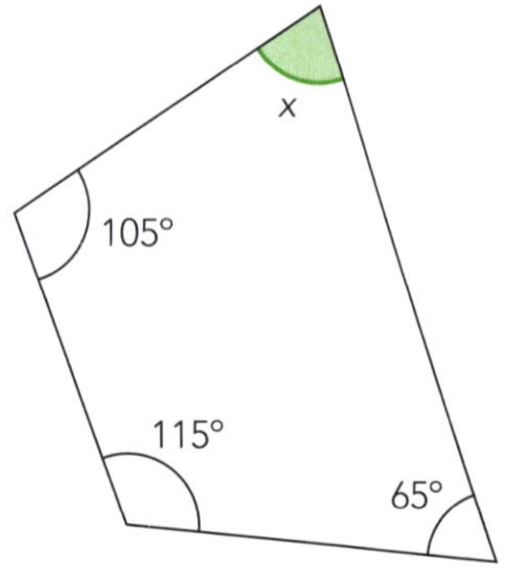


______________________________

______________________________

Reason(s): ______________________________

**2**

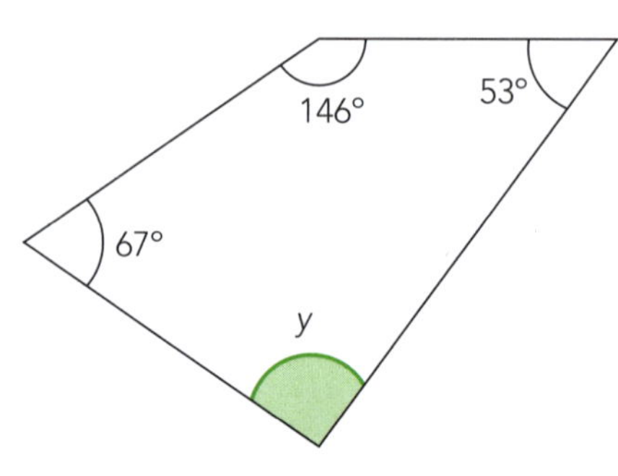


______________________________

______________________________

Reason(s): ______________________________



ISBN: 9780170451543

3

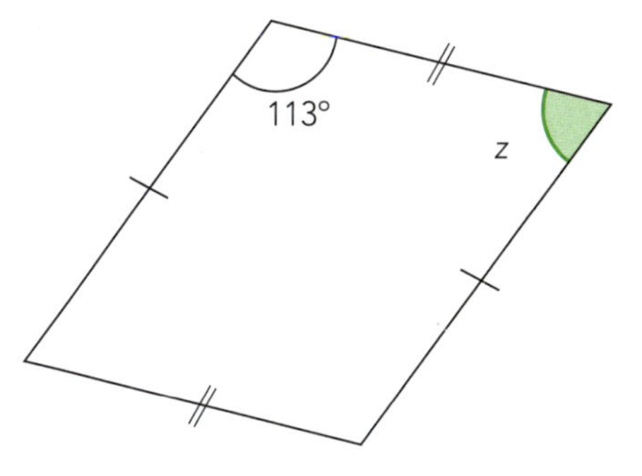


Reason(s):

4

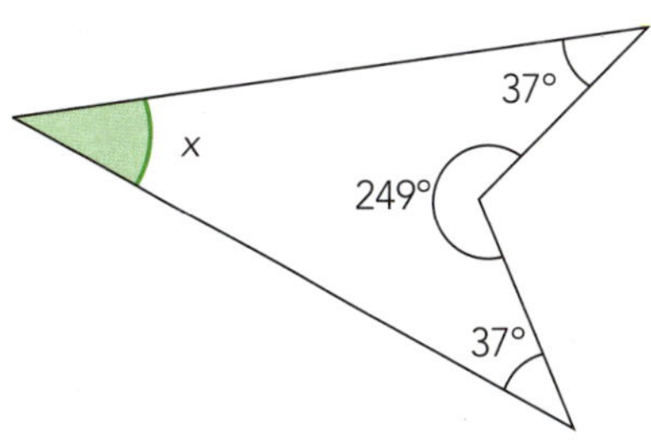


Reason(s):

5

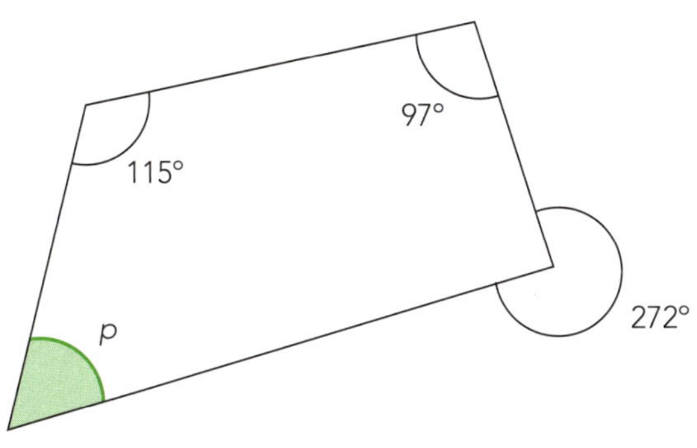


Reason(s):

6

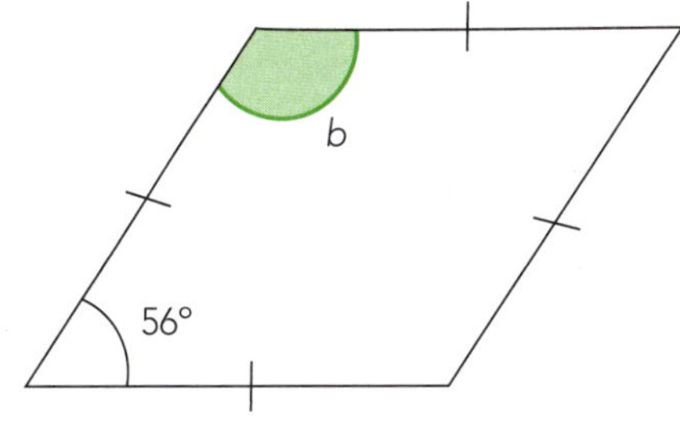


Reason(s):

7

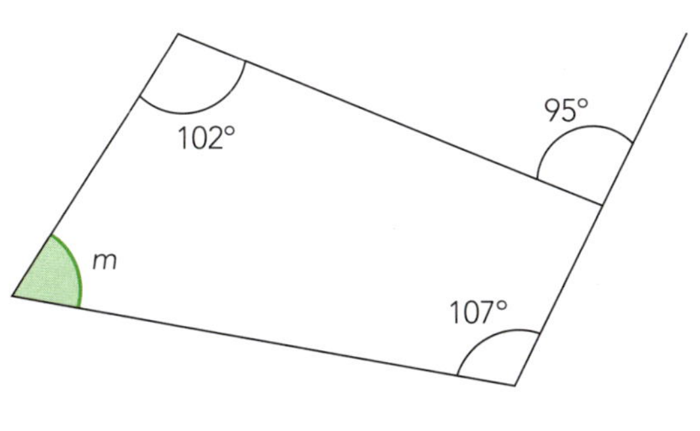


Reason(s):

8

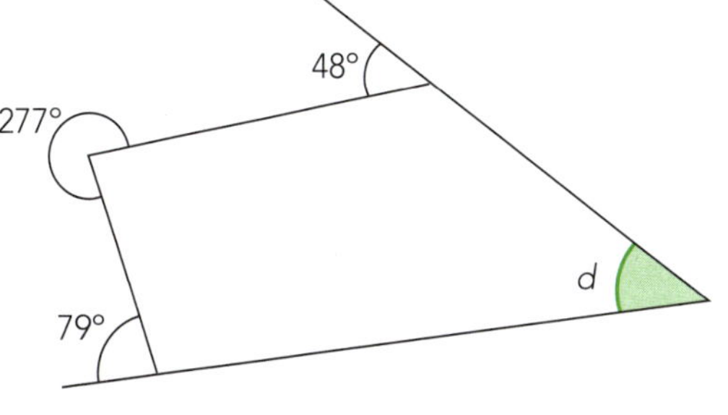


Reason(s):

ISBN: 9780170451543  

# Polygons

- There are different rules for exterior and interior angles in polygons.

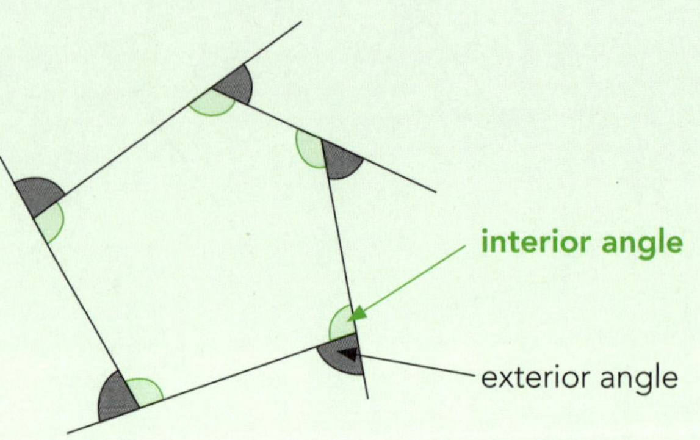


## Exterior angles

- Exterior angles of a polygon **always add to 360°**.

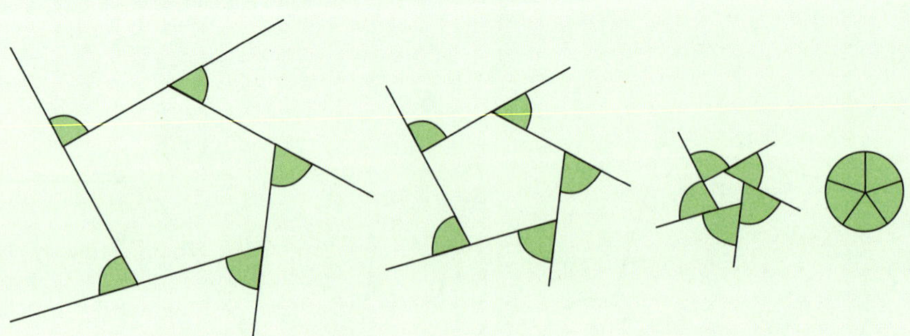

**Example:** Find the value of *b*.

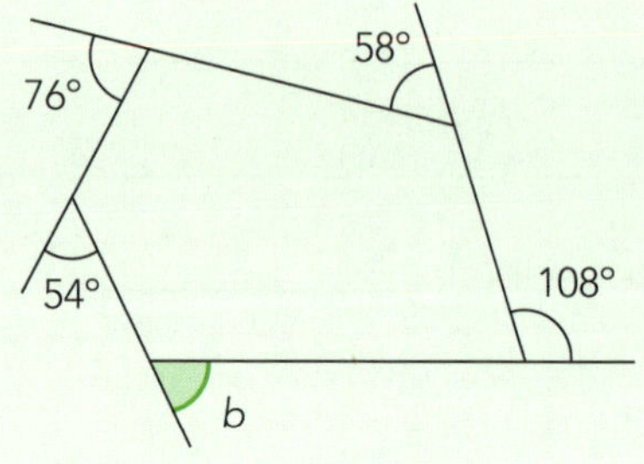


$108° + 58° + 76° + 54° + b = 360°$
$b = 360° - 108° - 58° - 76° - 54°$
$b = 64°$

**Reason:** Ext ∠s of polygon = 360°.

Calculate the missing angles.

**1**

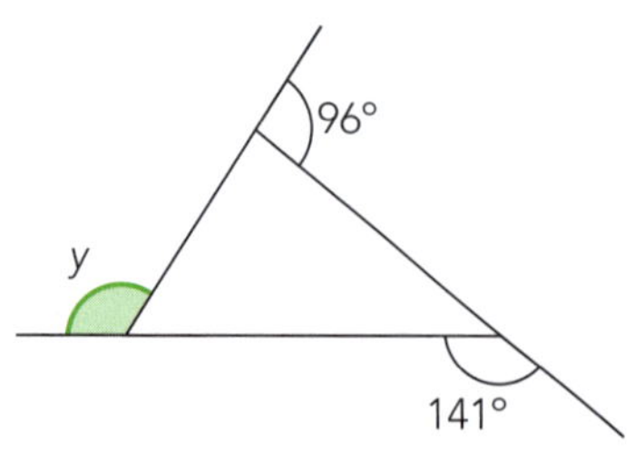


**2**

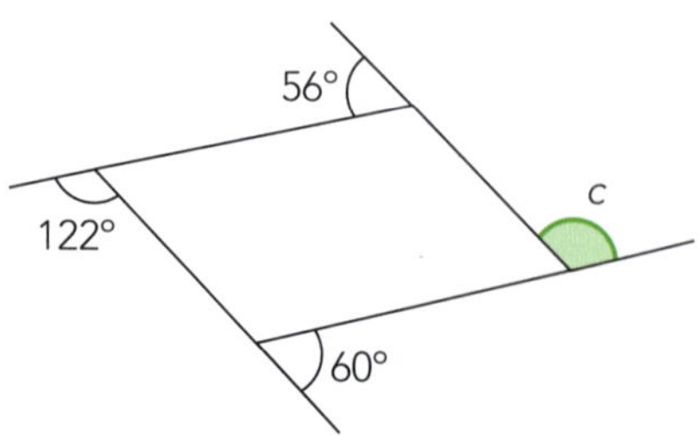




 ISBN: 9780170451543

**3**

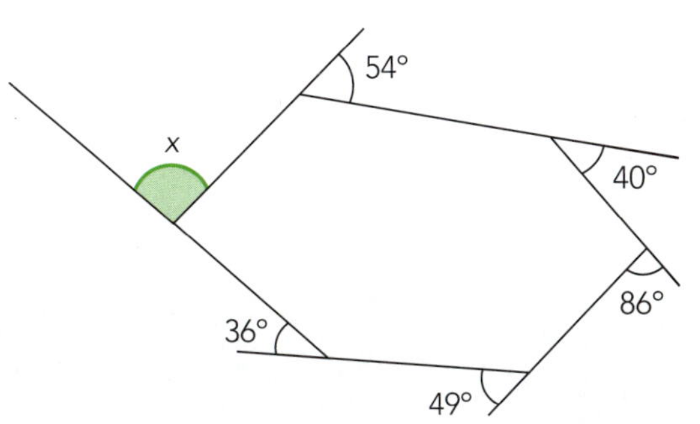


**4**

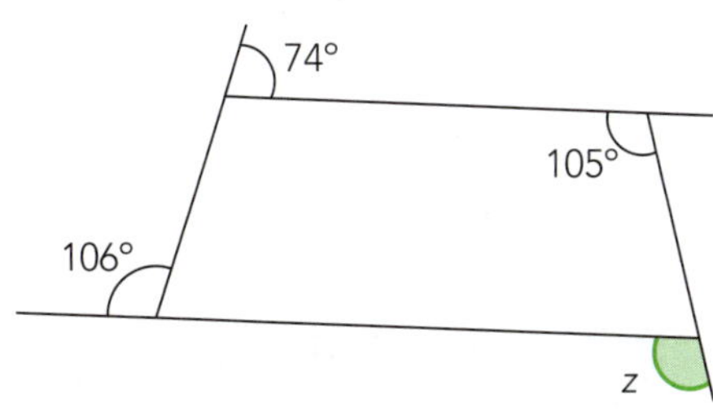


**5**

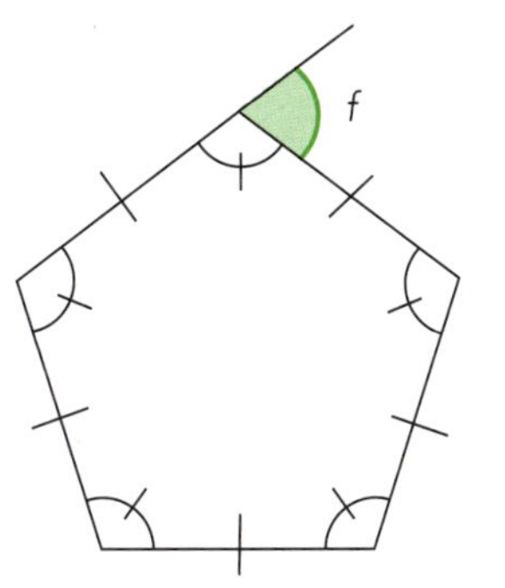


**6**

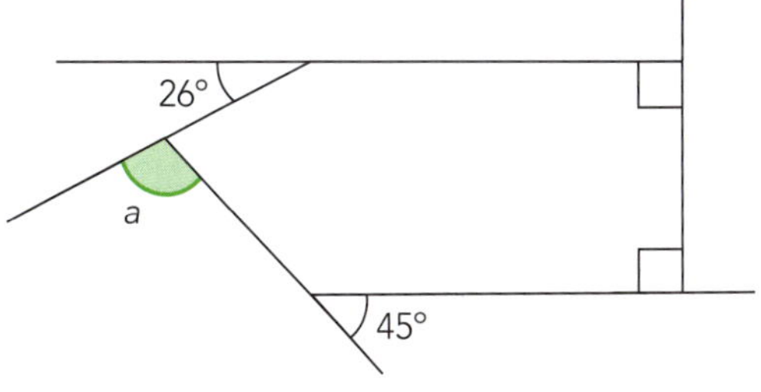


**7**

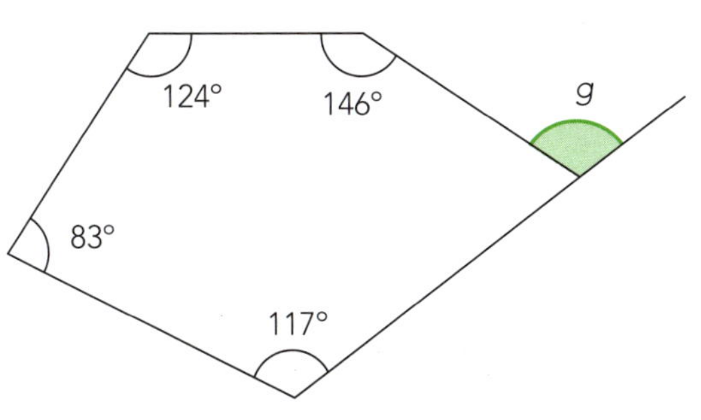


**8**

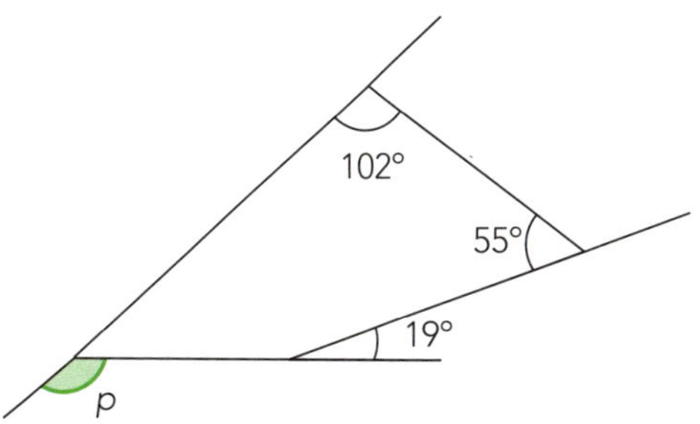


 

## Interior angles

- The sum of interior polygon angles depends on the number of sides.
- Calculate the sum of the interior angles by dividing the polygon into triangles.
- You know the interior angles of a triangle add to 180°.

| Name | Number of sides | Diagram | Sum of interior angles | Size of each interior angle of a *regular* polygon |
|---|---|---|---|---|
| Quadrilateral | **4** | 1, 2 | 2 x 180° = 360° | $\frac{360°}{4} = 90°$ |
| Pentagon | **5** | 1, 2, 3 | 3 x 180° = 540° | $\frac{540°}{5} = 108°$ |
| Hexagon | **6** | 1, 2, 3, 4 | 4 x 180° = 720° | $\frac{720°}{6} = 120°$ |
| Heptagon | **7** | 1, 2, 3, 4, 5 | 5 x 180° = 900° | $\frac{900°}{7} = 128.6°$ |
| Octagon | **8** | 1, 2, 3, 4, 5, 6 | 6 x 180° = 1080° | $\frac{1080°}{8} = 135°$ |
| Any polygon | ***n*** | The number of triangles is always 2 fewer than the number of sides. | **($n$ – 2) x 180°** | $\frac{(n-2) \times 180°}{n}$ |

**Example:**
Find the value of $x$.

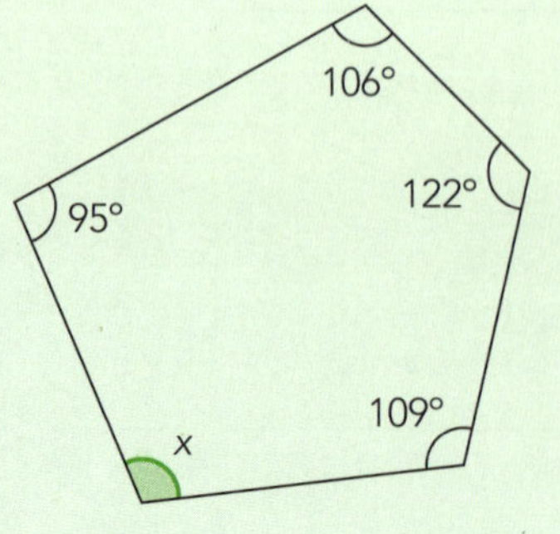


Sum of interior angles = $(n - 2) \times 180°$
= $(5 - 2) \times 180°$
= 540°

$x = 540° - 95° - 106° - 122° - 109°$
$x = 108°$


 ISBN: 9780170451543

Calculate the missing angles.

**1**

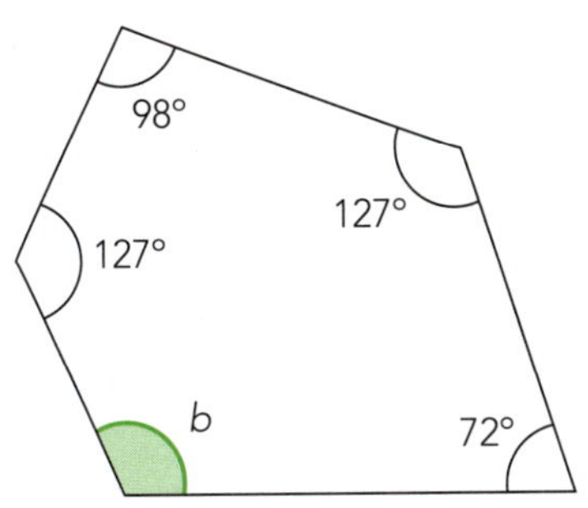


**2**

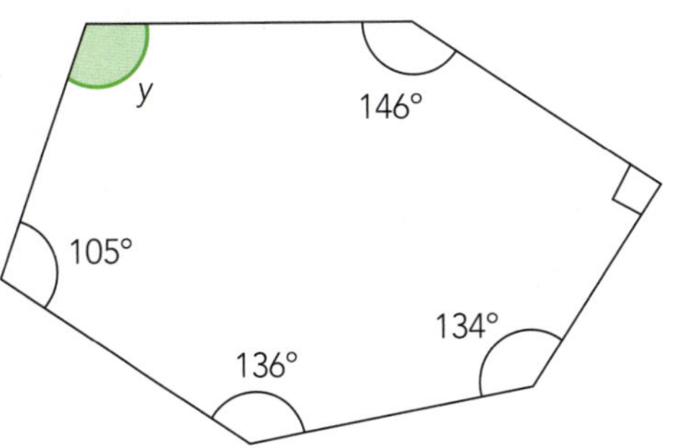


**3**

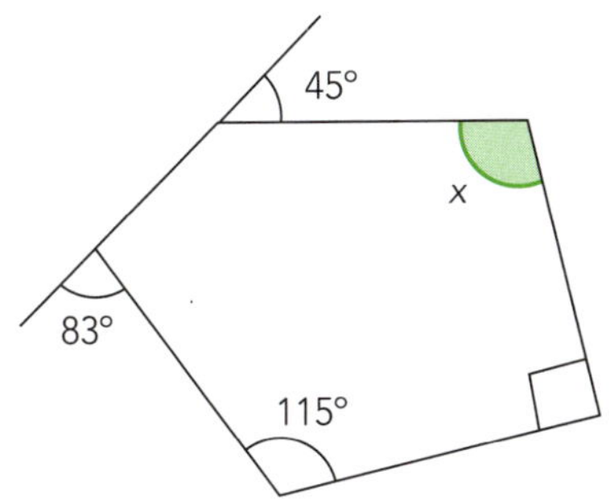


**4**

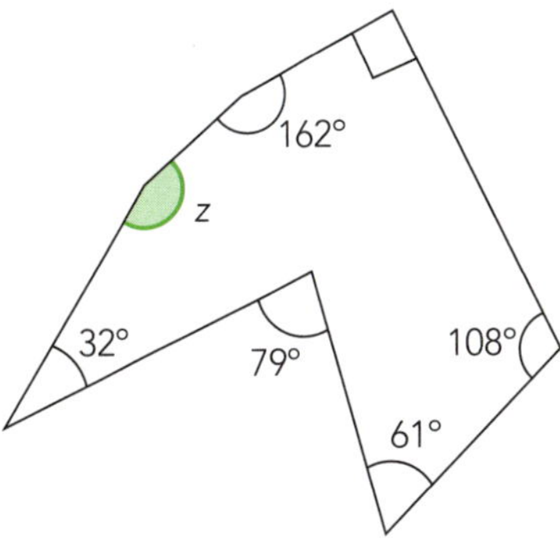


**5**

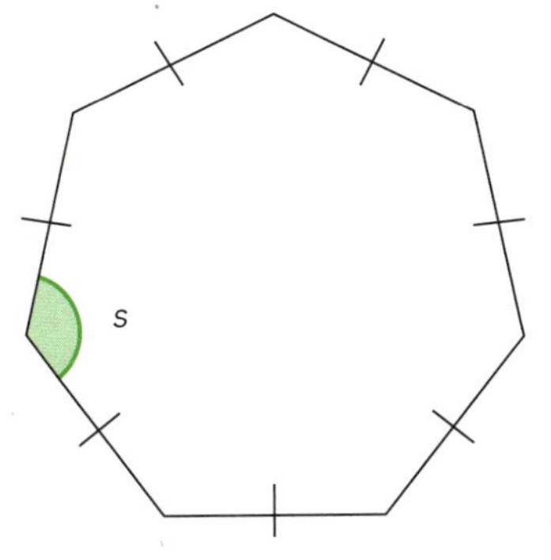


**6**

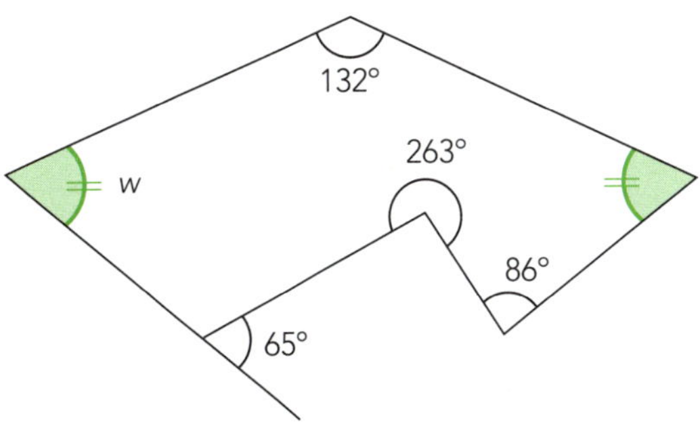


ISBN: 9780170451543 

# Parallel lines

- You will often need to **give reasons** for your answers.

## Alternate angles

- Alternate angles on parallel lines are **equal**.
- These form a '**Z**'.

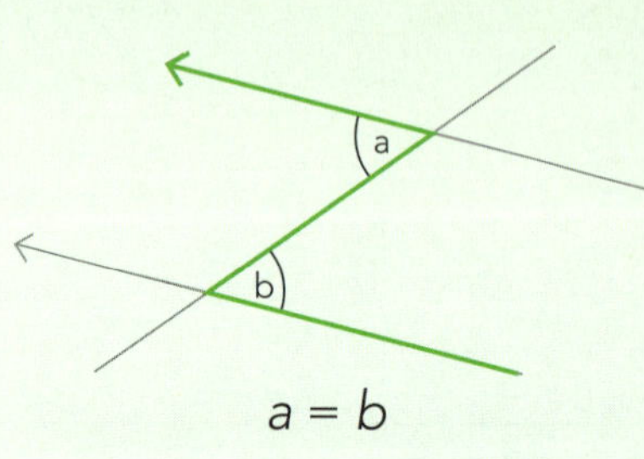


$a = b$

**Example:**
Find the value of $x$.

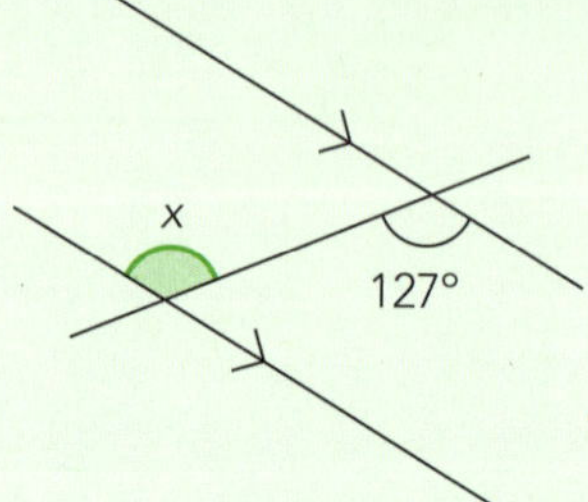


$x = 127°$

You are allowed to shorten 'Alternate angles are equal, parallel lines' to this:

**Reason:** Alt ∠s =, ∥ lines.

## Corresponding angles

- Corresponding angles on parallel lines are **equal**.
- These form an '**F**'.

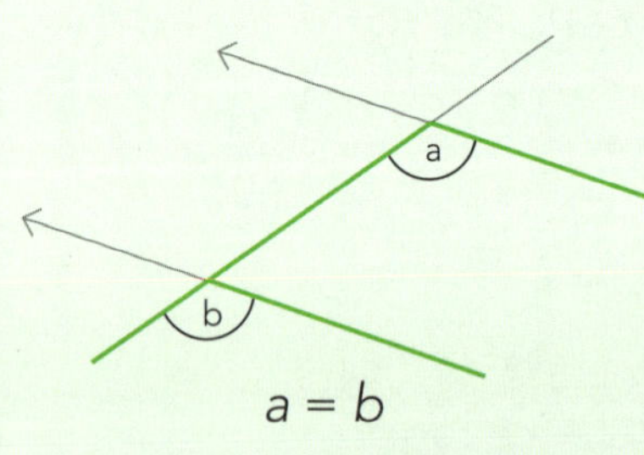


$a = b$

**Example:**
Find the value of $y$.

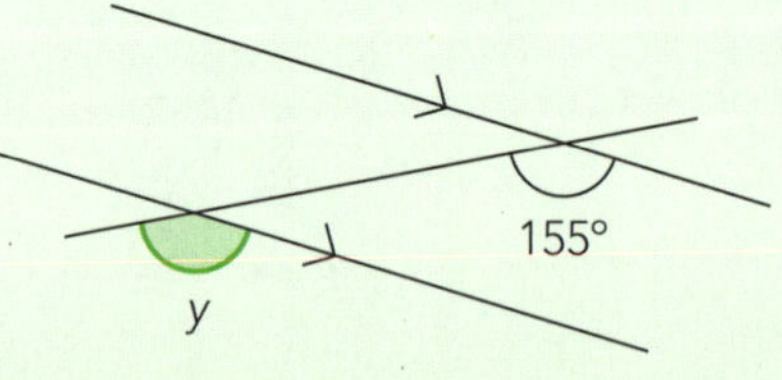


$y = 155°$

'Corresponding angles are equal, parallel lines':

**Reason:** Corr ∠s =, ∥ lines.

## Co-interior angles

- Co-interior angles on parallel lines **add to 180°**.
- These form a '**C**'.

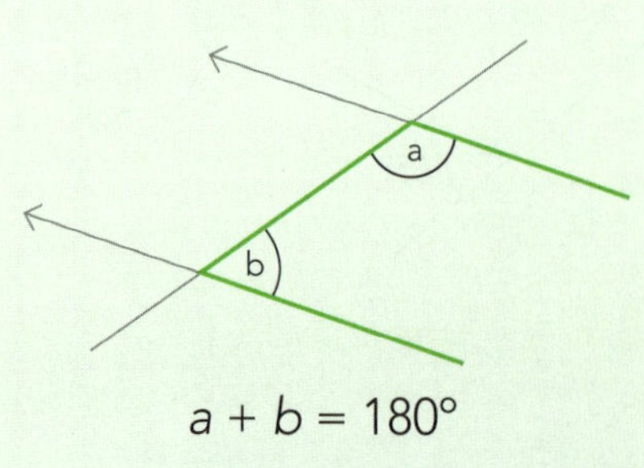


$a + b = 180°$

**Example:**
Find the value of $z$.

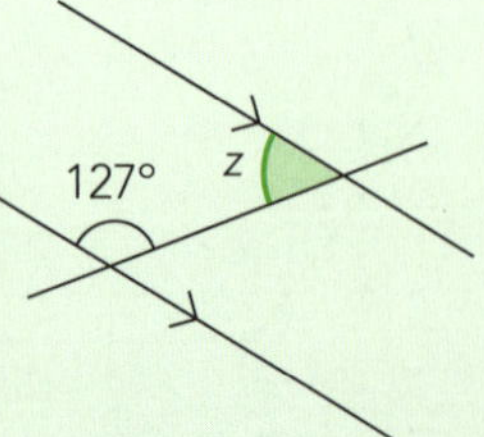


$z = 180° - 127°$
$z = 53°$

'Co-interior angles add to 180°, parallel lines':

**Reason:** Co-int ∠s add to 180°, ∥ lines.



ISBN: 9780170451543

State whether these angles are alternate, corresponding or co-interior.

**1**

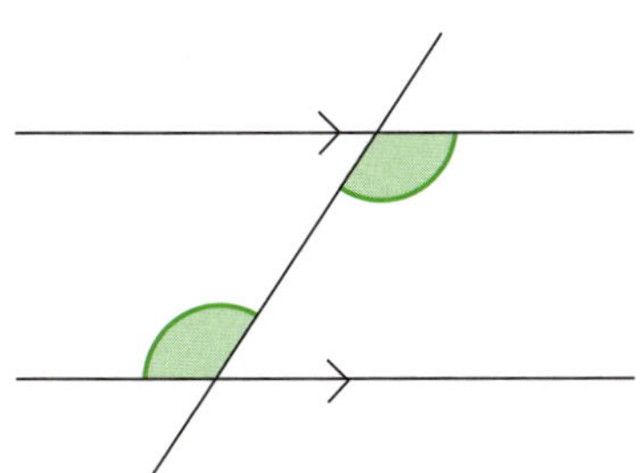

**2**

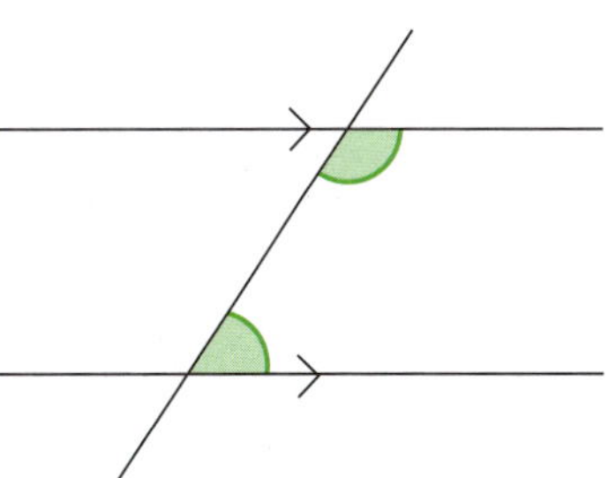

**3**

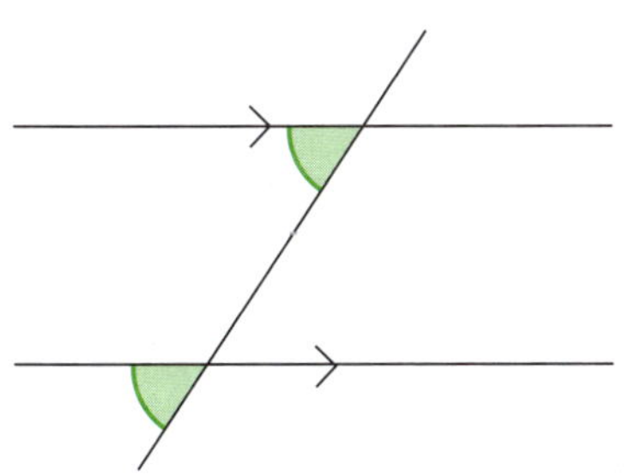

**4**

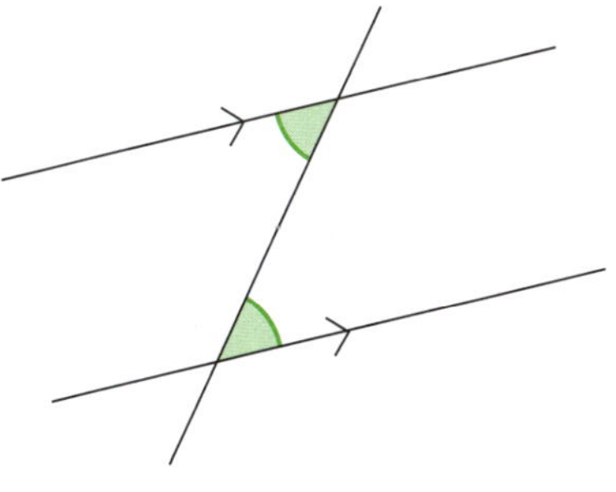

**5**

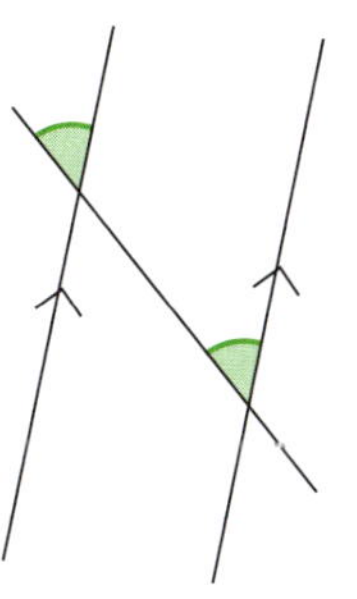

**6**

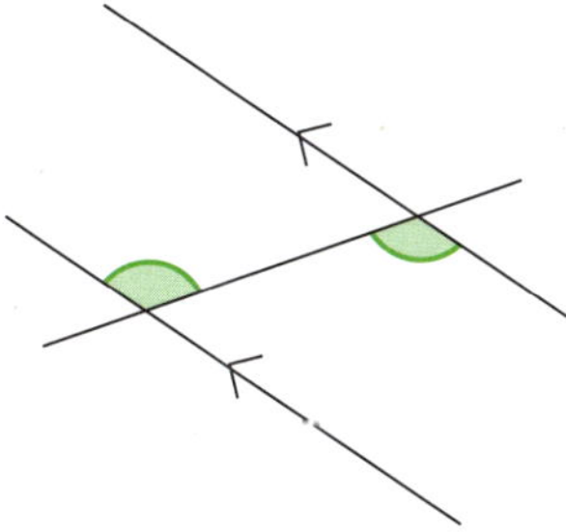

**7**

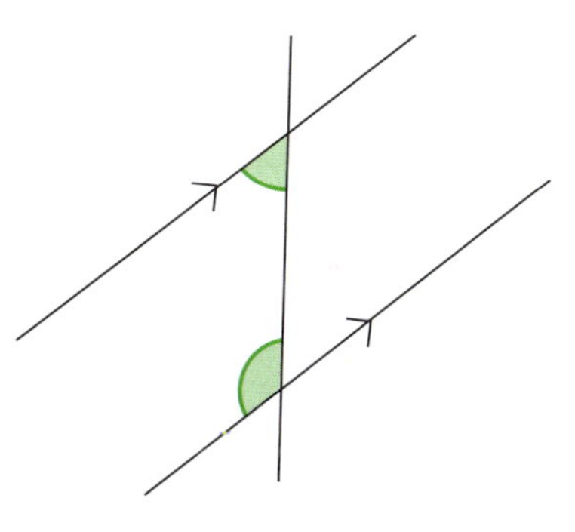

**8**

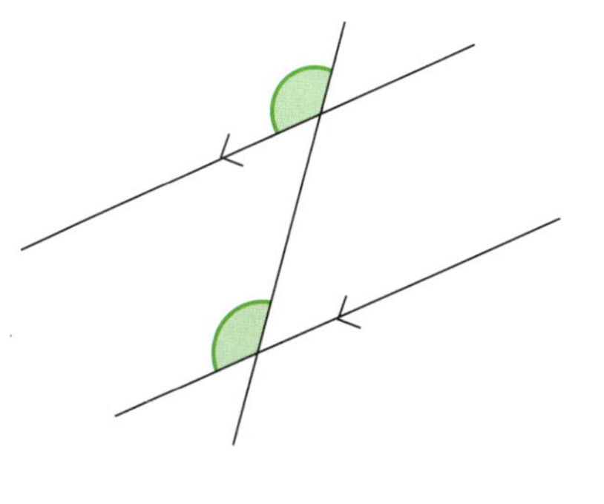

ISBN: 9780170451543 

Calculate the missing angles and give the reason.

**9**

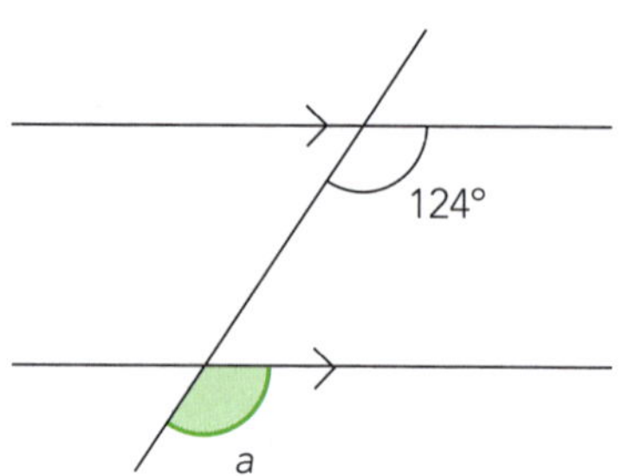


Reason:

**10**

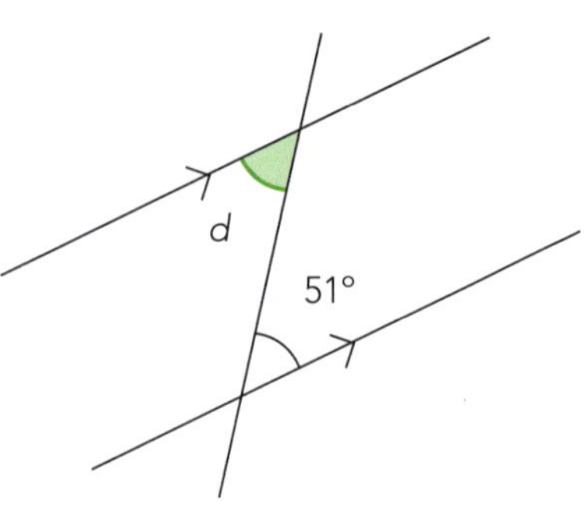


Reason:

**11**

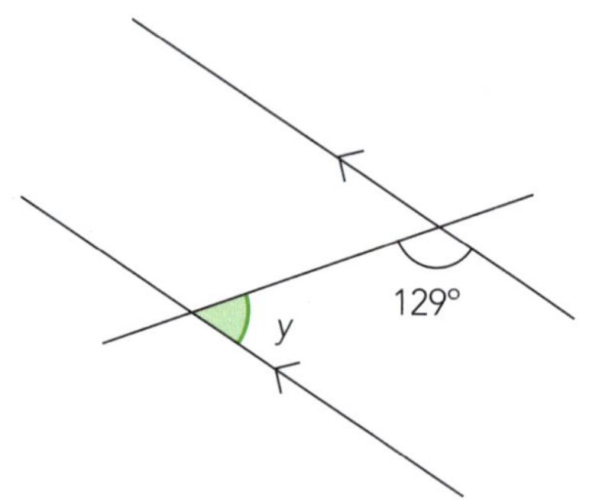


Reason:

**12**

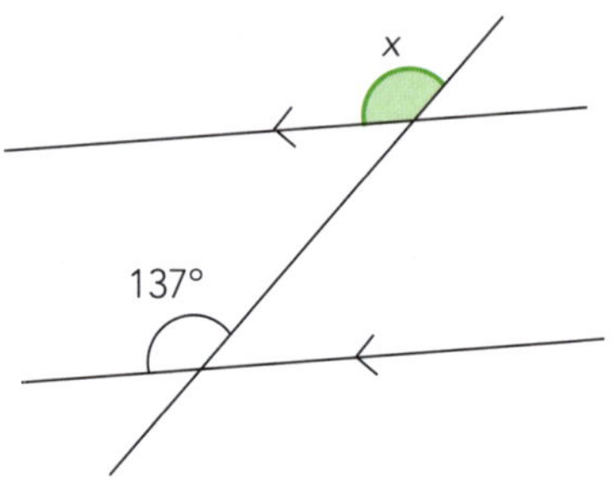


Reason:

**13**

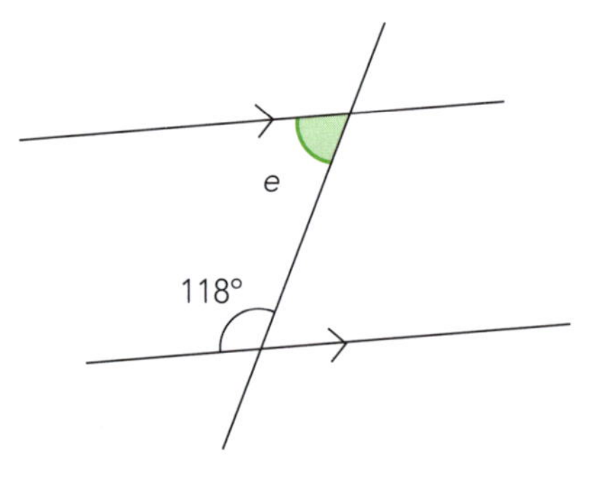


Reason:

**14**

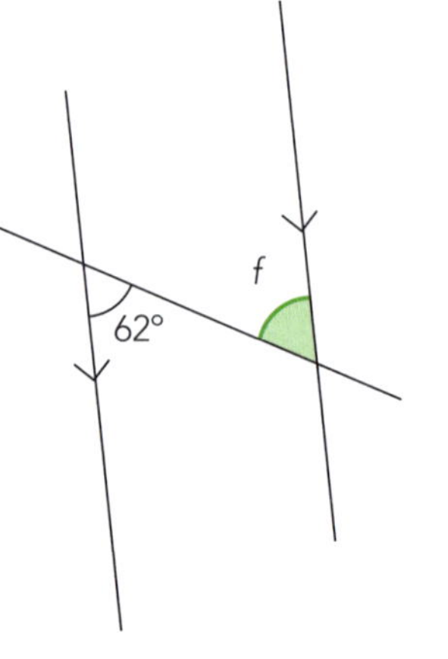


Reason:



 ISBN: 9780170451543

# Mixing it up

Calculate the missing angles and give the reason(s).

**1**

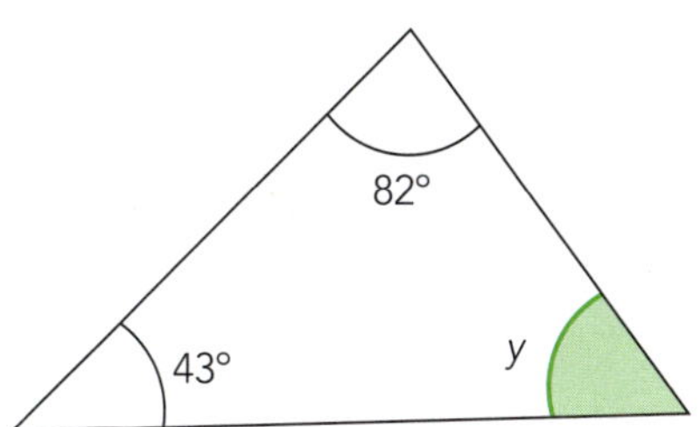


Reason(s):

**2**

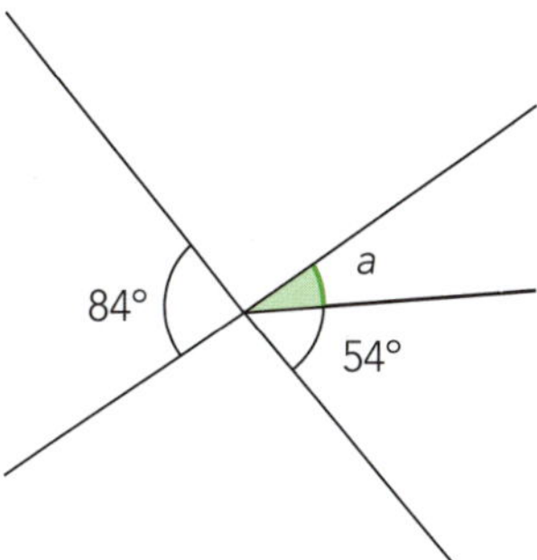


Reason(s):

**3**

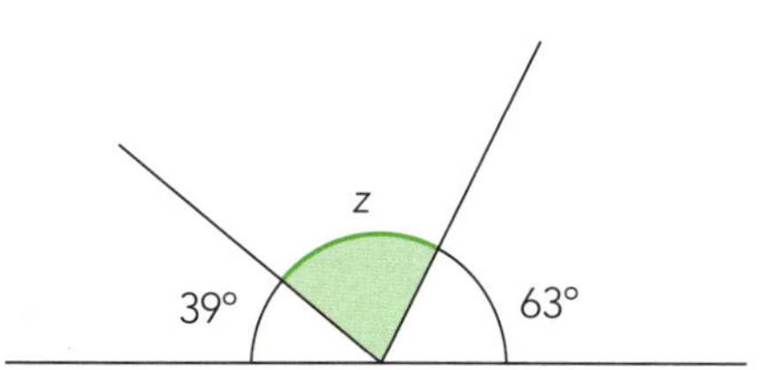


Reason(s):

**4**

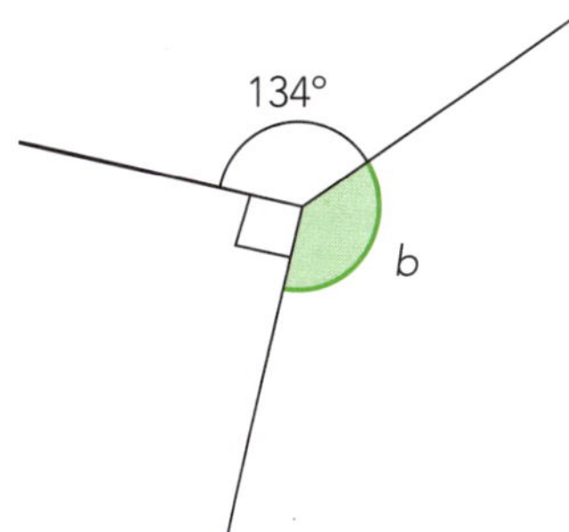


Reason(s):

**5**

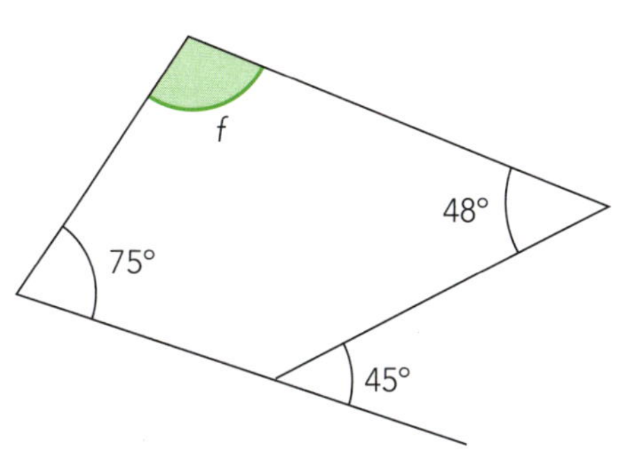


Reason(s):

**6**

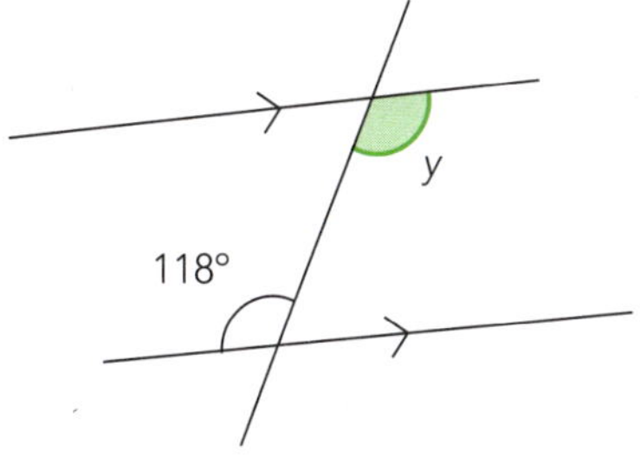


Reason(s):

ISBN: 9780170451543  

**7**

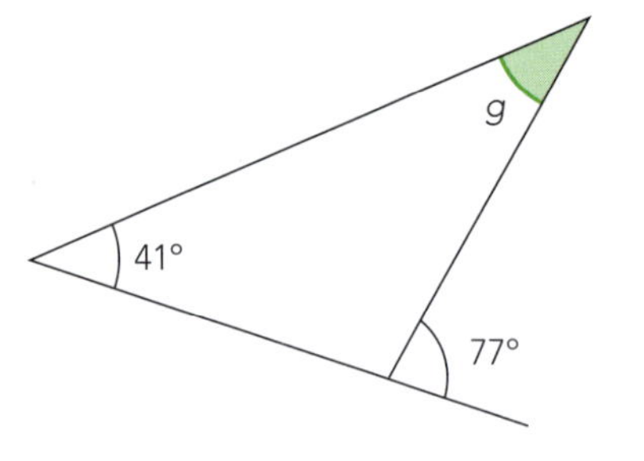


Reason(s):

**8**

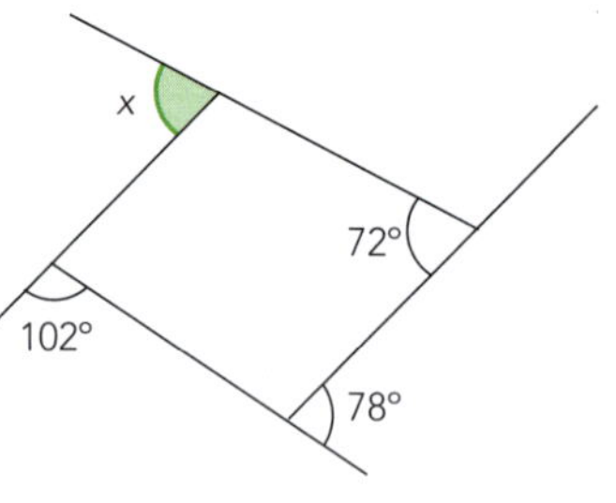


Reason(s):

**9**

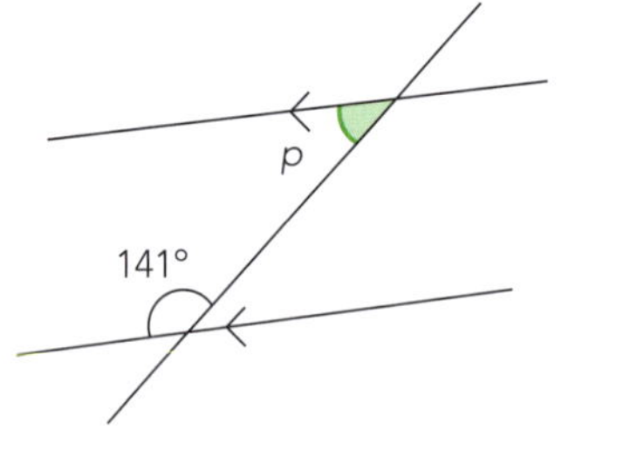


Reason(s):

**10**

Reason(s):

**11** This pentagon is regular.

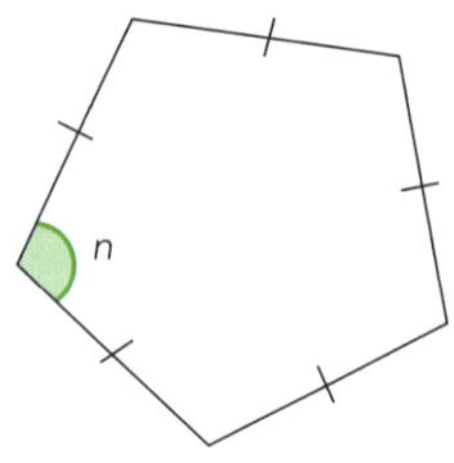


Reason(s):

**12**

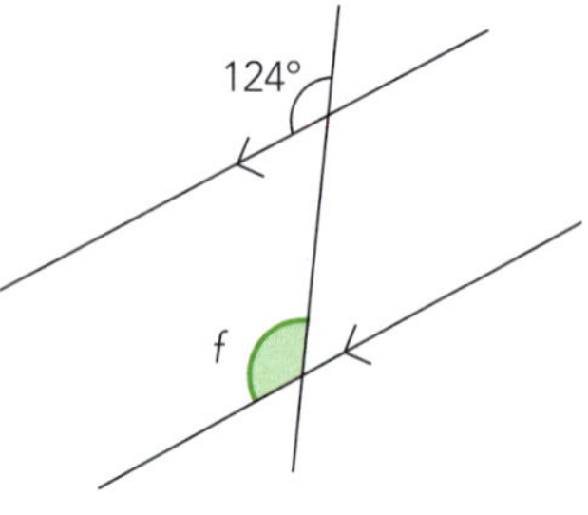


Reason(s):

**13**

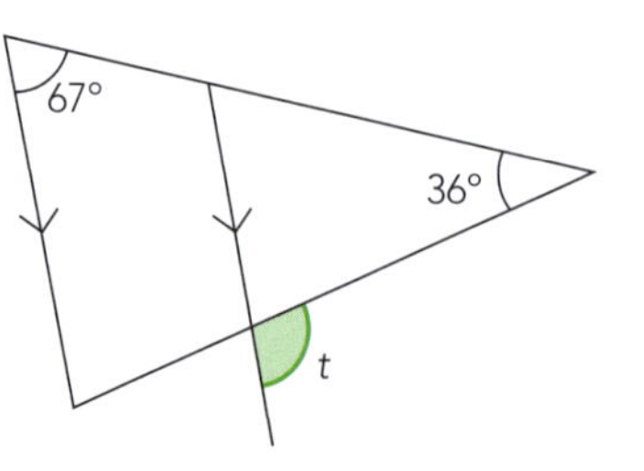


Reason(s):

**14**

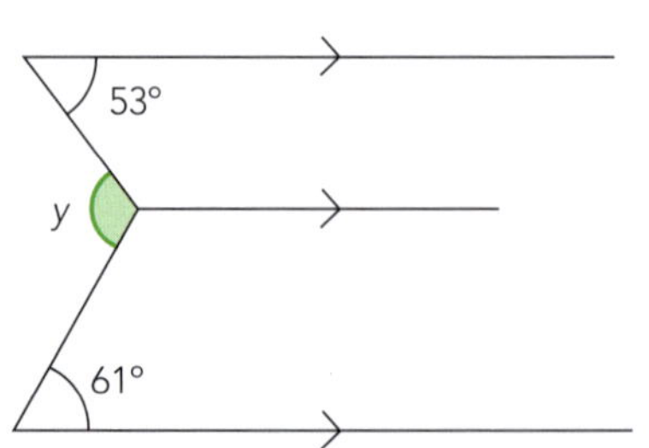


Reason(s):



 ISBN: 9780170451543

# Isometrics

**1** Copy this shape, showing the junctions between each block.

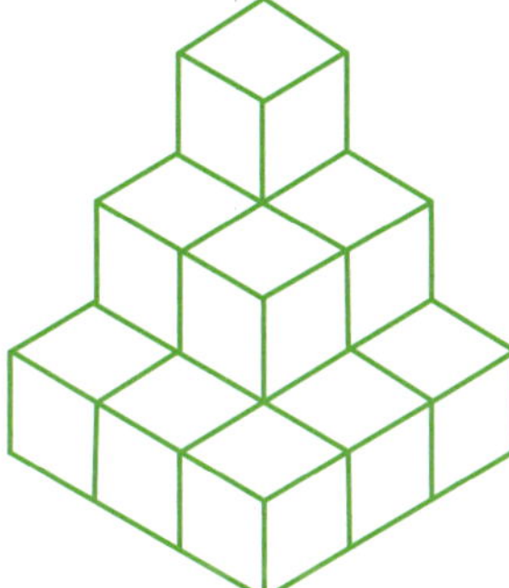

**2** Copy this shape, without showing the junctions between each block.

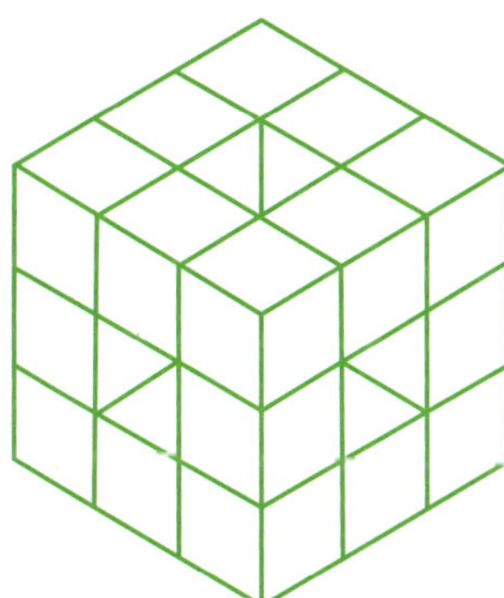

**3** Write down the number of blocks in each column of this shape.

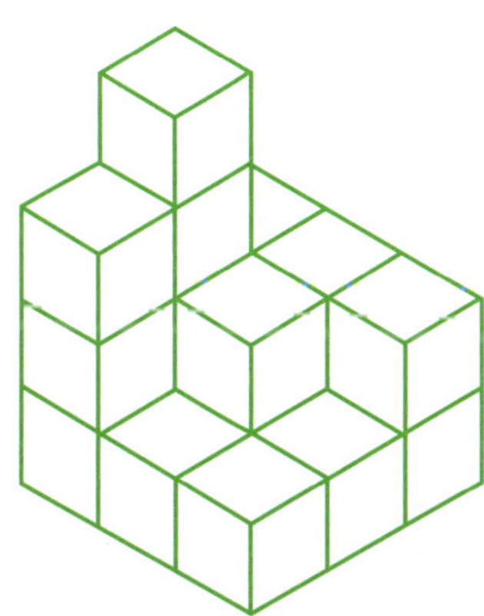

| 3 | | |
|---|---|---|
| | | |
| | | |

ISBN: 9780170451543 

**4** Draw this structure on the isometric grid.

| 1 | 2 | 2 |
|---|---|---|
| 1 | 2 | 3 |
| 1 | 1 | 1 |

Match these shapes with their 2D views.

A

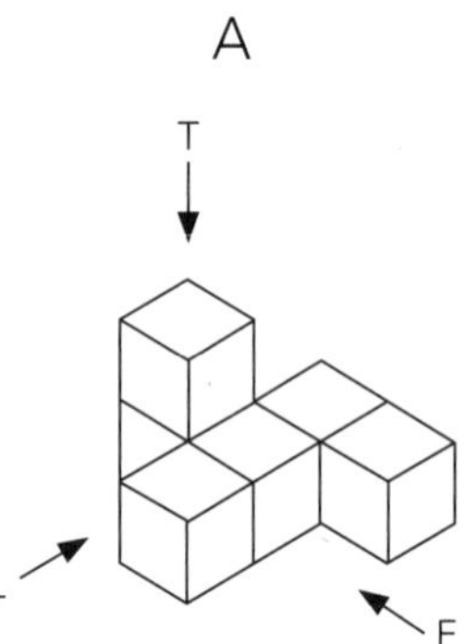


B

C

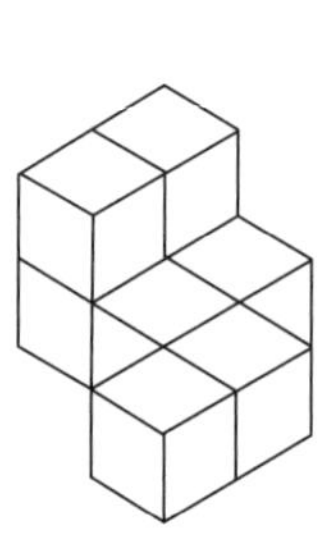

**5** ________

Top

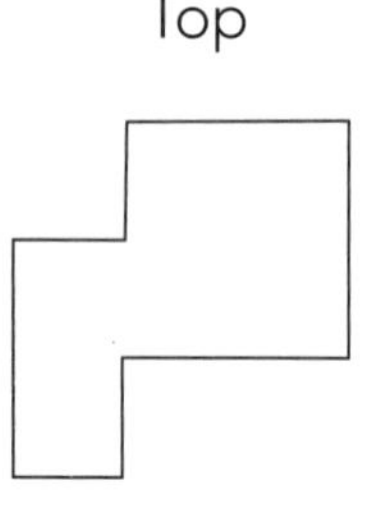

Left

Front

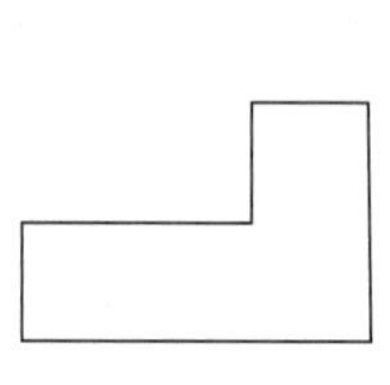

**6** ________

Top

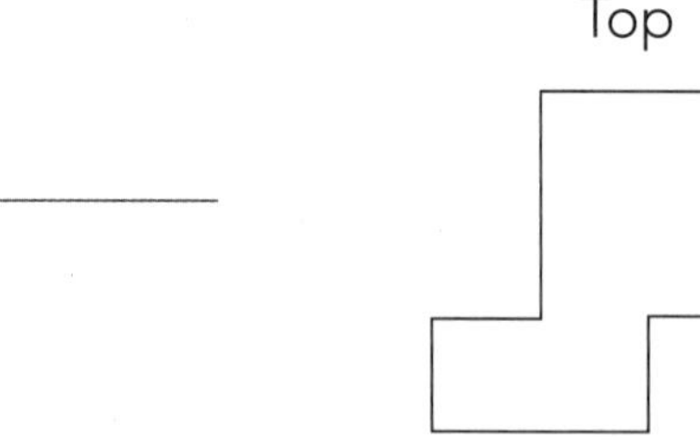

Left

Front

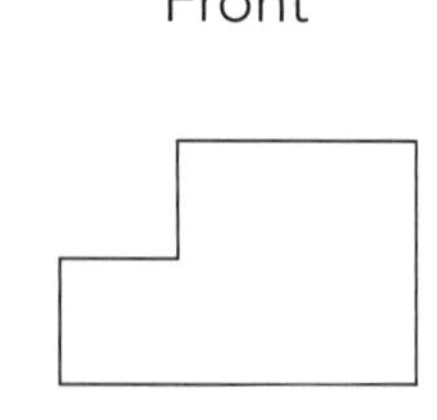

**7** ________

Top

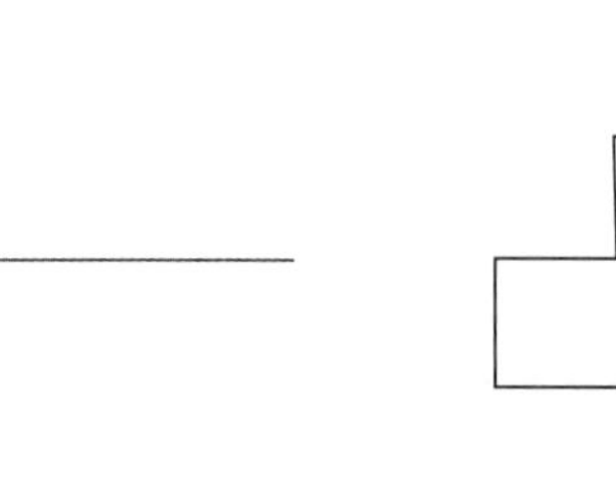

Left

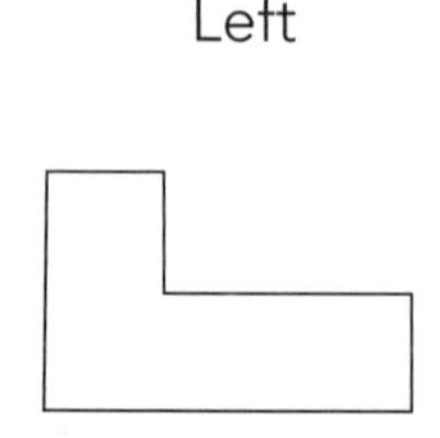

Front



 ISBN: 9780170451543

# Challenge 1

This is a different type of isometric paper. There are 24 ways of drawing this figure on isometric paper. Three are done for you. See how many you can draw.

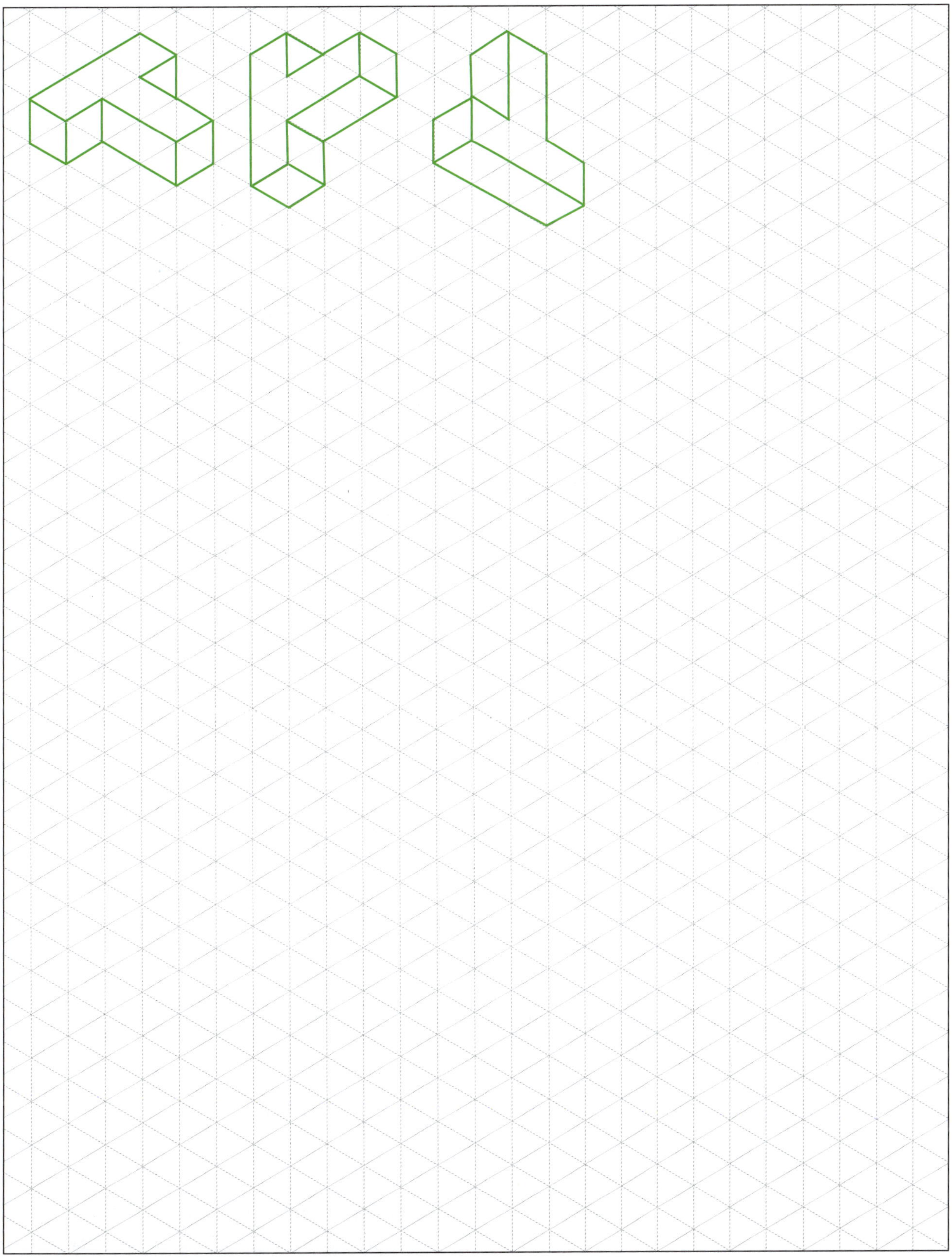

ISBN: 9780170451543

# Position and orientation

## Direction: bearings

- Bearings are used in navigation to define **direction** in a **horizontal** plane.
- Direction can be given in terms of north, south, east and west.
- North is always given as the starting point.

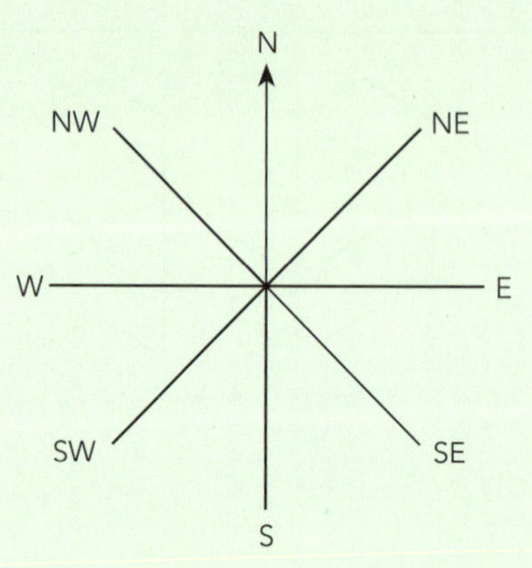


- Bearings are measured in **degrees** in a **clockwise direction from north (000° or 360°)**.
- All bearings must have **three digits**.

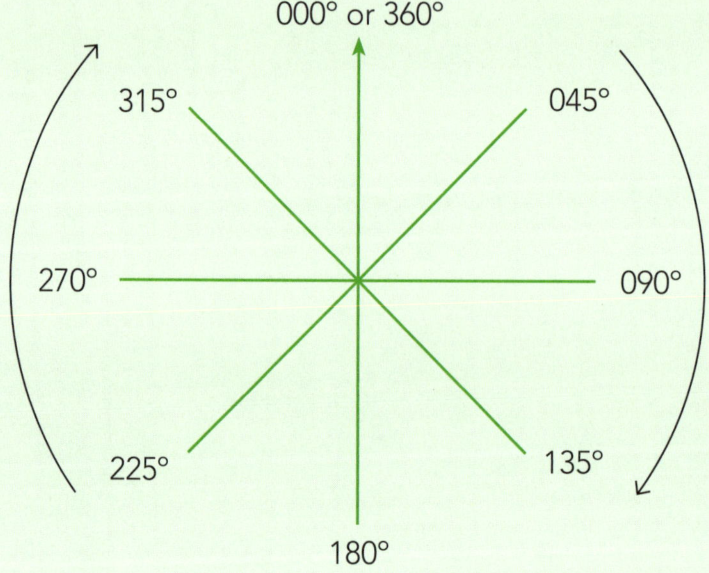


**Examples:**

**1**

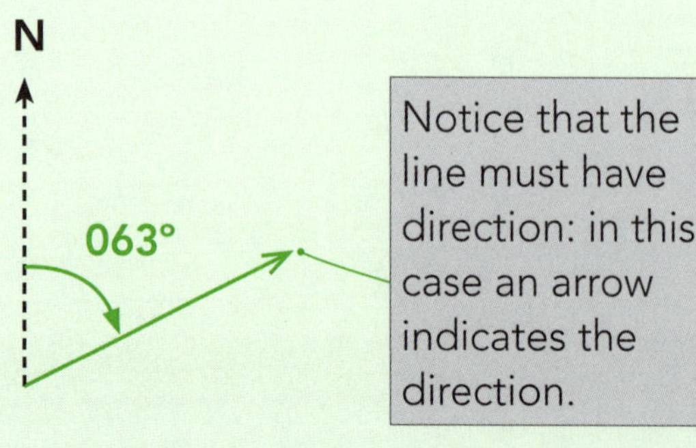


**2**

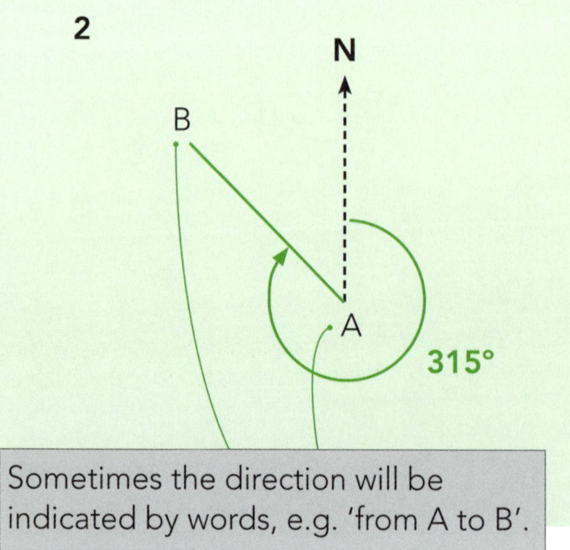




 ISBN: 9780170451543

Without using a protractor, match the bearings in the list to each of the diagrams. They are either in the direction of the arrow or from A to B. The dashed line points to north.

| 239° | 017° | 281° | 202° | 155° | 068° | 114° | 329° |
|---|---|---|---|---|---|---|---|

**1** ________ **2** ________ **3** ________ **4** ________

**5** ________ **6** ________ **7** ________ **8** ________

**9** Ngaire walks anticlockwise around this path, starting at point A. Write the bearings she will need to walk for each stretch of path. Select your answers from the list below.

| | |
|---|---|
| 263° | 126° |
| 037° | 318° |
| 247° | 114° |
| 096° | 288° |

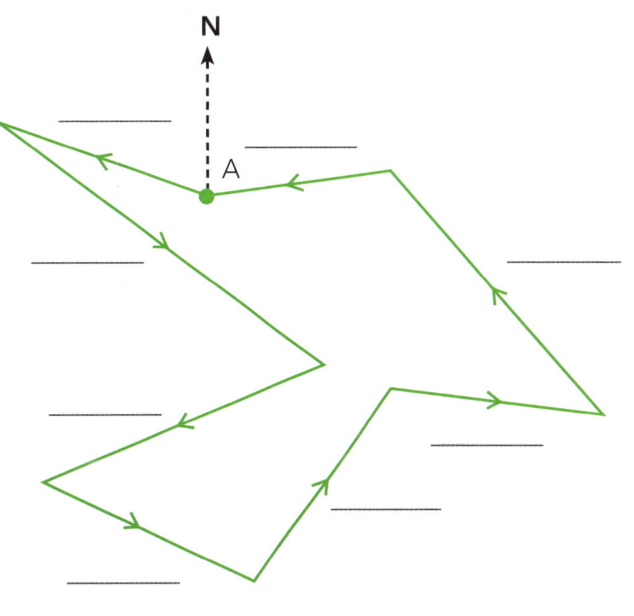


ISBN: 9780170451543 

# Using a protractor to find bearings

- You will need a ruler and, ideally, a 360° protractor.

**Example:** Find the location that is at a bearing of 215° from point A and 137° from point B.

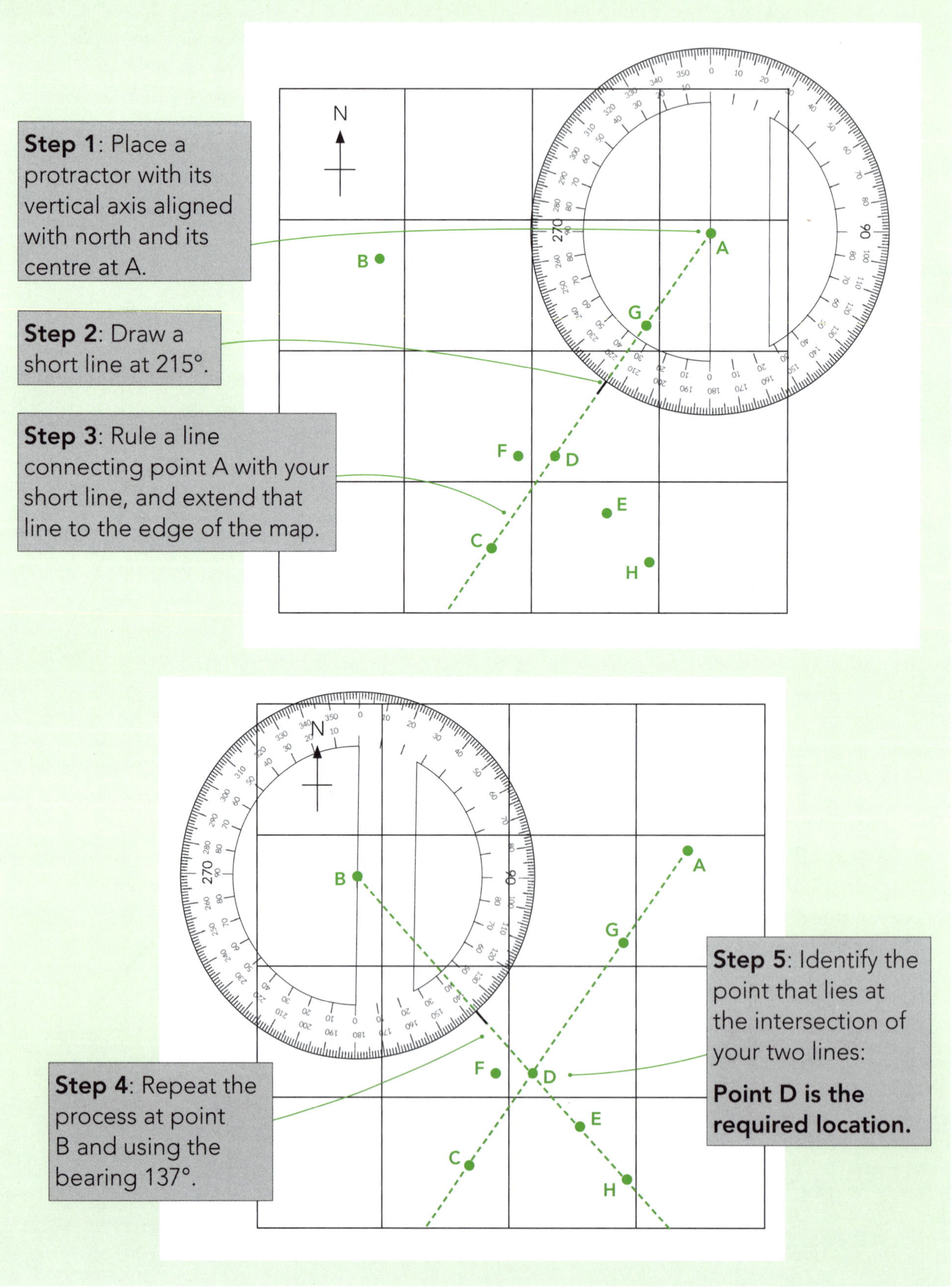




ISBN: 9780170451543

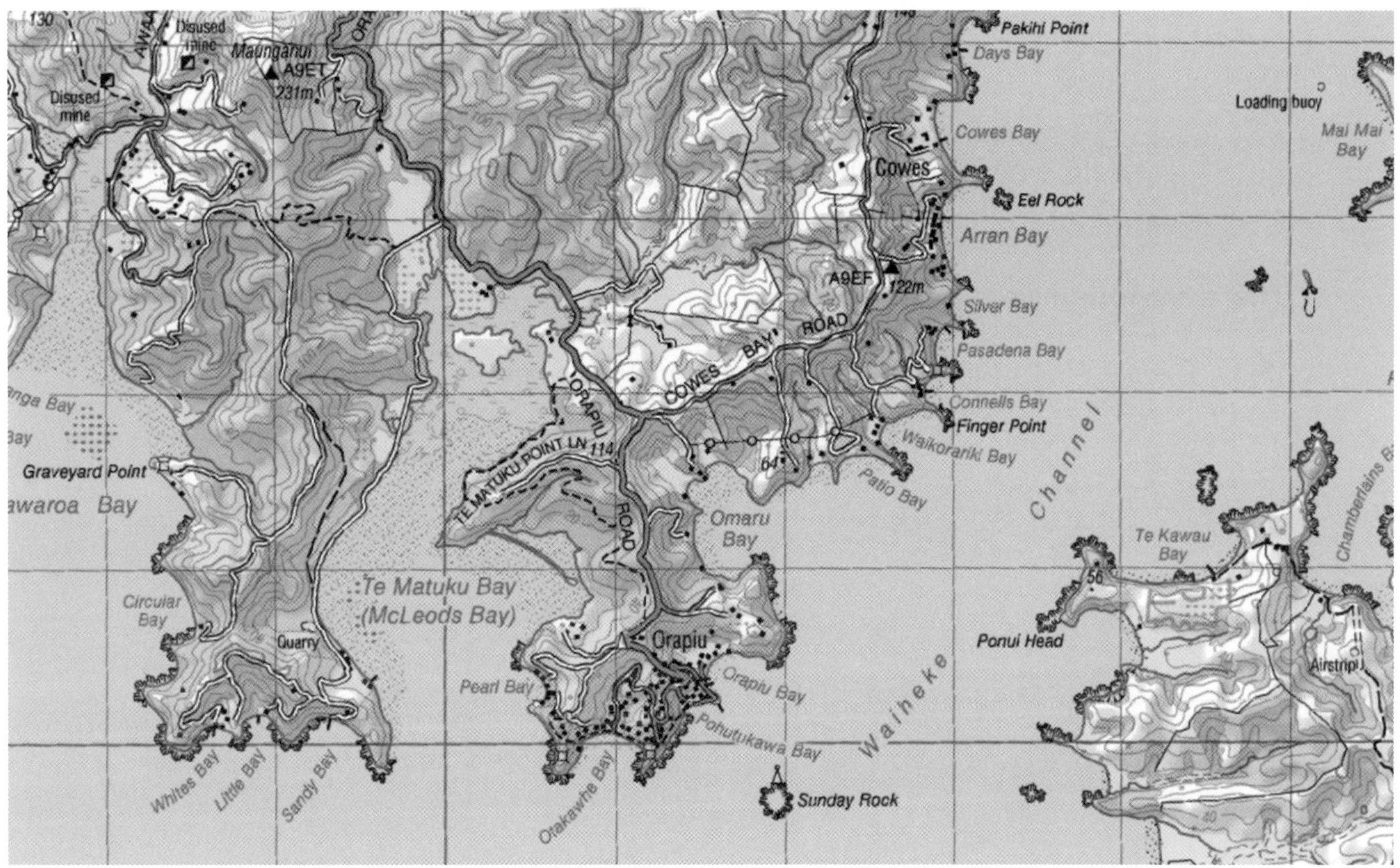


Identify the following locations.

1 A bearing of 090° from Maunganui (top left) and 049° from Finger Point. ____________________

2 A bearing of 240° from Ponui Head and 145° from the wharf on the point between Orapiu and Pohutukawa Bay. ____________________

3 A bearing of 197° from Maunganui and 295° from Sunday Rock. ____________________

4 A bearing of 075° from Graveyard Point and 330° from the wharf in Te Kawau Bay. ____________________

5 A bearing of 355° from Graveyard Point and 316° from the wharf on the point between Orapiu Bay and Pohutukawa Bay. ____________________

6 A bearing of 014° from Sunday Rock and 047° from the wharf in Sandy Bay. ____________________

7 A bearing of 270° from Ponui Head and 135° from Graveyard Point. ____________________

ISBN: 9780170451543  

# Location: loci

- A **locus** is a **set of points**.
- The plural of locus (when we have more than one locus) is **loci**.
- A locus describes **the set of all the points that satisfy certain conditions**.

**There are four main types of locus:**

**1** The set of all points that are the same distance from **one fixed point**.

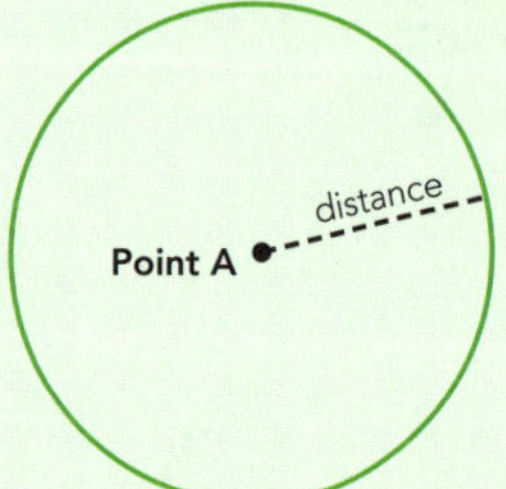


**The locus is a circle.**
The fixed point (A) = centre.
The same distance = radius.

**2** The set of all points that are the same distance from **a line**.

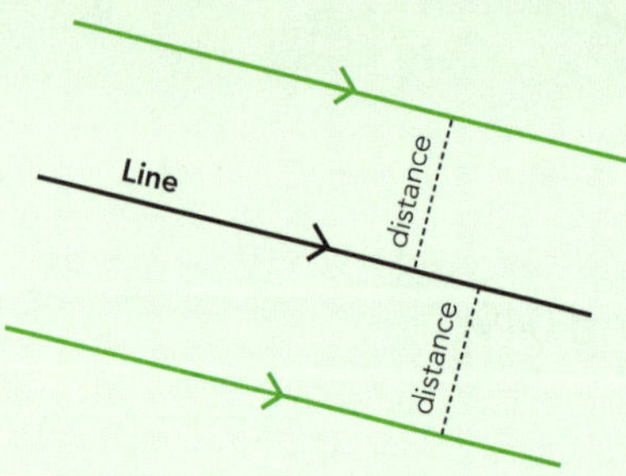


**The locus is a pair of parallel lines.**

**3** The set of all points that are the same distance from **two fixed points**.

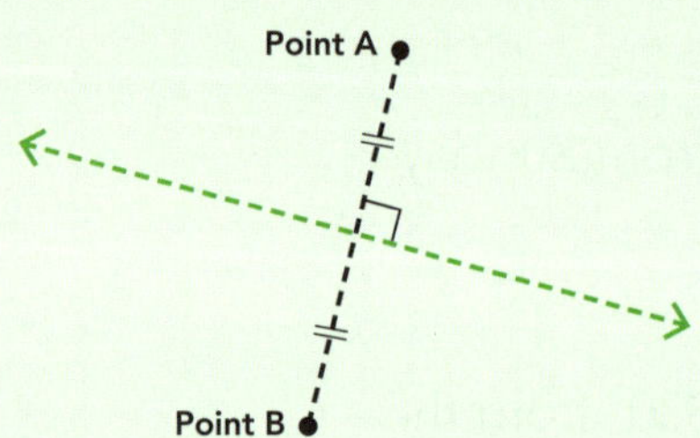


**The locus is the perpendicular bisector of the line (AB) joining the points.**

**4** The set of all points that are the same distance from **two fixed lines**.

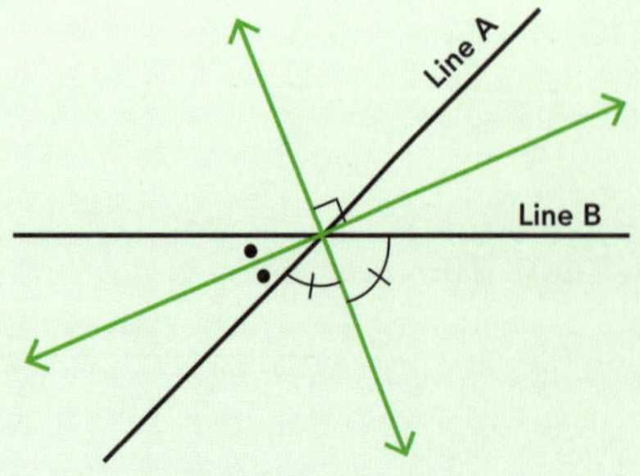


**The locus is a pair of angle bisectors that are perpendicular to each other.**


 ISBN: 9780170451543

**Examples:**

1 A fireplace (F) has been installed in the corner of a room that is 5 m long and 3 m wide. There is a guard to keep the children at least 1 m away from the fire. Their mum has also said that they must not play in the area where the door swings open. The diagram shows the locus of points for the area where the children can play.

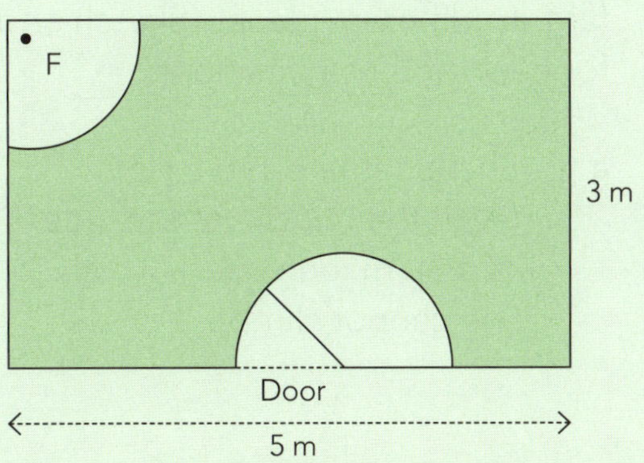


2 A rectangular section is 30 m wide on the side that borders the road and the other side is 20 m long. The building regulations say that the owners are not allowed to build within 4.5 m of the road. Nor are they allowed to build within 3 m of the remaining boundaries. The diagram shows the locus of points for the area that can be built on.

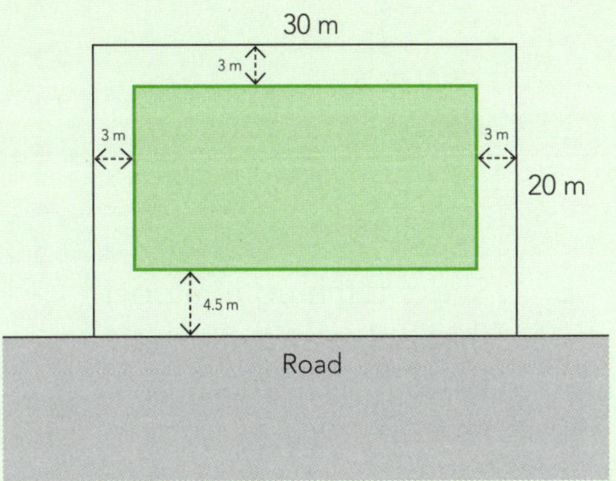


3 Five pairs of buoys mark the approach to a port entrance. The deepest part of the approach is halfway between each pair. The diagram shows the locus for the deepest line of approach to the port.

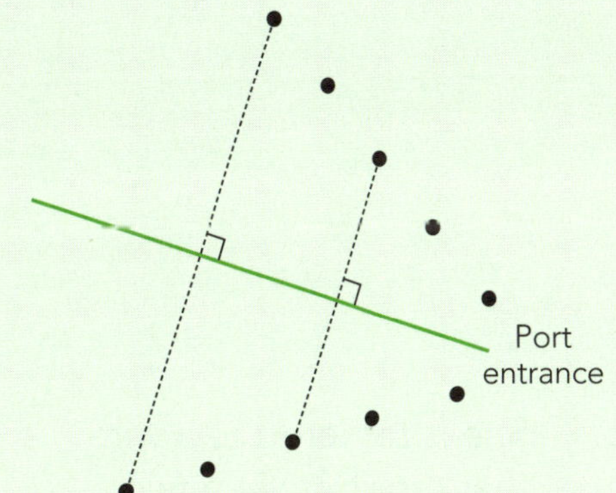


4 Two strings of decorations are fastened between the corners of a rectangular room. The diagram shows the locus for two more strings that are to be located at equal distances from the original two strings.

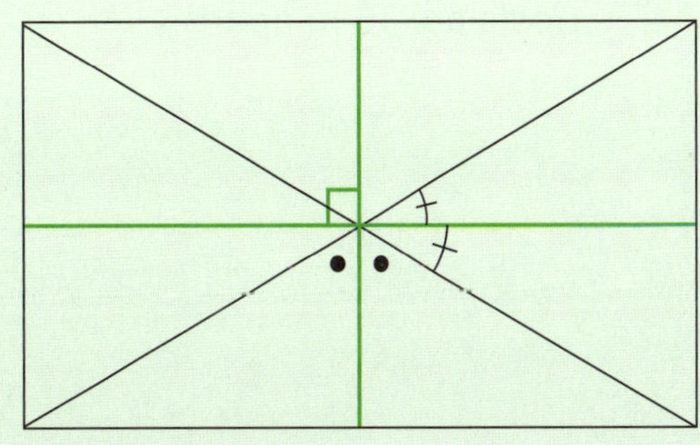

ISBN: 9780170451543 

Answer the following.

1 Gurtee the goat has a tether that is 4 m long. She needs to be moved around the farm to different places. Sketch and shade the locus of all the points she can reach for each of these positions.

a She is tethered to a point (A) in the middle of the side of a 10 m long shed (which she cannot climb).

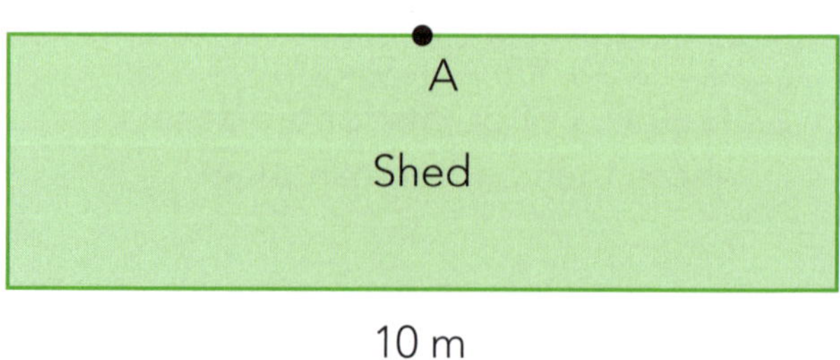


b She is tethered to a post that is 3 m away from a fence (which she cannot jump).

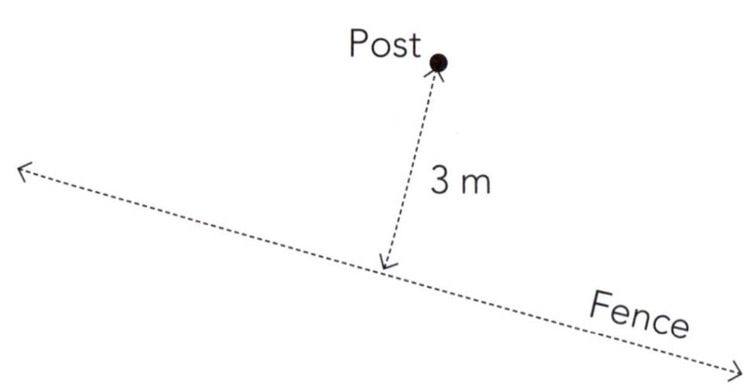


c She is tethered to a wire that runs between two posts (A and B) in the middle of a paddock. The posts are 16 m apart.

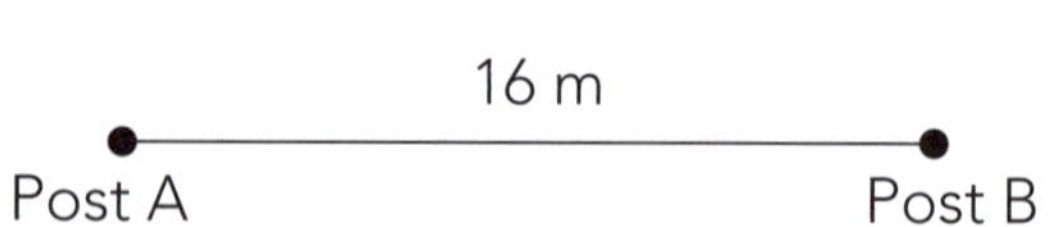




ISBN: 9780170451543

**d** At night, Gurtee is tethered to a point (A). The point is at the midpoint of one side. There is a delicious thistle (✶) 1 m from the midpoint of the back wall of her shed. Sketch the locus of the area that she can reach. (She cannot climb over the shed.)

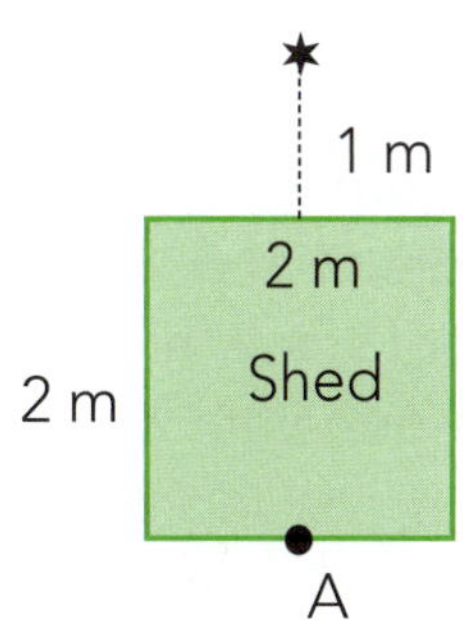


Can she reach the thistle?

______________________________

**2** Kara is making a star. It has six arms, and she wants to add six additional shorter arms that must be the same distance from each adjacent original arm. Sketch the locus for the new shorter arms.

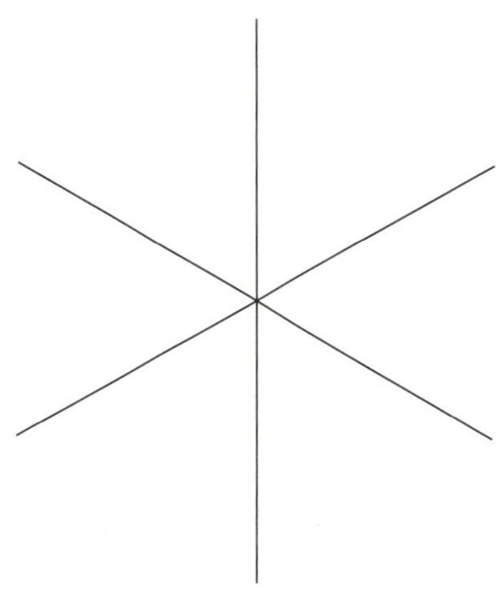

**3** During a PE class, the students are asked to take any position they like, provided they are the same distance from two points. One point is at the corner of a classroom block, and the other is a tree. Sketch the locus for the places they can stand.

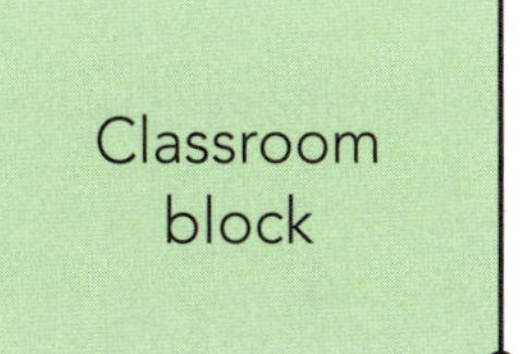


● Tree

ISBN: 9780170451543  

# Distances: scales on maps and diagrams

- Using the terminology of transformation geometry, maps are **enlargements** with scale factors of **less than 1**.
- Diagrams of small things are **enlargements** with scale factors of **more than 1**.
- Scales are generally expressed using **whole numbers**, one of which is **1**.
- Scales on maps and diagrams can come in several forms:

**1 Ratios**

**For maps or large objects:**

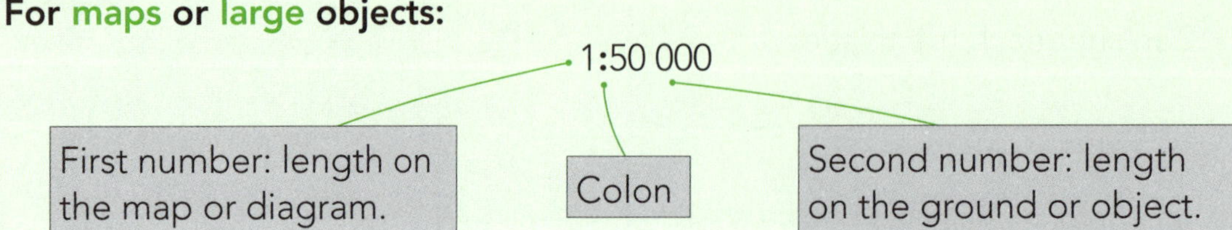


So, 1 cm on the map ≡ 50 000 cm on the ground or object.

≡ 500 m

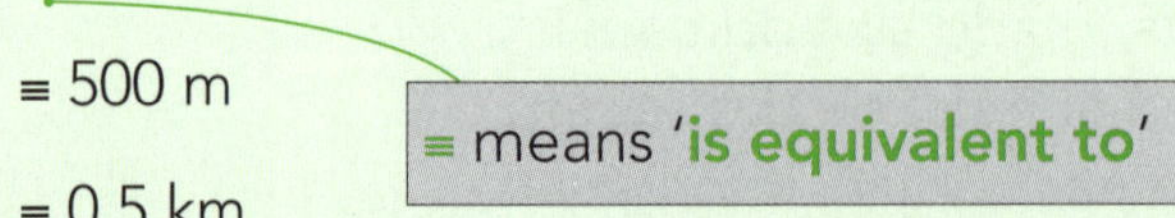


≡ 0.5 km

**For small objects:**

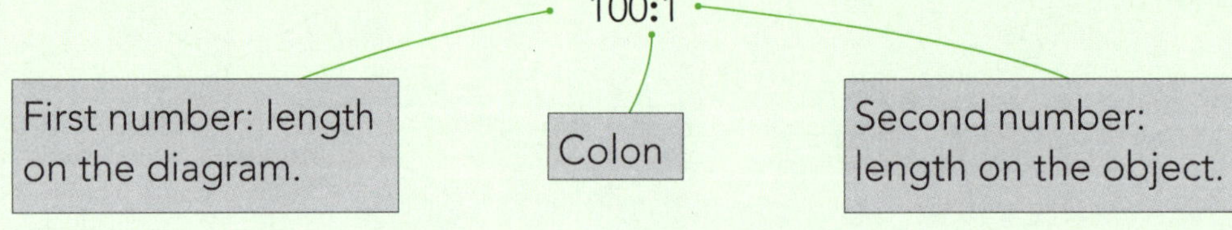


So, 100 cm on the diagram ≡ 1 cm on the object.

1 cm ≡ 0.01 cm

1 cm ≡ 0.1 mm

**2 Diagrams**

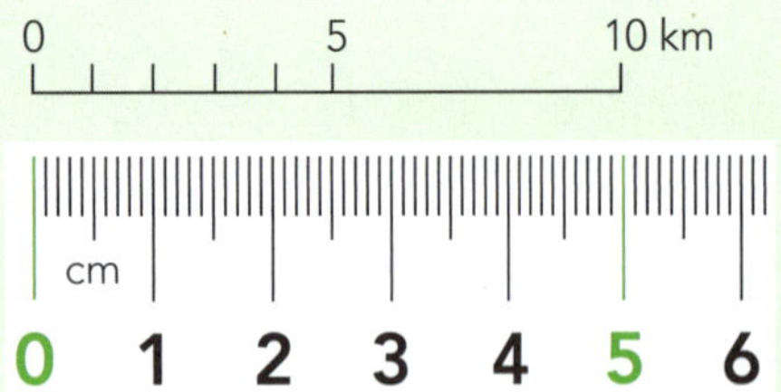


5 cm on the map ≡ 10 km on the ground
1 cm on the map ≡ 2 km on the ground

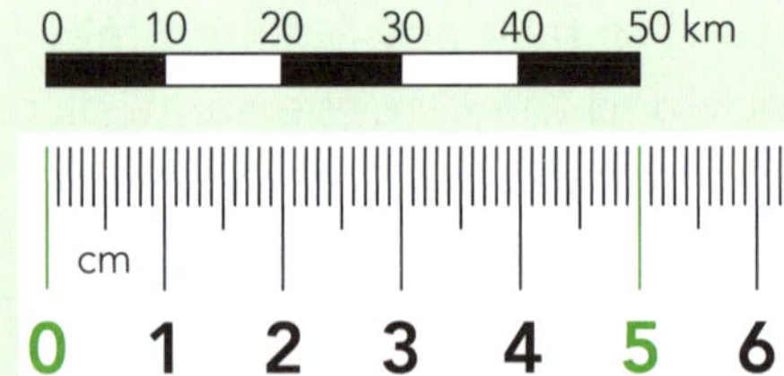


5 cm on the map ≡ 50 km on the ground
1 cm on the map ≡ 10 km on the ground

**3 Sometimes you will be told the scale**

**Example:** 1 cm = 1.5 km

So, 1 cm on the diagram ≡ 1.5 km on the object.



ISBN: 9780170451543

**Examples:** Calculate the distance between points A and B.

**1**

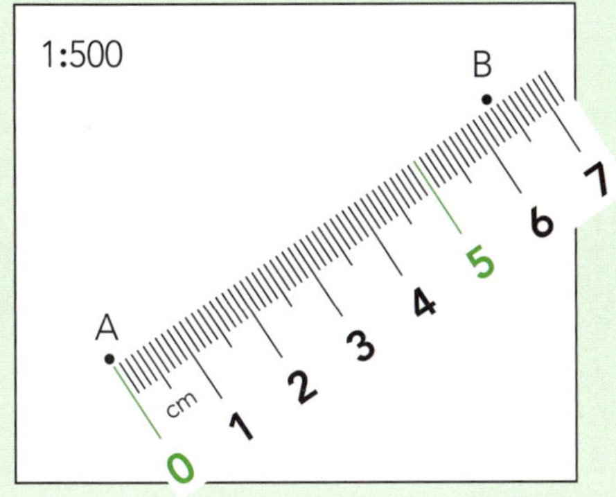


1:500 means 1 cm ≡ 500 cm

∴ 6.3 cm ≡ 6.3 x 500 cm

≡ 3150 cm

≡ 31.50 m

∴ is a short way of writing 'therefore'.

**2**

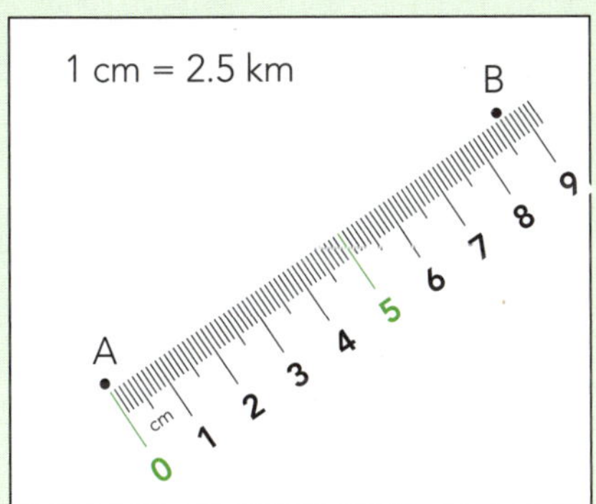


1 cm ≡ 2.5 km

∴ 8.6 cm ≡ 8.6 x 2.5 km

≡ 21.5 km

**3**

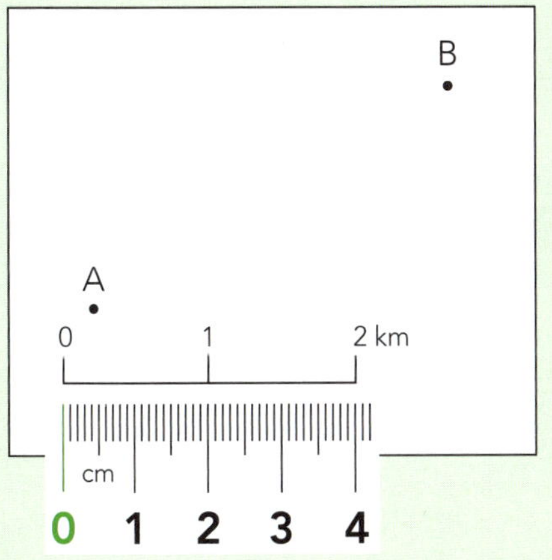


**Step 1: Calculate scale**

4 cm ≡ 2 km

∴ 1 cm ≡ 0.5 km

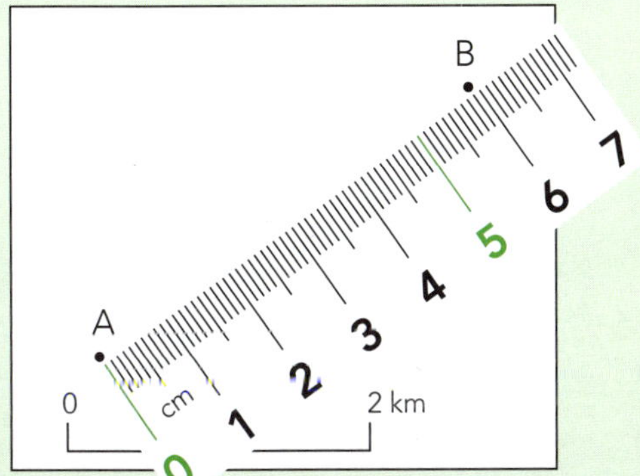


**Step 2: Calculate distance**

1 cm ≡ 0.5 km

∴ 5.9 cm ≡ 5.9 x 0.5 km

≡ 2.95 km

ISBN: 9780170451543 

4

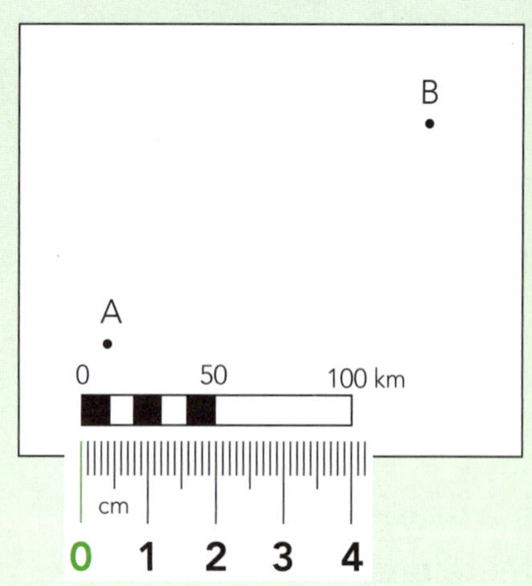


**Step 1: Calculate scale**

4 cm ≡ 100 km

∴ 1 cm ≡ 25 km

**Step 2: Calculate distance**

1 cm ≡ 25 km

∴ 5.8 cm ≡ 5.8 x 25 km

≡ 145 km

For each of the following ratios, calculate what length 1 cm would represent on a diagram or map.

**1** 1:100

______ 1 cm ≡ ______

______

**2** 1:1 000 000

______ 1 cm ≡ ______

______

**3** 1:5000

______ 1 cm ≡ ______

______

**4** 1:2500

______ 1 cm ≡ ______

______

**5** 20:1

20 cm ≡ 1 cm 1 cm ≡ 0.5 mm

1 cm ≡ $\frac{1}{20}$ cm

**6** 5:1

______ 1 cm ≡ ______

______



 ISBN: 9780170451543

Using a ruler, measure the distances between A and B on this page. Then calculate the distance between the points. Round your answers to the nearest metre.

**7**

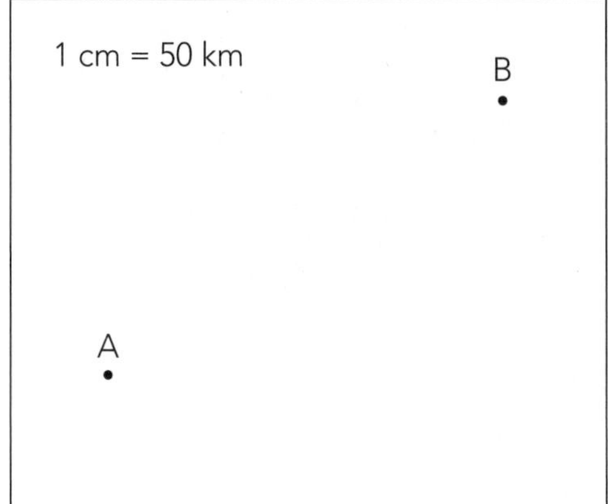


**8**

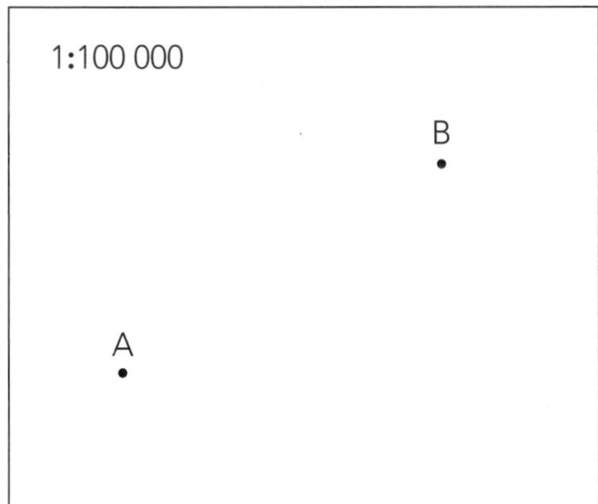


**9**

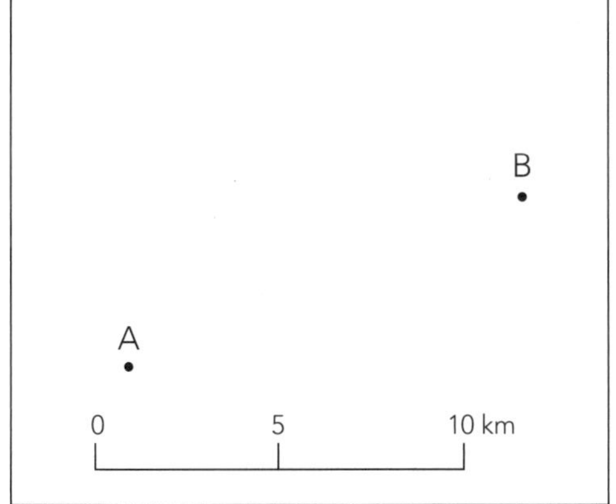


**10**

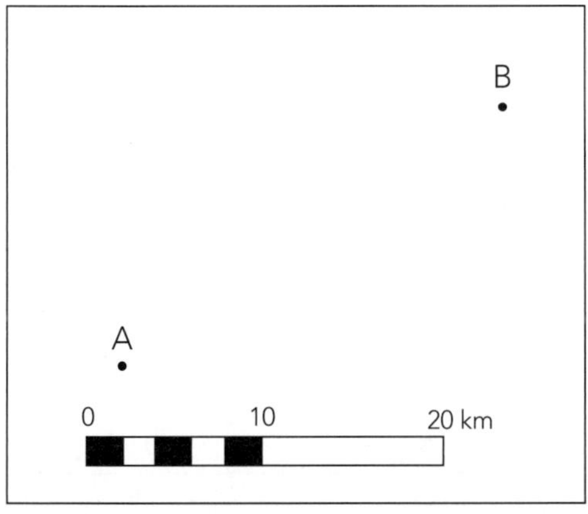

Find the direct distances between the centres of the green crosses on the map. The scale is 1:500 000.

**11 a** Between Fort Francis and Castleton.

**b** Between the northern tip of the Snake Islands and the chin of Skull Rock.

**c** Between the door of Midland Port and the treasure chest.

**d** Between the top of Devil's Mouth and the top of the 'Maya Ruines'.



 ISBN: 9780170451543

**12** The scale for this house plan is 1:100. Find the following, rounding your answers to the nearest 0.1 m.

**a** The external dimensions of the house (including the terrace).

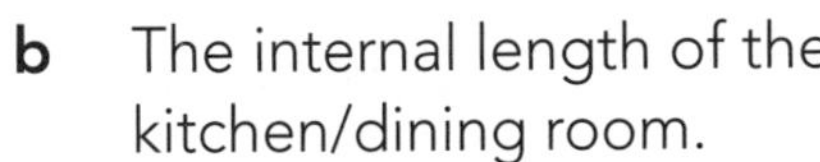

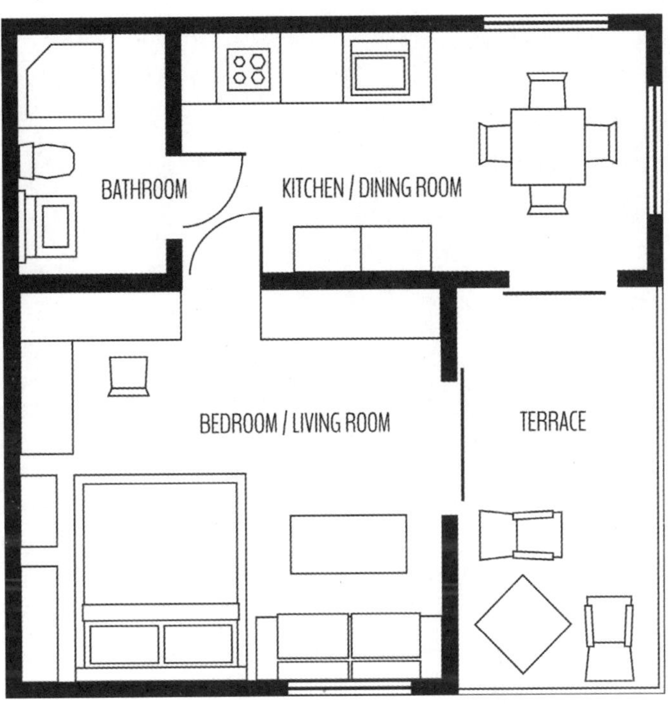


**b** The internal length of the kitchen/dining room.

**c** The outer dimensions of the bed.

**13** The scale for this diagram of a fly is 10:1.

**a** How long is the body (including the head)?

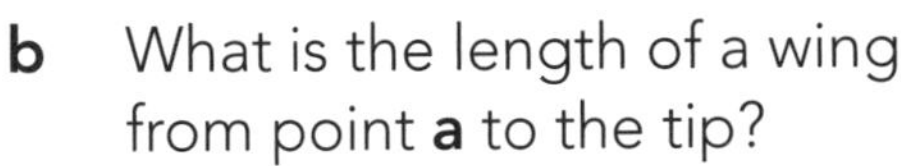

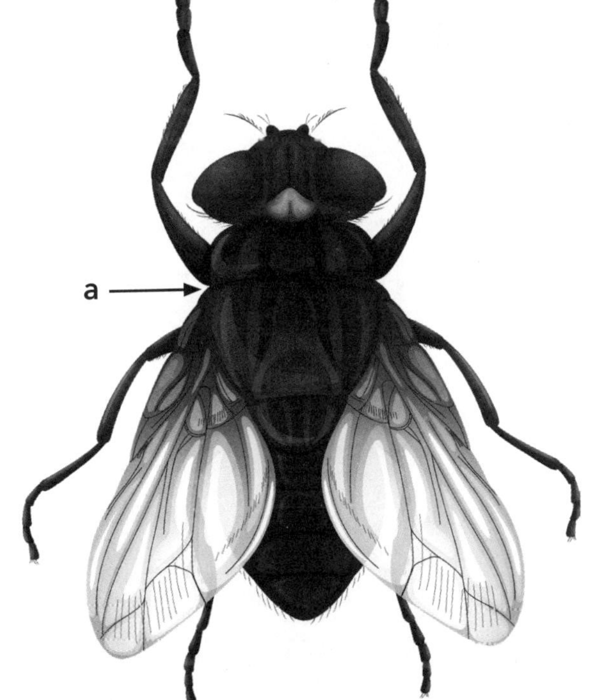


**b** What is the length of a wing from point **a** to the tip?

**c** What is the width of its head?

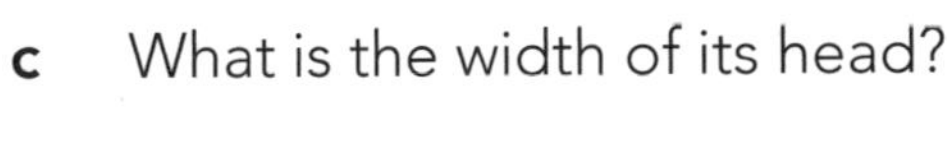

ISBN: 9780170451543 

# Mixing it up

 ISBN: 9780170451543

Without using a protractor, estimate the bearings between each of the following pairs of points (places). Then use a ruler along with the scale to estimate the distances to the nearest 10 km. Select your bearings from the list below. Some values may be used more than once, and some may not be needed.

Bearings:

| 045° | 225° | 315° | 135° | 180° | 090° | 000° | 270° |
|---|---|---|---|---|---|---|---|

**1** Reefton to Hokitika

Bearing: ________

Distance: ________

**2** Gisborne to Kaikoura

Bearing: ________

Distance: ________

**3** Hāwera to Napier

Bearing: ________

Distance: ________

**4** Christchurch to Greymouth

Bearing: ________

Distance: ________

**5** Invercargill to Timaru

Bearing: ________

Distance: ________

**6** Whakatāne to Whangārei

Bearing: ________

Distance: ________

**7** Picton to Otiria

Bearing: ________

Distance: ________

**8** Whakatāne to Gisborne

Bearing: ________

Distance: ________

**9** Wellington to Gisborne

Bearing: ________

Distance: ________

**10** Whangārei to Gisborne

Bearing: ________

Distance: ________

**11** Ashburton to Haast

Bearing: ________

Distance: ________

**12** Collingwood to Blenheim

Bearing: ________

Distance: ________

ISBN: 9780170451543 

# Transformation geometry

- Transformation geometry is changing figures by following certain rules.
- The transformed figure is called the **image**.
- A transformation may change the size, shape, or orientation of the image.
- Properties that **remain the same** when a figure is transformed are said to be **invariant**.

**Properties of transformations**

| | |
|---|---|
| **Size** | Is the image **bigger or smaller** than the original figure? |
| **Shape** | Are the **angles** within the image **different** from those of the original figure? |
| **Orientation** | Does the image **face a different direction** from that of the original figure? |

The property tables for Translation and Reflection have been filled in for you.

## Translation

- The figure is **shifted**.

**Properties**

| | Invariant |
|---|---|
| **Size** | ✓ |
| **Shape** | ✓ |
| **Orientation** | ✓ |

## Reflection

- The figure is **reflected in a mirror** line.

**Properties**

| | Invariant |
|---|---|
| **Size** | ✓ |
| **Shape** | ✓ |
| **Orientation** | × |

The hands on these clocks would move in opposite direction, so the orientation has changed.



 ISBN: 9780170451543

Fill in the property tables for Rotation and Enlargement.

**Rotation**

- The figure **rotates around a point**.

**Properties**

| | Invariant |
|---|---|
| Size | |
| Shape | |
| Orientation | |

Hint: Do the hands on these clocks move in the same direction or not?

**Enlargement**

- The figure **gets bigger or smaller**.

**Properties**

| | Invariant |
|---|---|
| Size | |
| Shape | |
| Orientation | |

Answer the following questions.

1 Which transformation(s) result in a change of size? ________________

2 Which transformation(s) result in a change of shape? ________________

3 Which transformation(s) result in a change of orientation? ________________

ISBN: 9780170451543

# Revision of translation, reflection and rotation

Answer the following.

**1** Write vectors for the following word descriptions. (Remember: Translation)

**a** Right four and down three. $\begin{pmatrix} \\ \end{pmatrix}$

**b** Left two and up one. $\begin{pmatrix} \\ \end{pmatrix}$

**2** Write the vector for the translation of this figure. The green shape is the original.

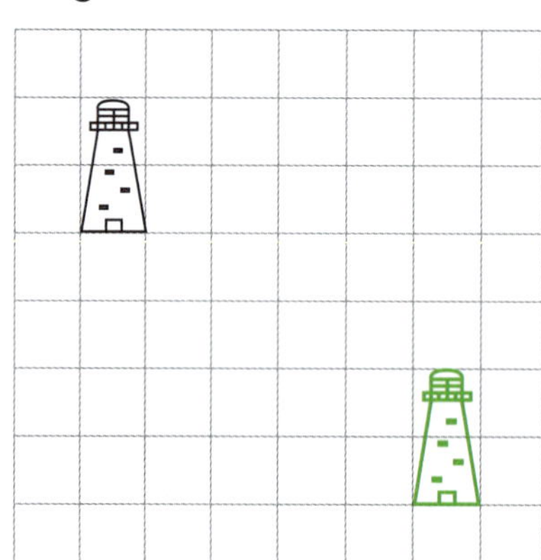

$\begin{pmatrix} \\ \end{pmatrix}$

**3** Draw the image of the figure after it has been translated by the given vector.

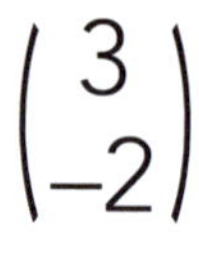

$\begin{pmatrix} 3 \\ -2 \end{pmatrix}$

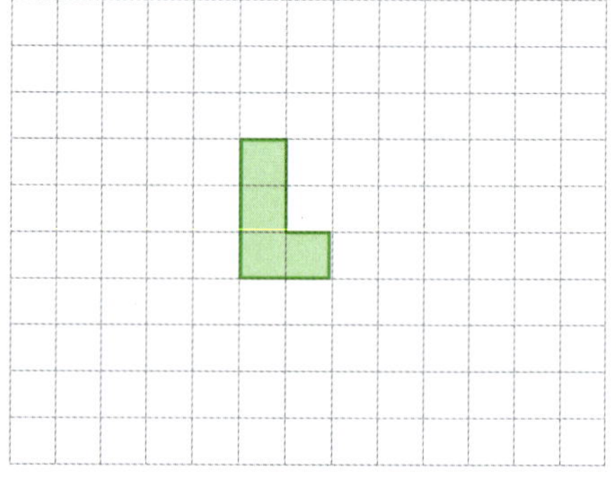

**4** Draw the mirror lines for these reflections.

**a**

**b**

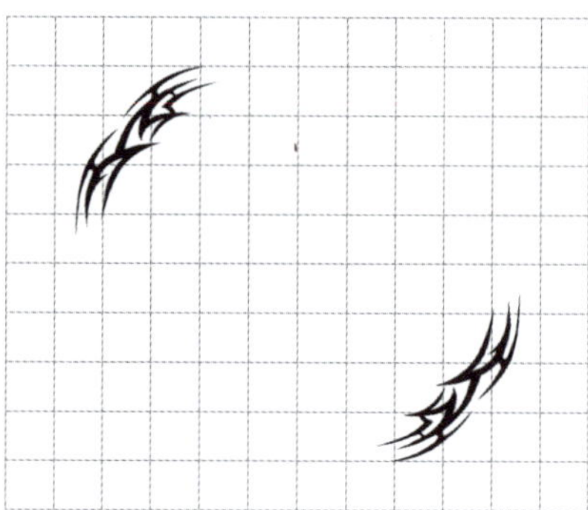

**5** Reflect the figure in the mirror line. Label any invariant points.

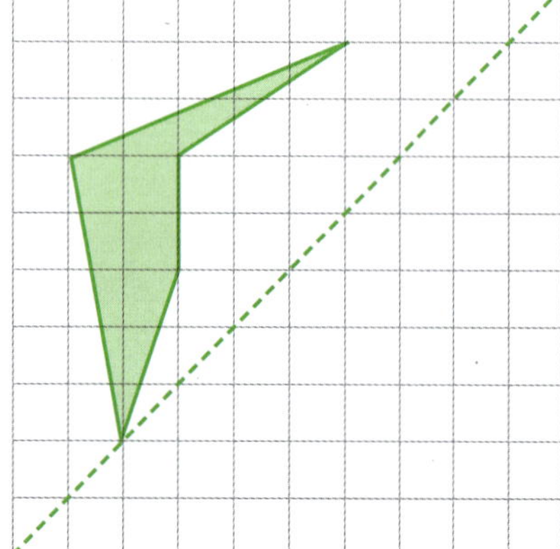

**6** Reflect each of the shaded squares in both mirror lines, and shade them appropriately.

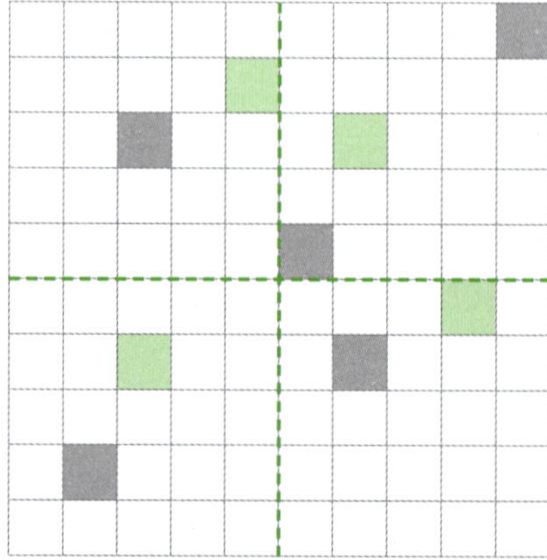



 ISBN: 9780170451543

**7** Write the order of line symmetry for these images.

**a**

Order of line symmetry = ________

**b**

Order of line symmetry = ________

**8** Write the angle of rotation for each of these figures. Remember: rotations are clockwise unless otherwise stated; the green shape is the original.

**a**

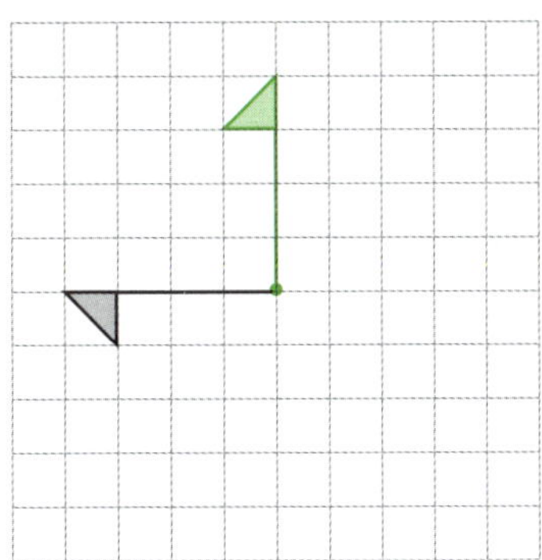

Angle of rotation = ________°

**b**

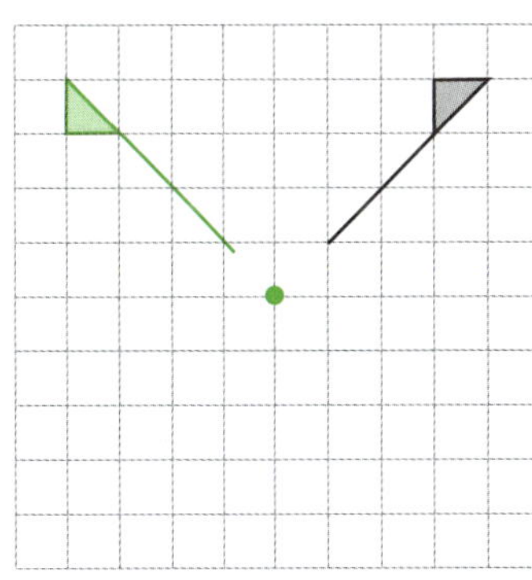

Angle of rotation = ________°

**9** **a** Rotate this figure 180° around the point.

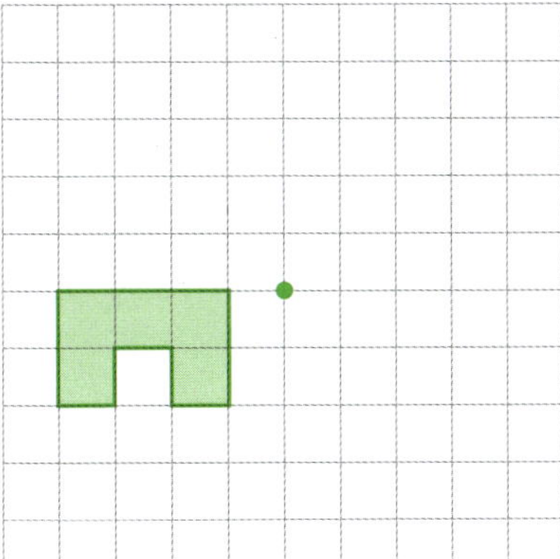

**b** Rotate this figure 270° around the point.

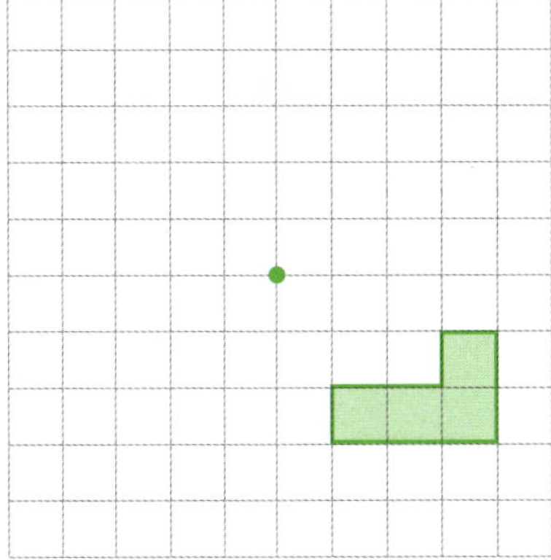

**10** Write the order of rotational symmetry for these images.

**a**

Order of rotational symmetry = ________

**b**

Order of rotational symmetry = ________

ISBN: 9780170451543 

# Enlargement

- The figure **gets bigger or smaller**.
- The **scale factor** tells us how much larger or smaller the lines in the figure become.
- The **centre** tells us the position of the image.

## Scale factor

$$\textbf{scale factor} = \frac{\textbf{length of image}}{\textbf{length of original figure}}$$

- Notice that the scale factor applies to the **lines**. The increase in **area** = (scale factor)$^2$.

**Examples:**

**1**

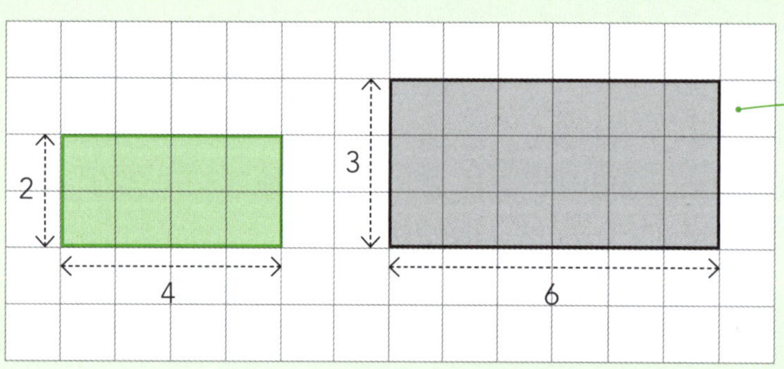


The increase to area $= \frac{18}{8} = 2.25 = \left(\frac{3}{2}\right)^2$. So the scale factor of $\frac{3}{2}$ means the area of the image is 2.25 times that of the original.

$$\text{scale factor} = \frac{\text{length of image}}{\textbf{length of original figure}} = \frac{6}{\mathbf{4}} = \frac{3}{\mathbf{2}}$$

You could write the answer as 1.5 or $1\frac{1}{2}$, but it is often more useful to leave it as a simplified improper fraction.

**2**

$$\text{scale factor} = \frac{\text{length of image}}{\textbf{length of original figure}} = \frac{4}{\mathbf{6}} = \frac{2}{\mathbf{3}}$$



ISBN: 9780170451543

Write the scale factor for these enlargements.

**1**

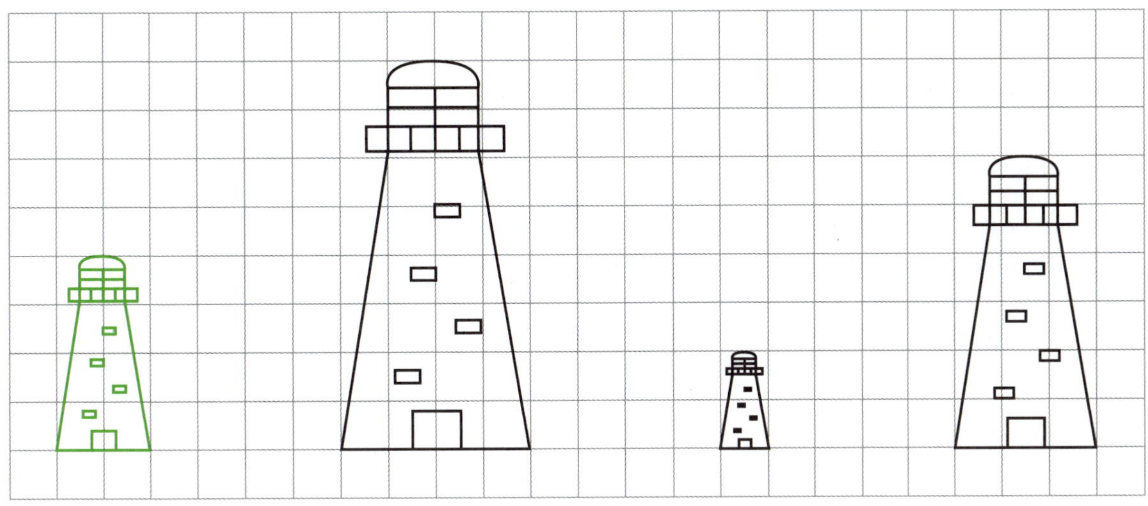

scale factor = __________ scale factor = __________ scale factor = __________

**2**

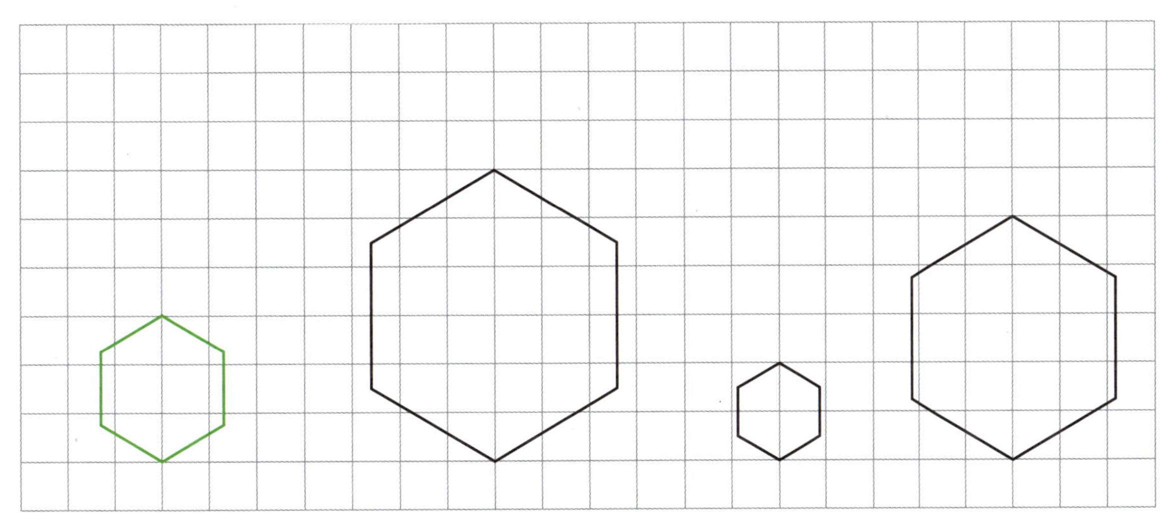

scale factor = __________ scale factor = __________ scale factor = __________

**3**

scale factor = __________ scale factor = __________ scale factor = __________ scale factor = __________

ISBN: 9780170451543 

## Finding the centre of enlargement

- The centre of englargement is the point where lines drawn through equivalent points on the figure and the image meet.

**Examples:**

**1**

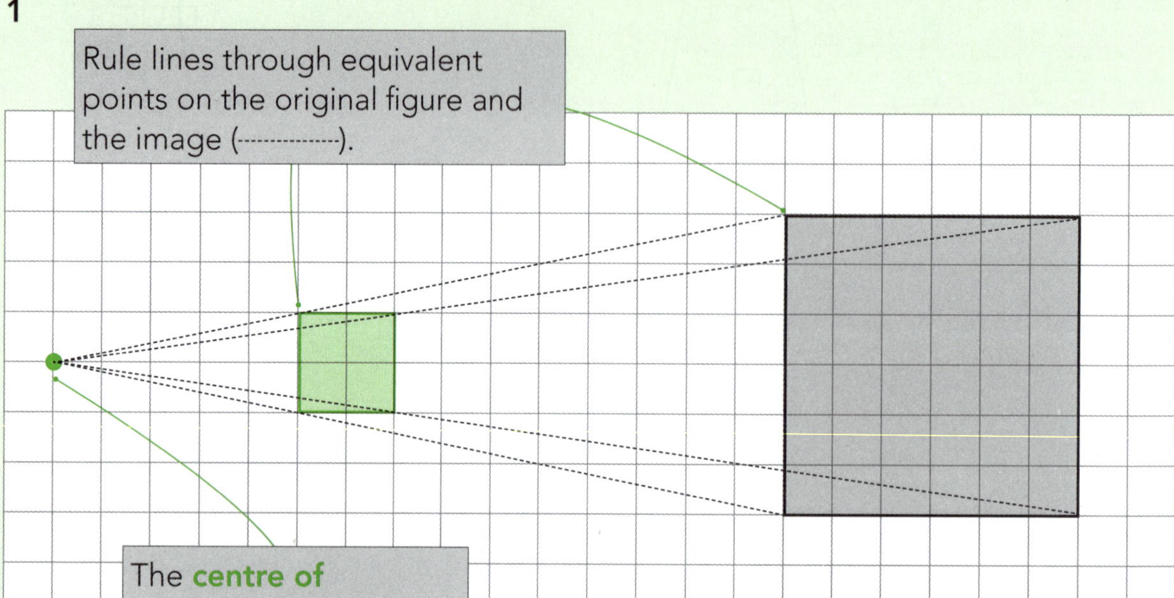


Notice that in this case, the image is **bigger** than the original figure, so the image is **beyond** both the centre of enlargement and the original figure.

**2**

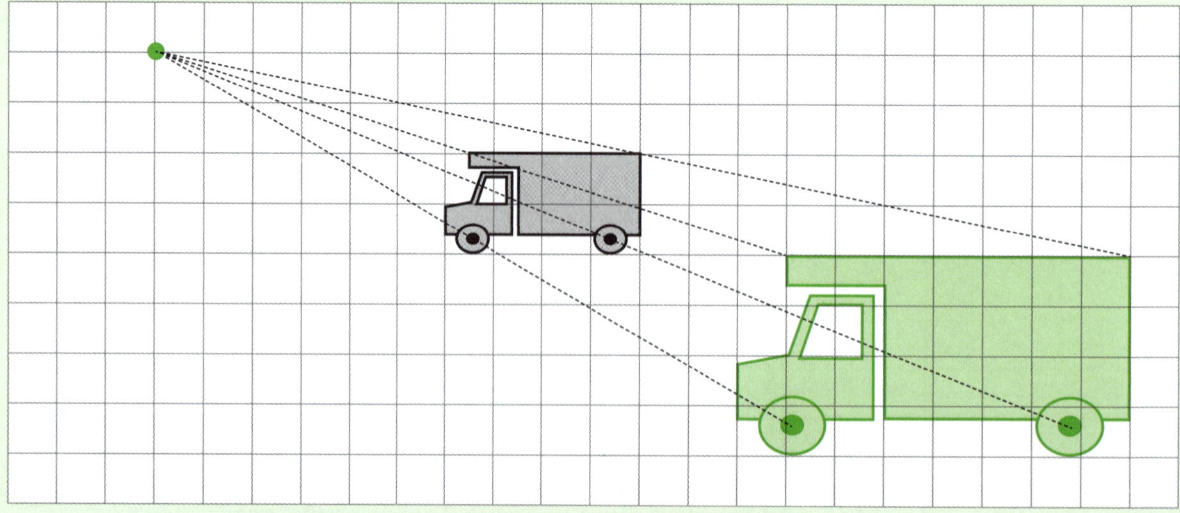

Notice that in this case, the image is **smaller** than the original figure, so the image is **between** the centre of enlargement and the original figure.



ISBN: 9780170451543

Find the centres of enlargement for these images.

**1**

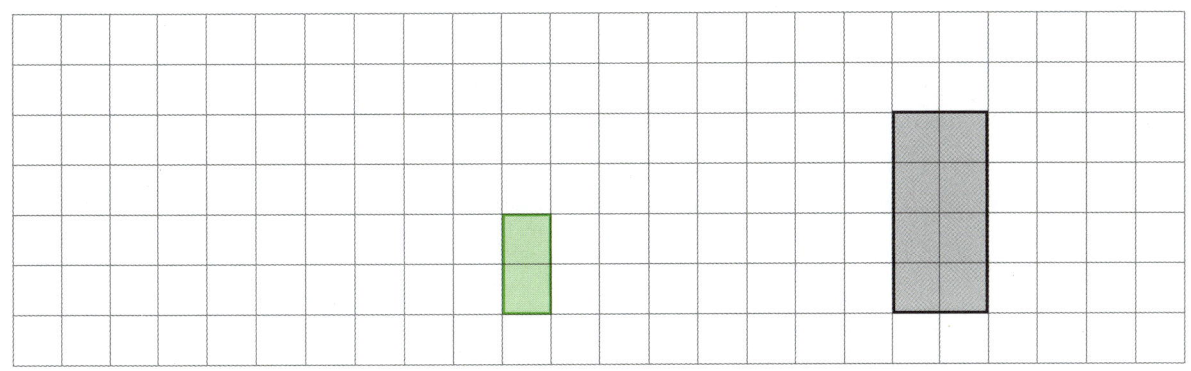

scale factor = ________

**2**

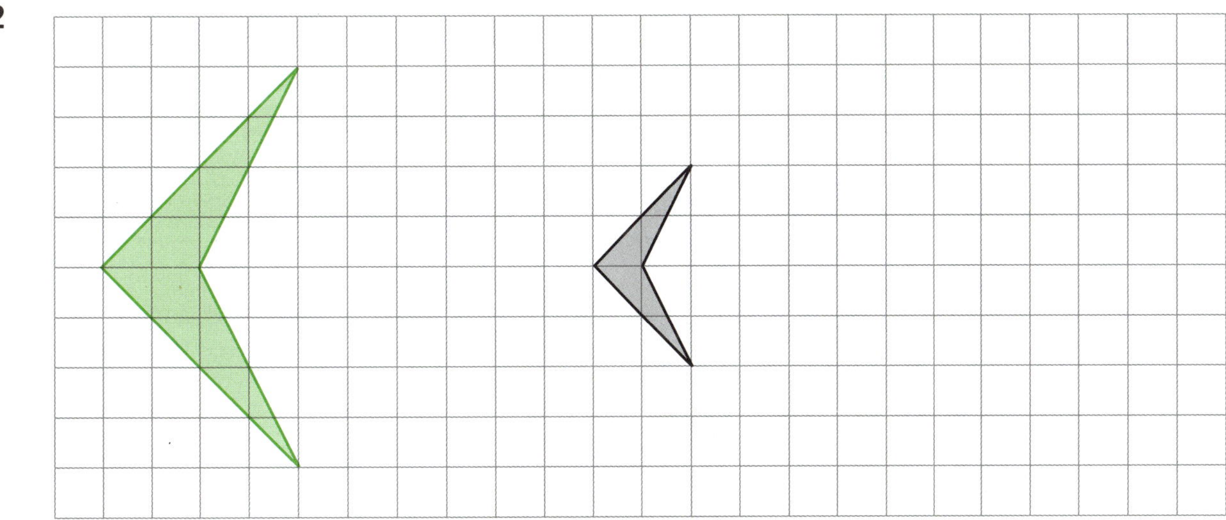

scale factor = ________

**3**

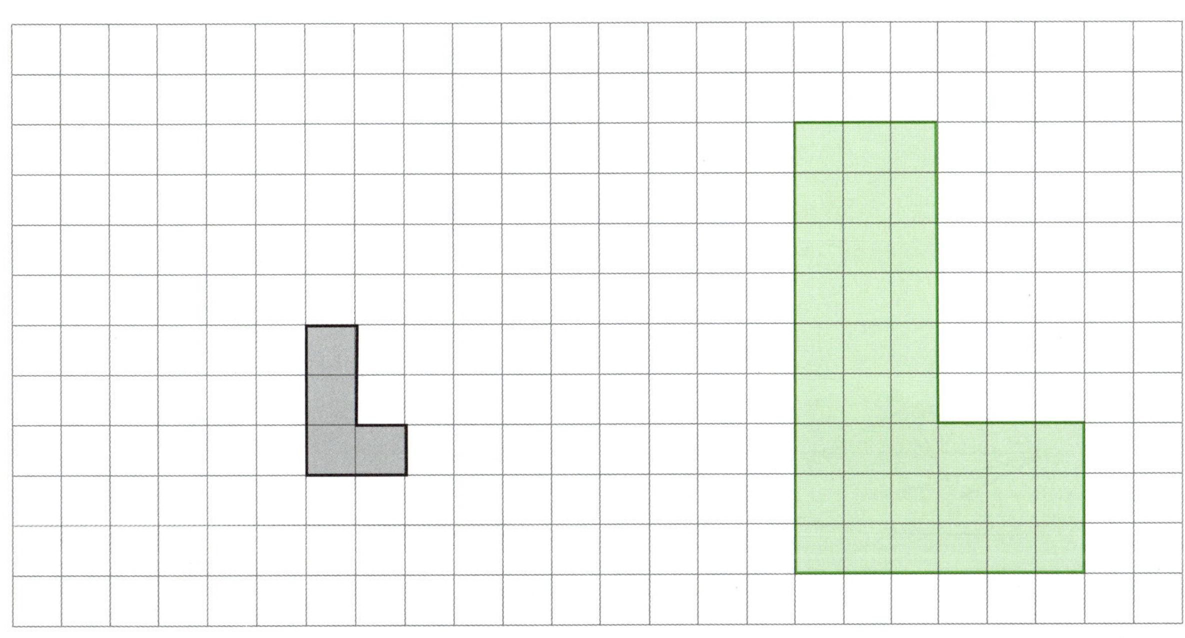

scale factor = ________

ISBN: 9780170451543

## Drawing enlargements

**Examples:**

**1** Enlarge the green triangle by a scale factor of **4**, using the green dot as the centre of enlargement.

**Step 1:** Write the distance and direction from the centre to points on the original figure.

Point **A**: $\begin{pmatrix} 4 \\ 1 \end{pmatrix}$ Point **B**: $\begin{pmatrix} 5 \\ -1 \end{pmatrix}$ Point **C**: $\begin{pmatrix} 3 \\ 0 \end{pmatrix}$

**Step 2:** Multiply each vector by the scale factor — in this case **4**.

x **4**

Point A: $\begin{pmatrix} 16 \\ 4 \end{pmatrix}$ Point B: $\begin{pmatrix} 20 \\ -4 \end{pmatrix}$ Point C: $\begin{pmatrix} 12 \\ 0 \end{pmatrix}$

**Step 3:** Draw the enlarged vectors, starting at the centre of enlargement. The points at the ends of these vectors are at the vertices of the enlarged figure.

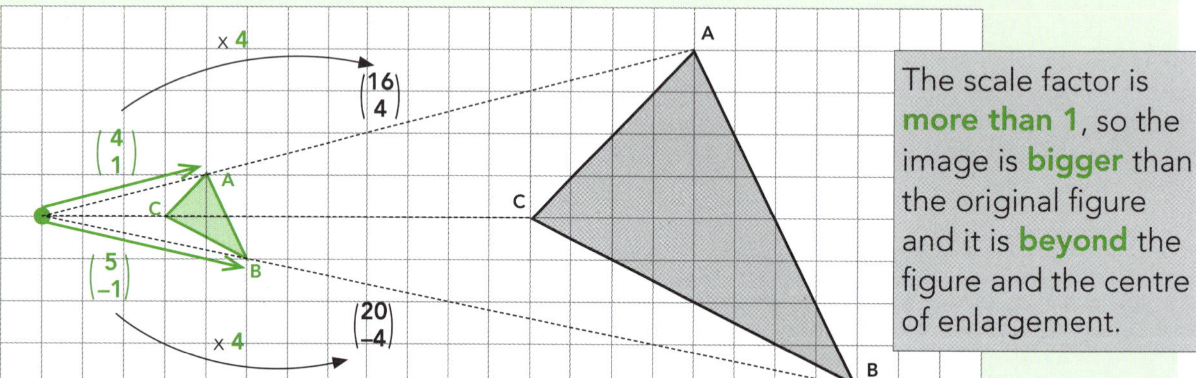


**2** Enlarge the green triangle by a scale factor of $\frac{1}{3}$.

Point **A**: $\begin{pmatrix} 9 \\ 3 \end{pmatrix}$ Point **B**: $\begin{pmatrix} 6 \\ -3 \end{pmatrix}$ Point **C**: $\begin{pmatrix} 12 \\ -3 \end{pmatrix}$ Point **D**: $\begin{pmatrix} 15 \\ 0 \end{pmatrix}$

x $\frac{1}{3}$

Point A: $\begin{pmatrix} 3 \\ 1 \end{pmatrix}$ Point B: $\begin{pmatrix} 2 \\ -1 \end{pmatrix}$ Point C: $\begin{pmatrix} 4 \\ -1 \end{pmatrix}$ Point C: $\begin{pmatrix} 5 \\ 0 \end{pmatrix}$

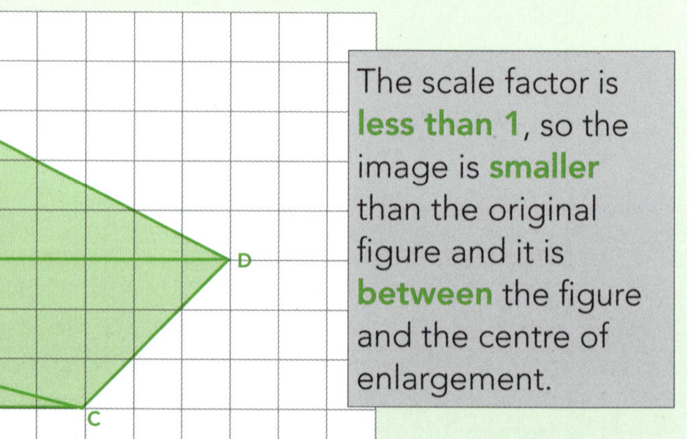


Note: You do not need to plot every point like this. Once you have one or two points, the shape will tell you where the rest are.



ISBN: 9780170451543

Some of these enlargements have been started for you. Complete them.

**1** scale factor = 3

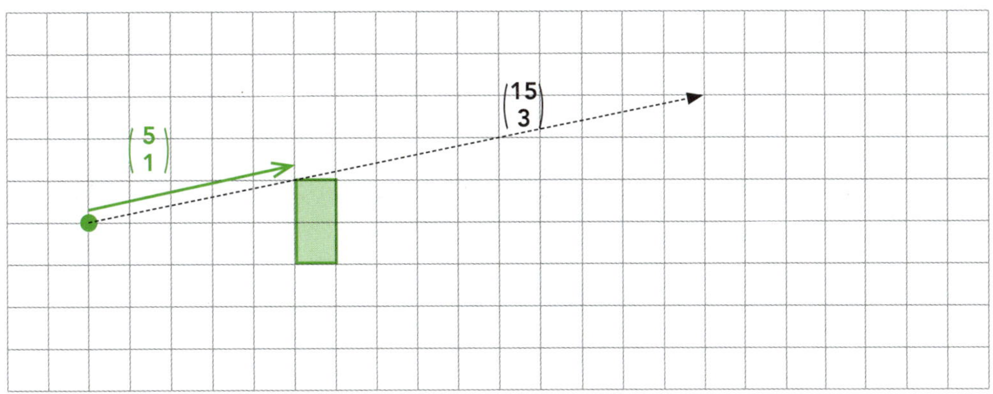


**2** scale factor = 2

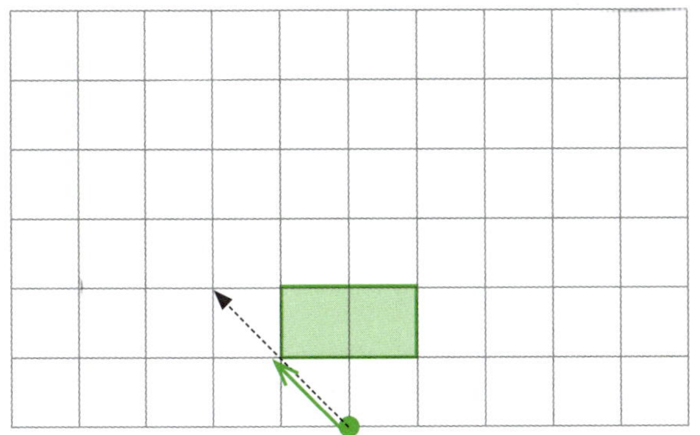

**3** scale factor = $\frac{1}{2}$

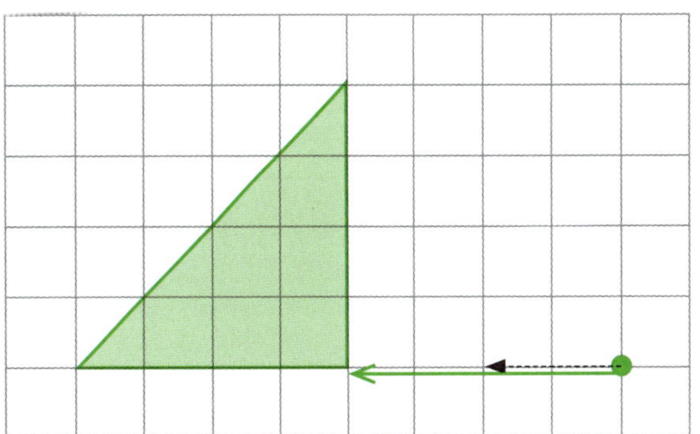

**4** scale factor = 4

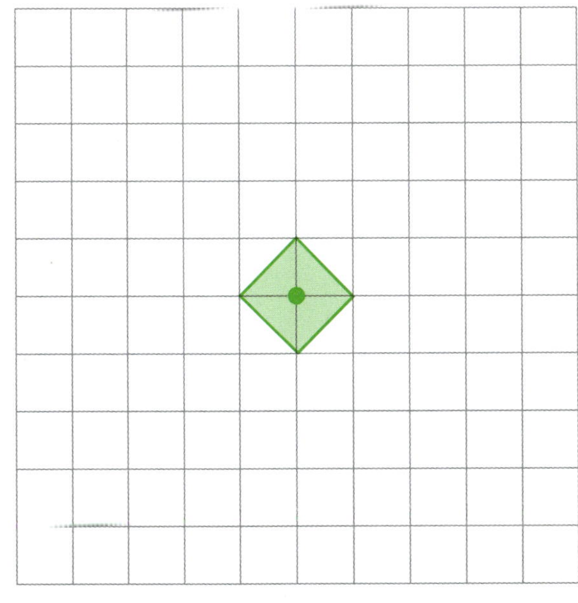

**5** scale factor = $\frac{3}{2}$

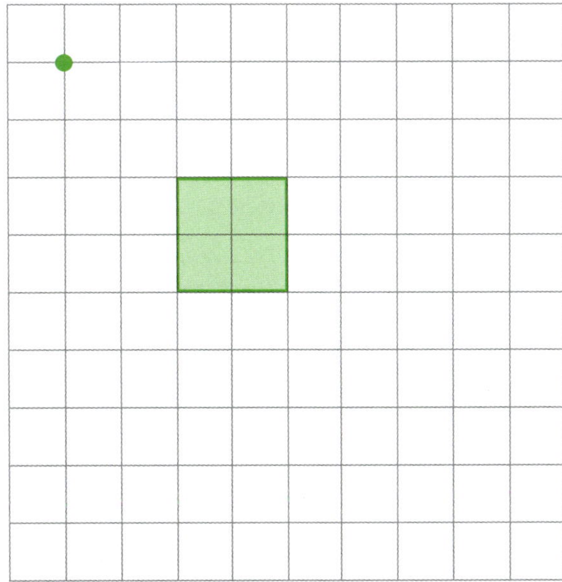

ISBN: 9780170451543 

# The theorem of Pythagoras

## Activity

**1** Trace the two grey squares containing the numbers 1–5 onto a piece of paper.

**2** Cut out your copies of these squares.

**3** Cut along the dotted lines on the bigger grey square.

**4** Like a jigsaw, fit pieces 1–5 onto the large (green) square, and stick them down.

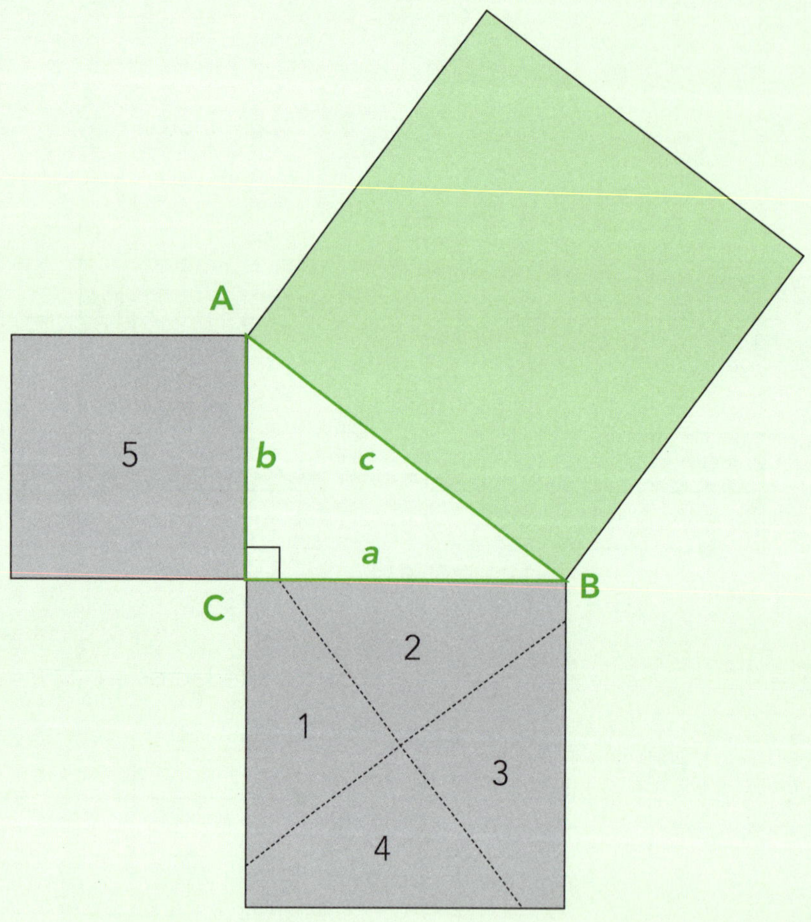


**Complete:**

- The area of the (green) square = $c^2$
- The area of the bottom square (containing 1, 2, 3 and 4) = ________
- The area of the smallest square (5) = ________

So $c^2$ = ________ + ________

**You have just illustrated the theorem of Pythagoras.**



ISBN: 9780170451543

- The theorem of Pythagoras applies to **right-angled** triangles only.
- The longest side of the triangle is called the **hypotenuse**.
- The hypotenuse is always **opposite the right angle**.
- The theorem of Pythagoras is used for finding **lengths** of sides.

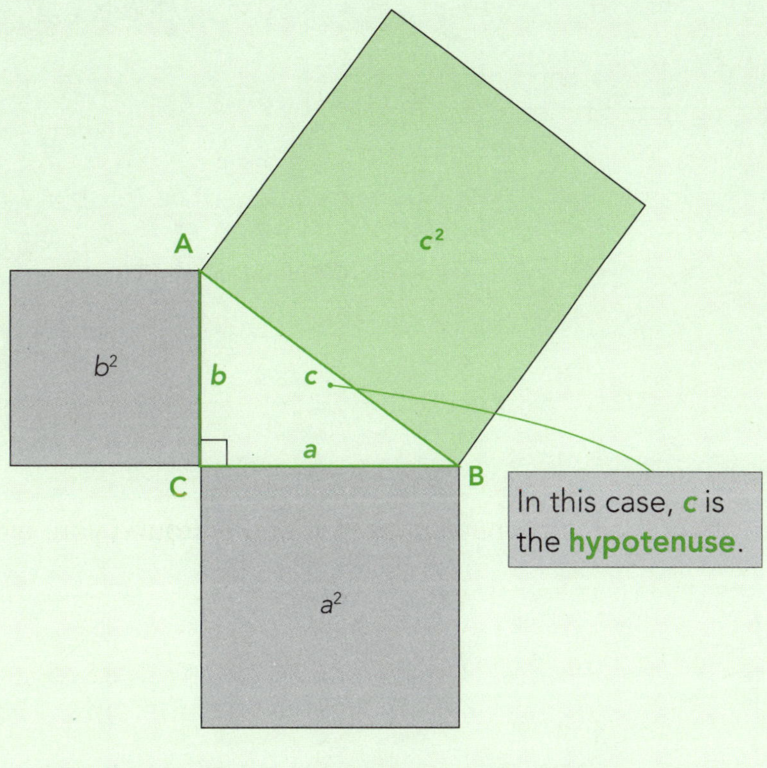


**hypotenuse² = short side² + short side²**

$$c^2 = a^2 + b^2$$

## Finding the length of the hypotenuse

**Examples:**

**1** Calculate the length of $c$.

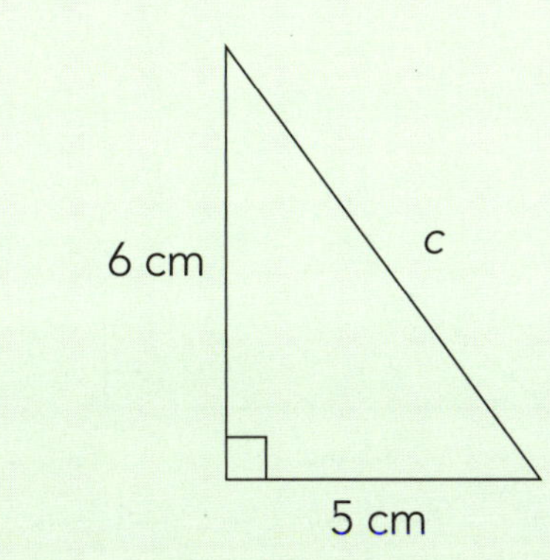


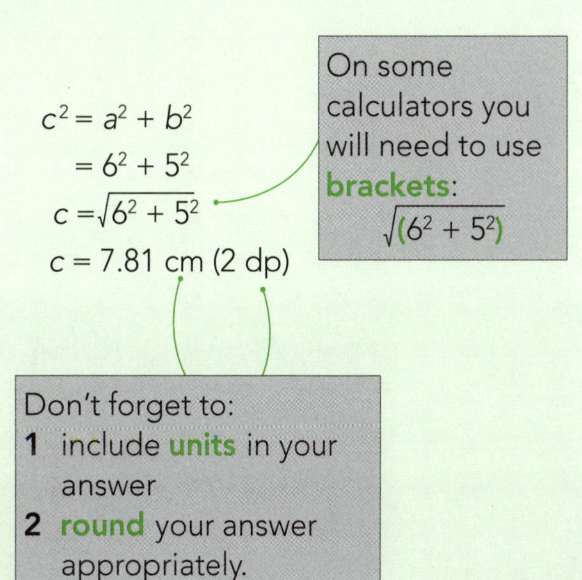

**2** Sometimes,
- the letters may **not** be *a*, *b* and *c*
- the triangle might be at a **different orientation**.

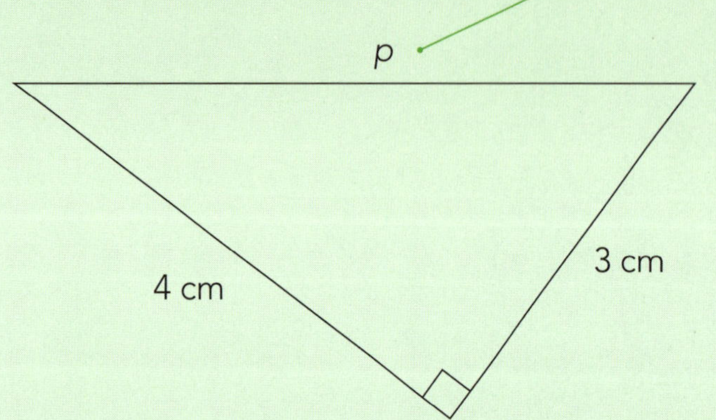


p is opposite the right angle, so ***p* is the hypotenuse**. This means that $p^2$ must be **on its own** on one side of the = sign.

$$p^2 = 4^2 + 3^2$$
$$p = \sqrt{4^2 + 3^2}$$
$$p = 5.00 \text{ cm (2 dp)}$$

**Think** about your answer. Does it seem about right?

Calculate the length of the hypotenuse in each triangle. Round your answers to 2 dp.

**1**

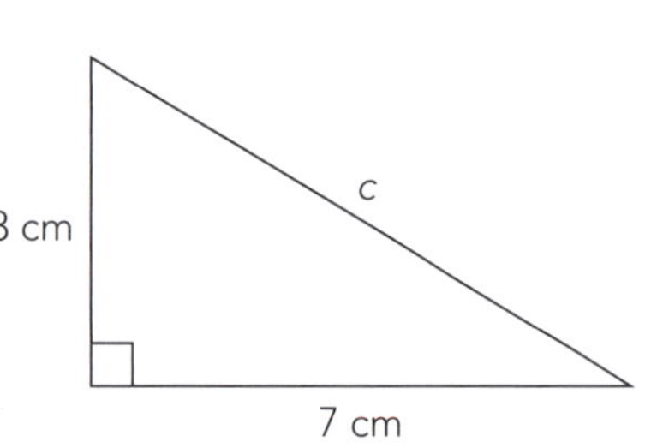


**2**

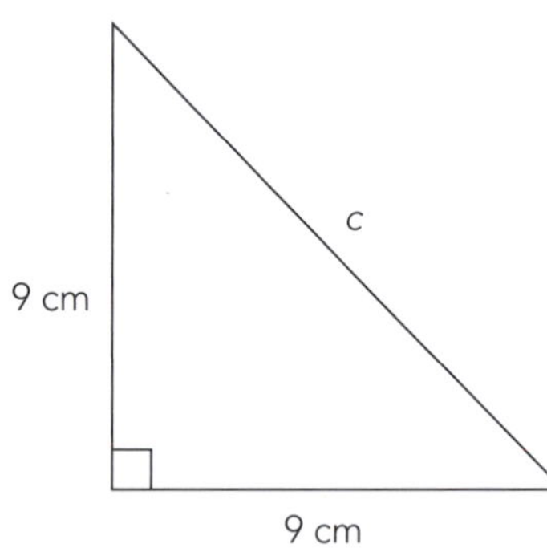


**3**

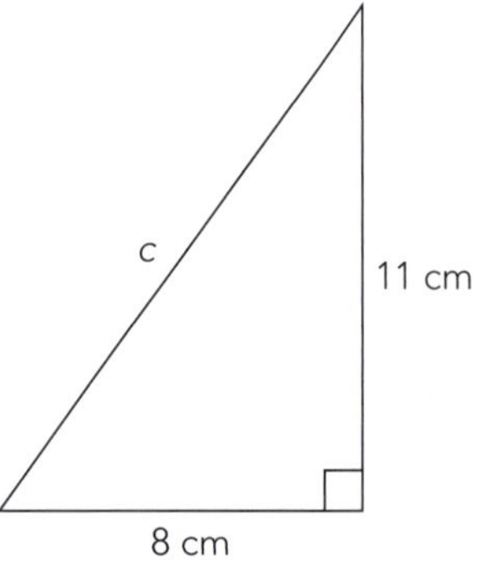


**4**

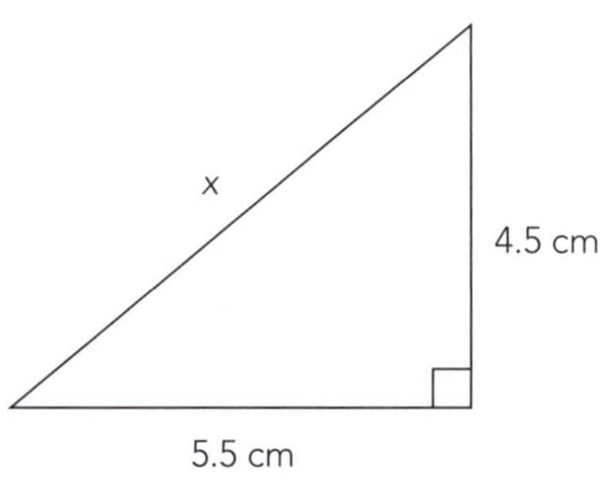




ISBN: 9780170451543

**5**

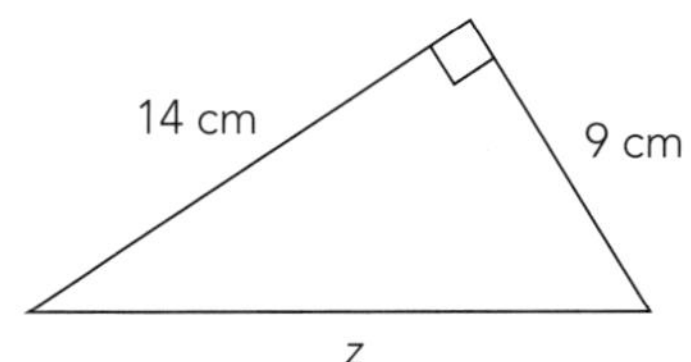


**6**

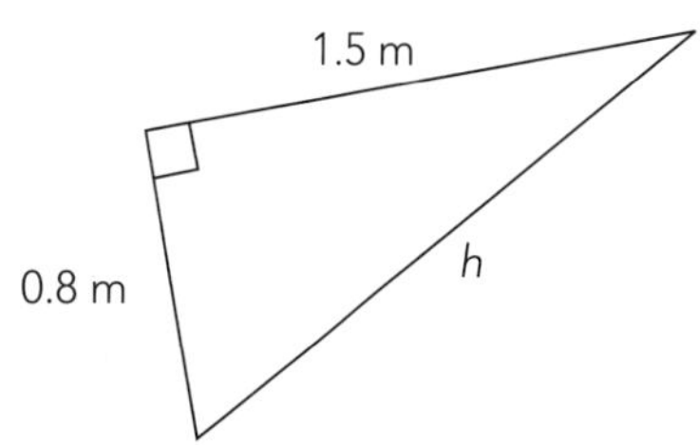


**7**

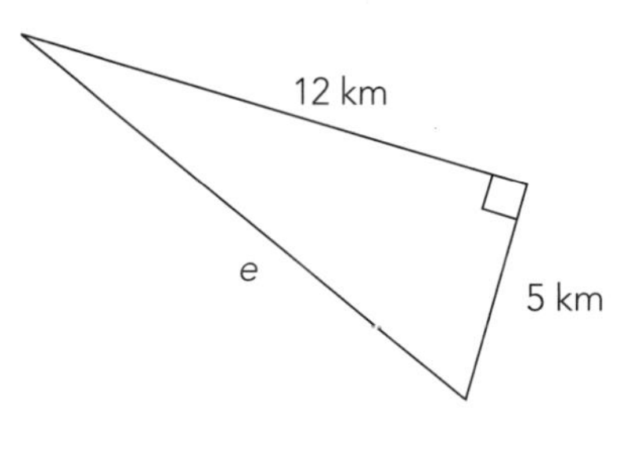


**8**

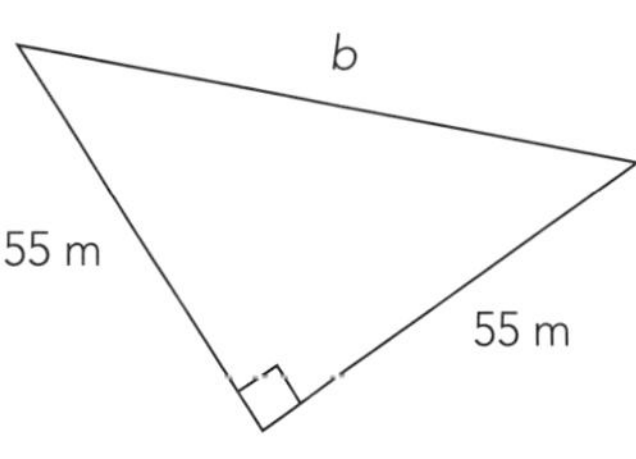


**9**

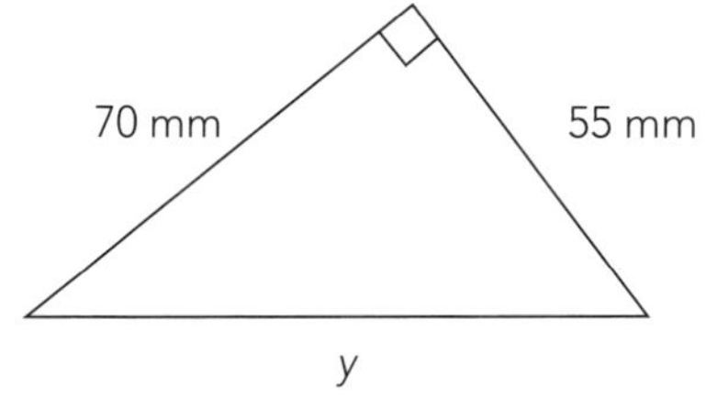


**10**

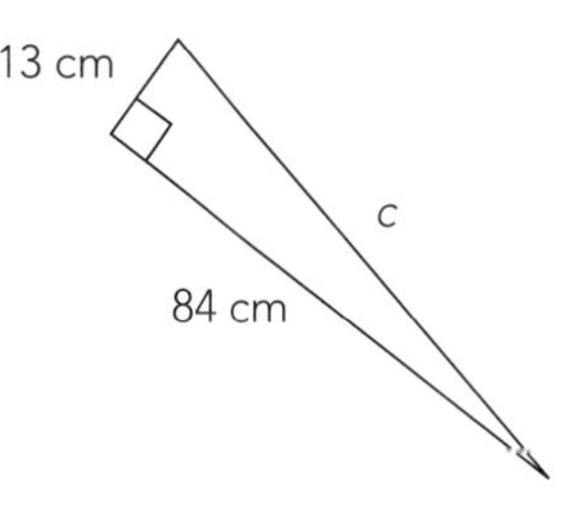


**11**

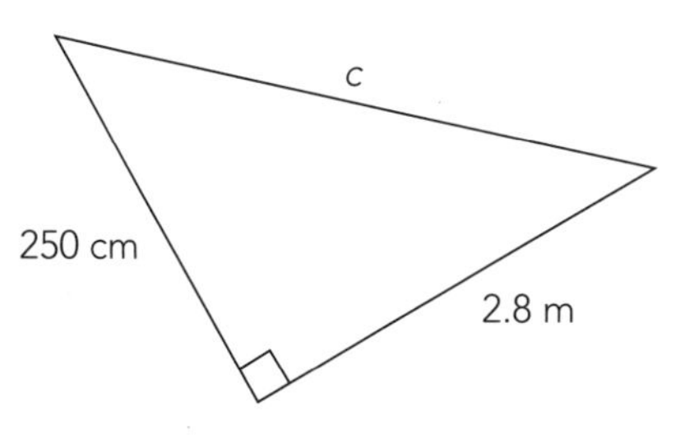


**12**

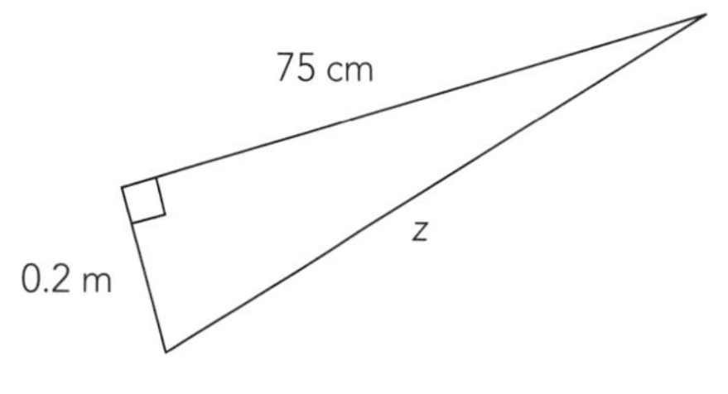


ISBN: 9780170451543

# Finding the lengths of short sides

**Example**: Calculate the length of *a*.

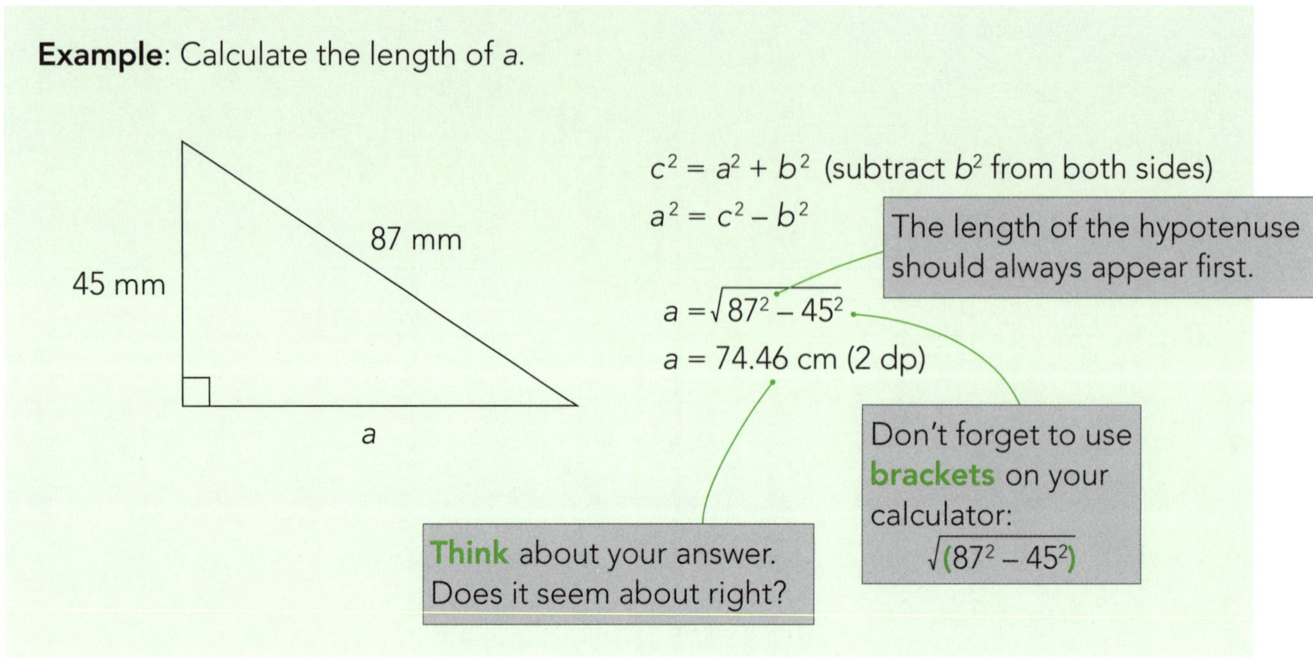


Calculate the unknown length of each triangle. Round your answers to 2 dp.

**1**

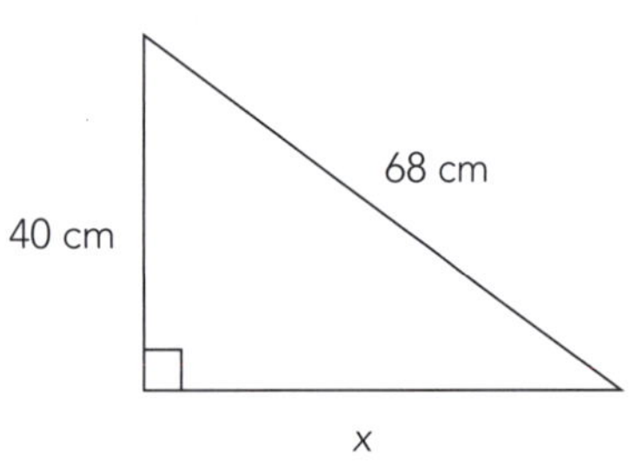


**2**

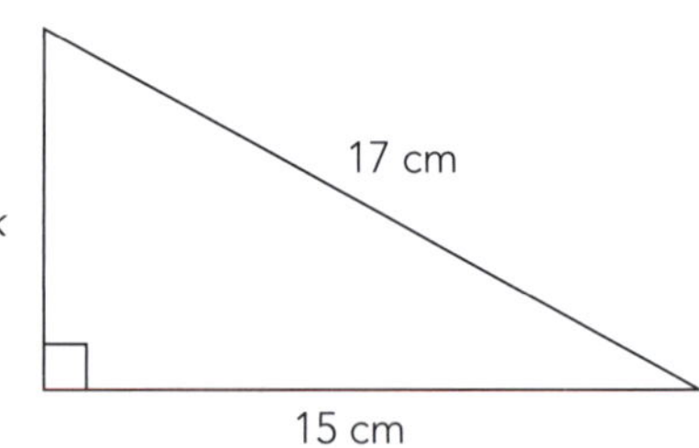


**3**

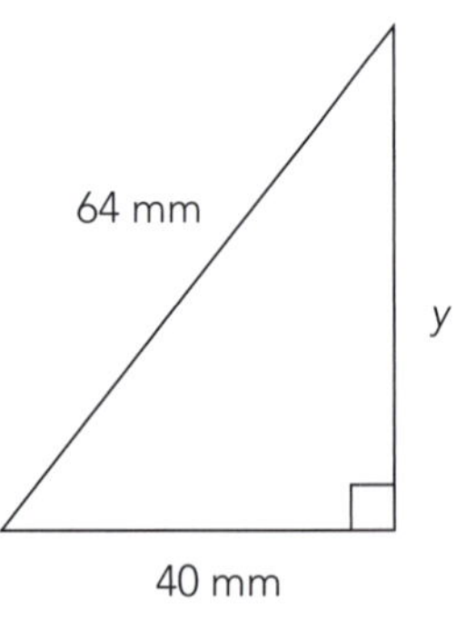


**4**

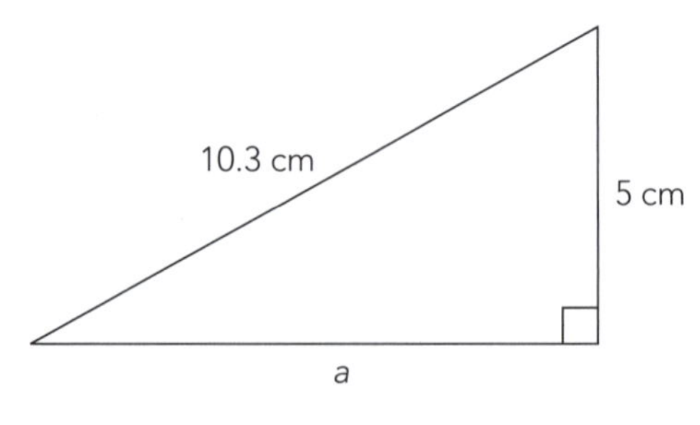




ISBN: 9780170451543

**5**

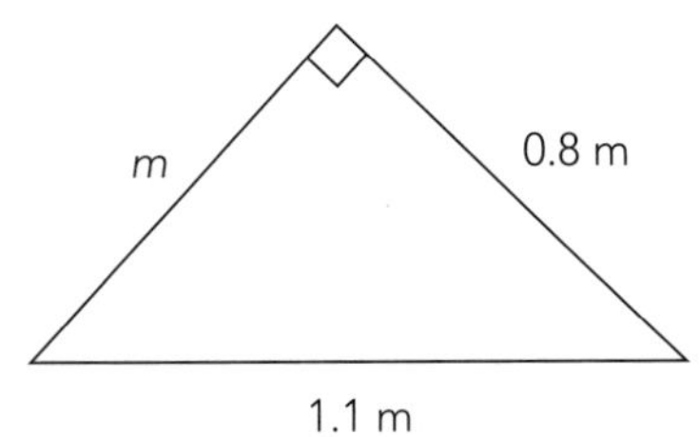


**6**

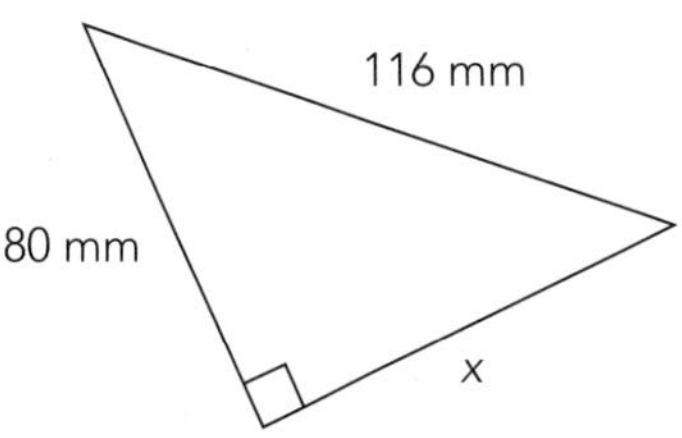


**7**

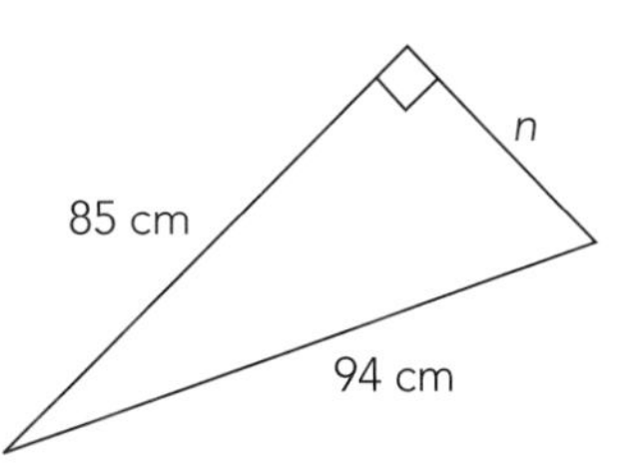


**8**

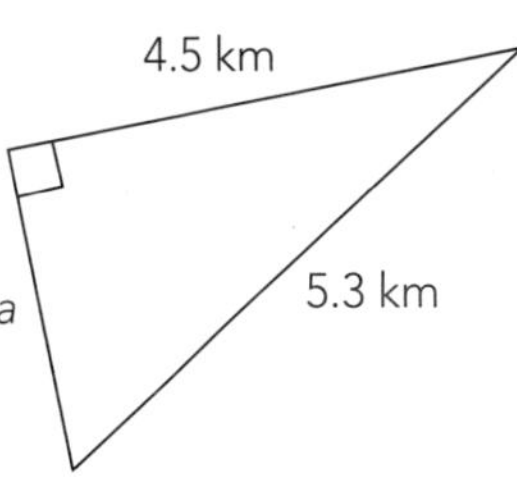


**9**

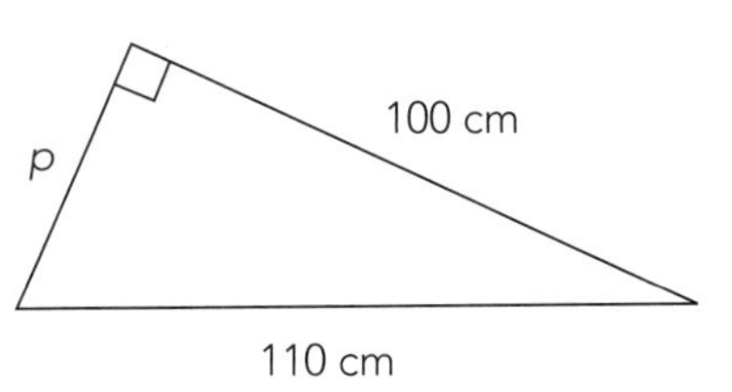


**10**

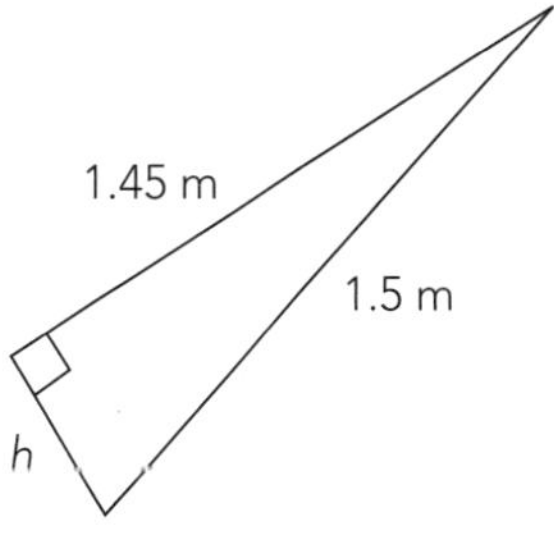


**11**

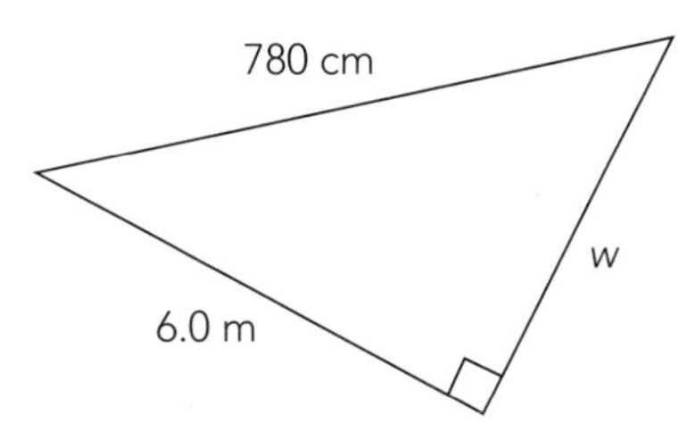


**12**

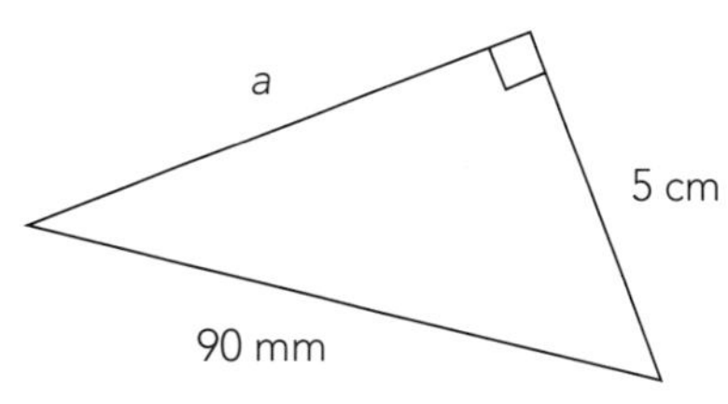

# Mixing it up

Calculate the unknown length of each triangle. Round your answers to 2 dp.

**1**

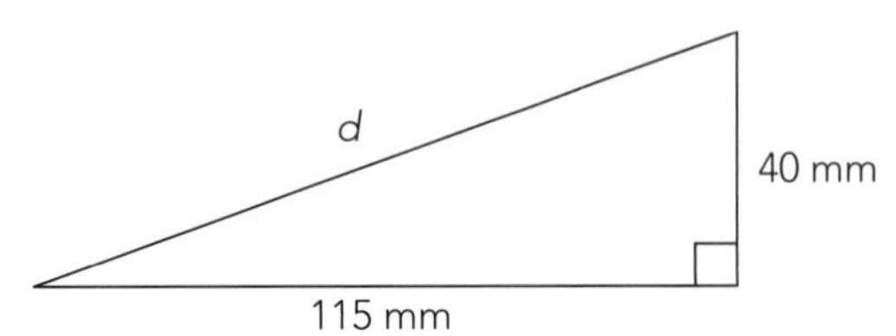


**2**

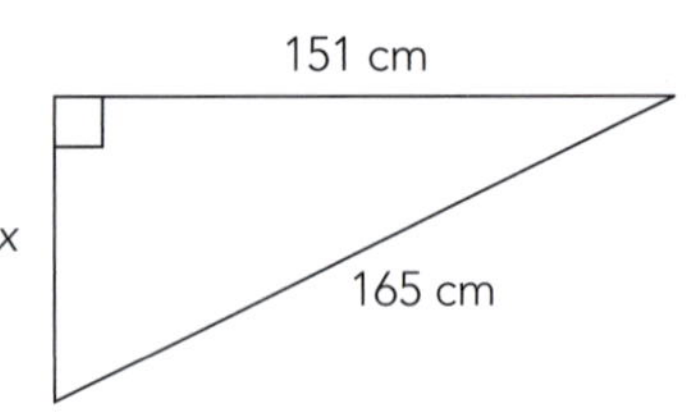


**3**

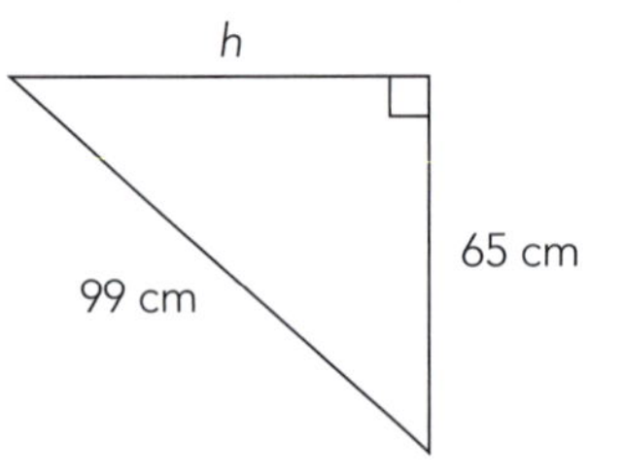


**4**

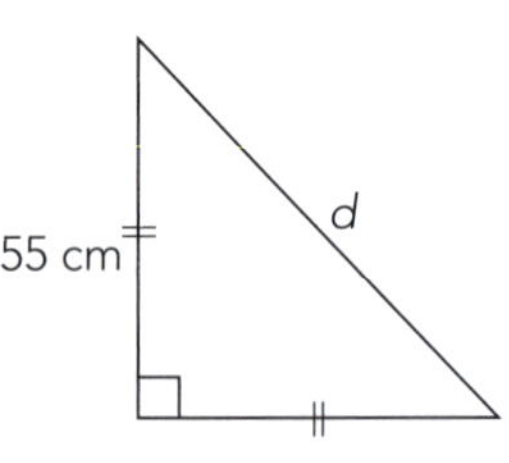


**5**

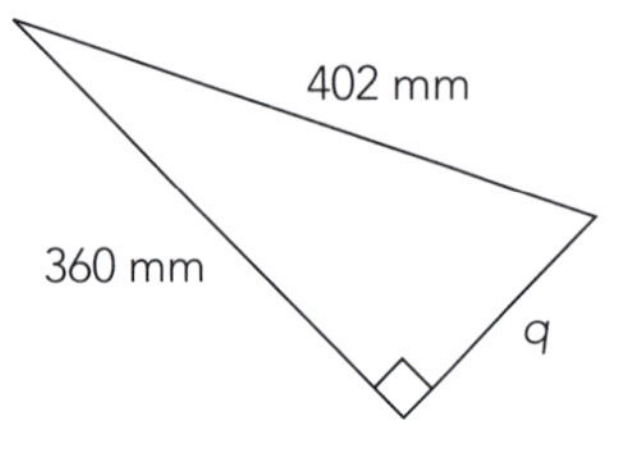


**6**

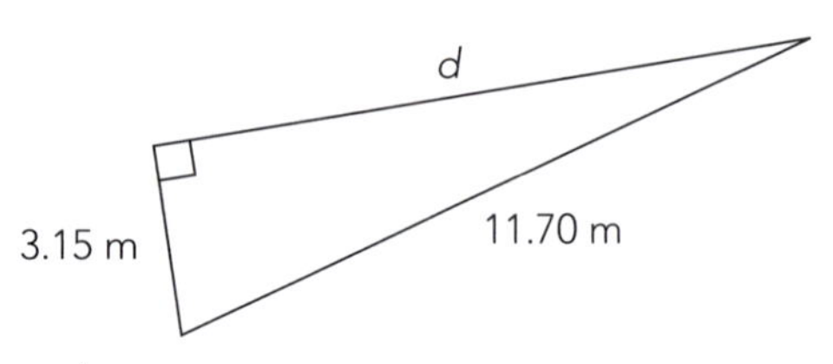


**7**

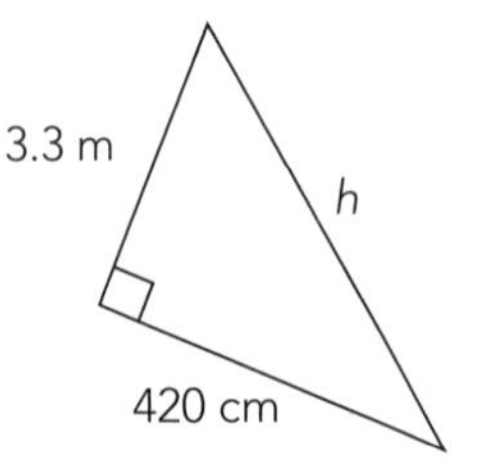


**8**

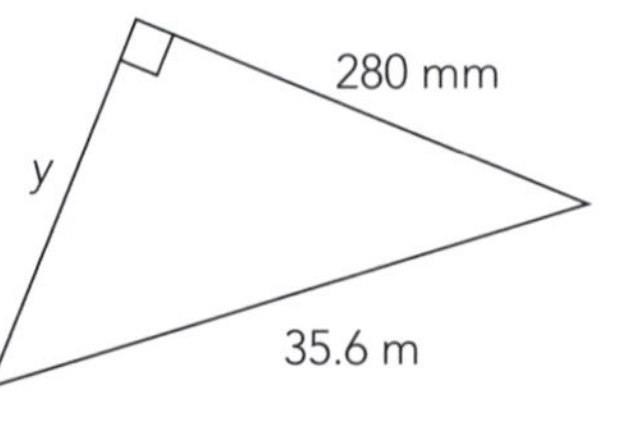




 ISBN: 9780170451543

# Mixing the theorem of Pythagoras with geometry

**1** Calculate the length of the diagonal of this square.

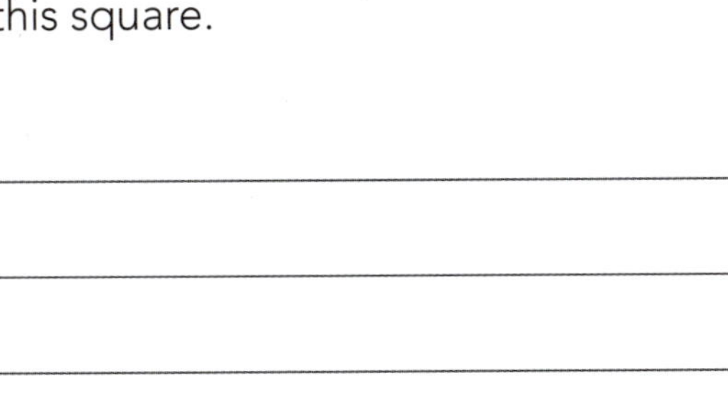

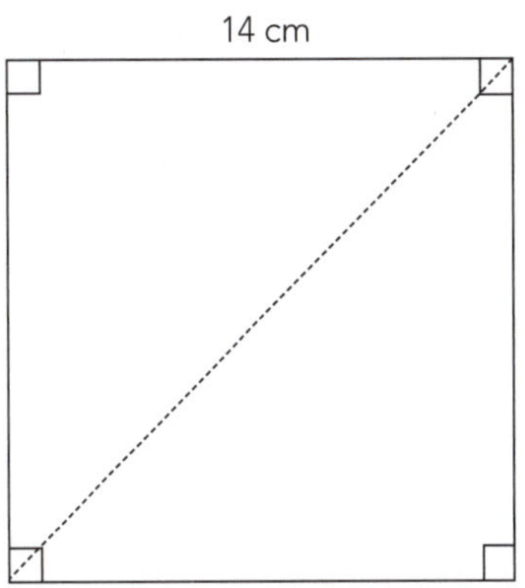


**2** Calculate the width ($w$) of this rectangle.

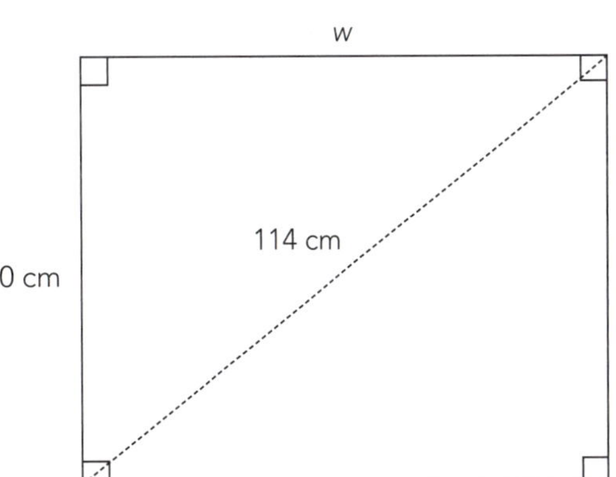


**3** Calculate the lengths of the two equal sides of this isosceles triangle.

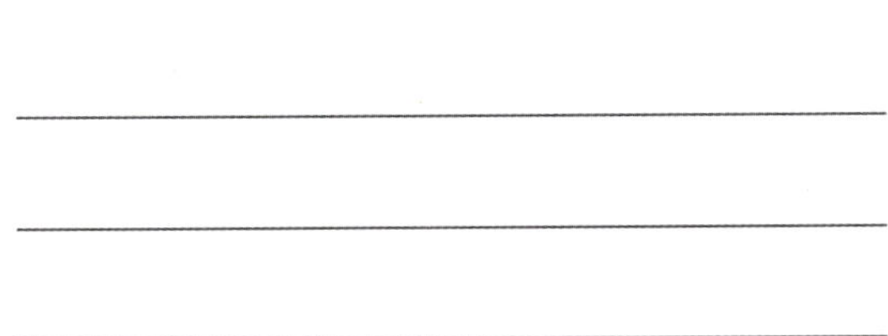

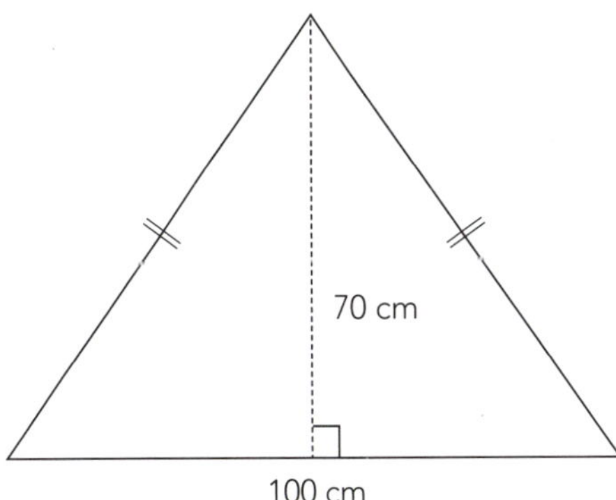


**4** A 3.5 m long ladder is leaning against a wall.
If the base of the ladder is 1.3 m from the wall, calculate how far up the wall ($h$) the ladder reaches.

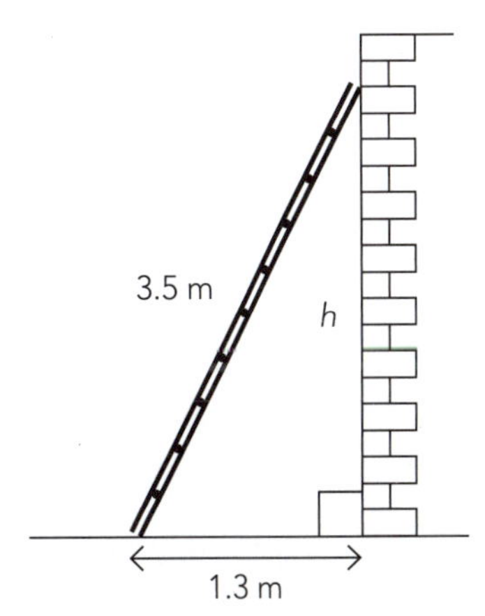


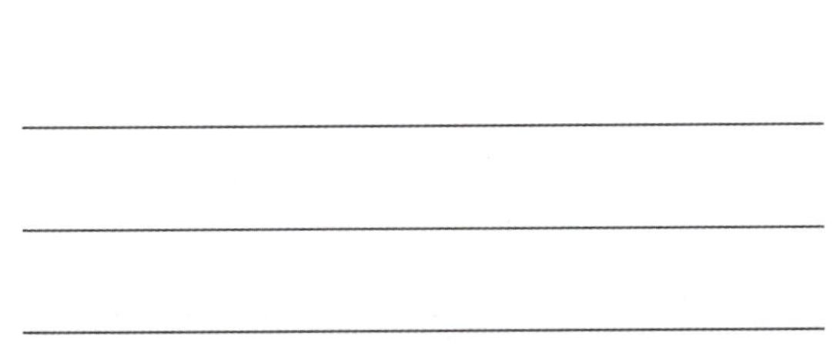

ISBN: 9780170451543  

**5** Max is making pennants (flags) in the shape of isosceles triangles. Each pennant is 16 cm wide and 22 cm deep. Calculate the length of binding needed to go around all three sides of each pennant.

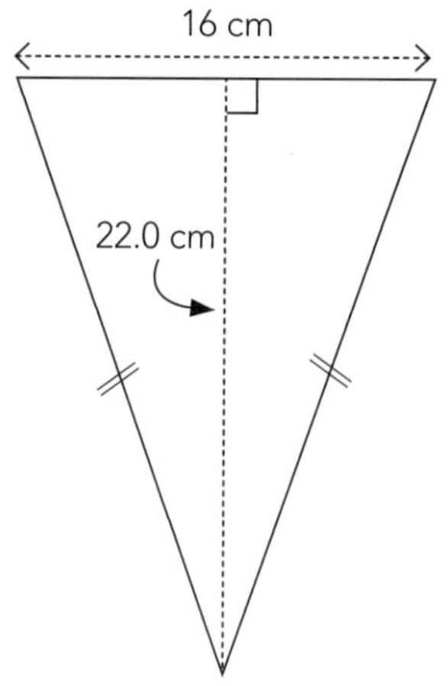

16 cm
22.0 cm

______________________________

______________________________

______________________________

**6** The diagram shows a right trapezium. Calculate the length of line *d*.

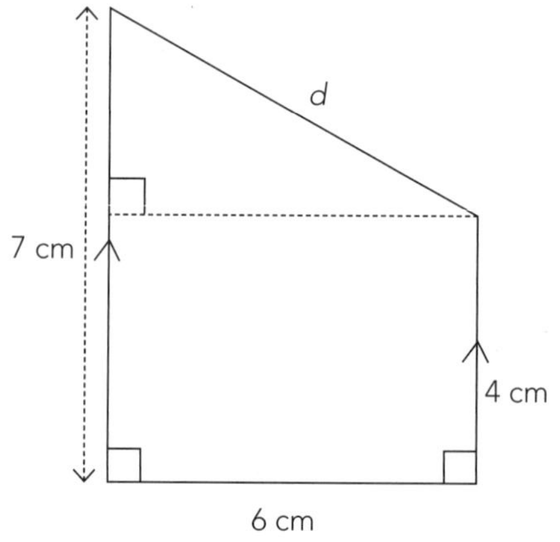

*d*
7 cm
4 cm
6 cm

______________________________

______________________________

______________________________

**7** The diagram shows a right trapezium. Calculate the length of the base (*b*).

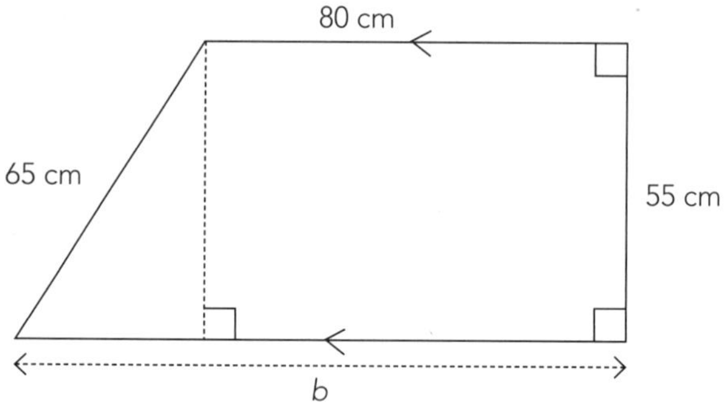

80 cm
65 cm
55 cm
*b*

______________________________

______________________________

______________________________

**8** The diagonal of a square is 10 cm long. Calculate the length of the sides of the square.

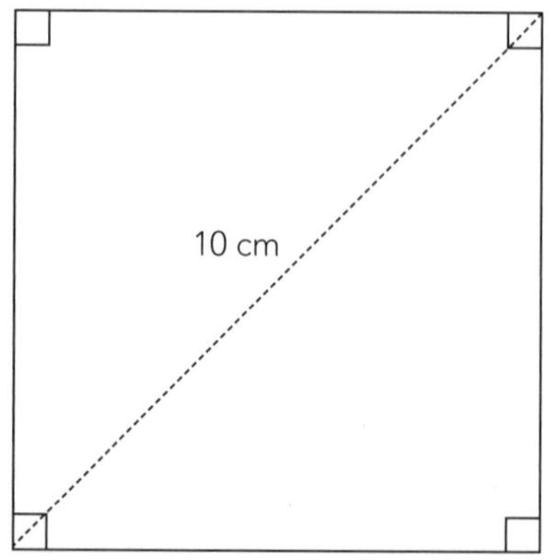

10 cm

______________________________

______________________________

______________________________


 ISBN: 9780170451543

# Trigonometry

## What is trigonometry?

Consider the lengths of the shadows cast by a tree, a goal post and a person at a particular time of day.

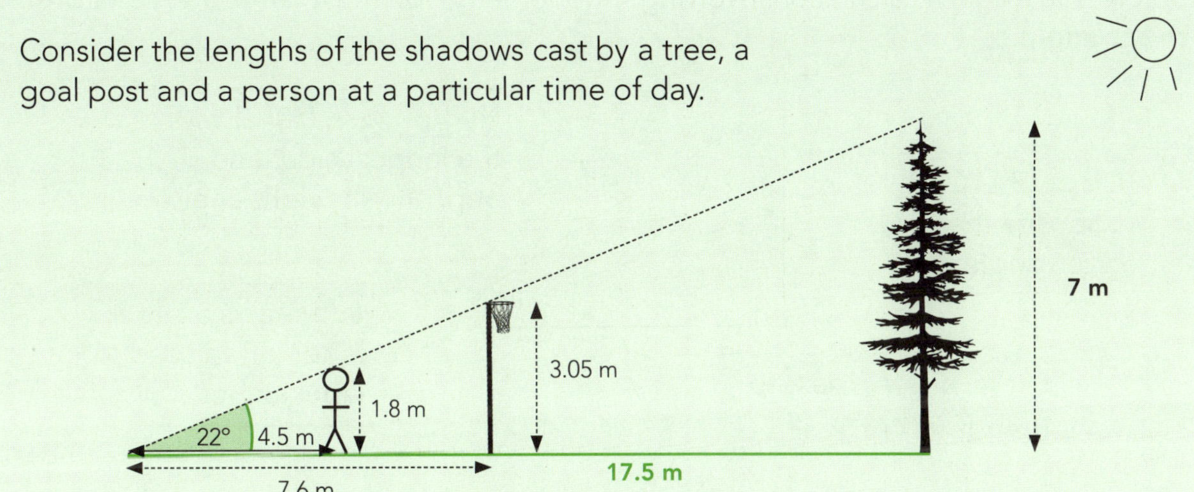


**For each, calculate the ratio of their height to the length of the shadow.**

For the tree: Ratio $= \dfrac{\text{height of tree}}{\text{length of its shadow}}$

$= \dfrac{7}{17.5}$

$= 0.40$ (2 dp)

For the goal post: Ratio $= \dfrac{\text{height of goal post}}{\text{length of its shadow}}$

$= \dfrac{\_\_\_}{\_\_\_}$

= ________ (2 dp)

For the person: Ratio $= \dfrac{\text{height of person}}{\text{length of their shadow}}$

$= \dfrac{\_\_\_}{\_\_\_}$

= ________ (2 dp)

- Notice that the ratios are ______________________.
- Because the angle between the sun's rays and the ground (22°) is the same for all three shadows, the triangles in the diagram are **similar**.
- For any given angle, these ratios in right-angled triangles are fixed.
- **Trigonometry is the use of these ratios to calculate the lengths of unknown sides and angles.**
- These ratios are stored in your calculator.
- In this case, tan 22° = 0.404.

ISBN: 9780170451543

## More about trigonometry

- Trigonometry is used for calculating lengths and angles in **right-angled triangles**.
- Unlike calculations using the theorem of Pythagoras, an **angle must be involved**.

Before you begin a calculation involving trigonometry, you must **label the sides of the triangle**.

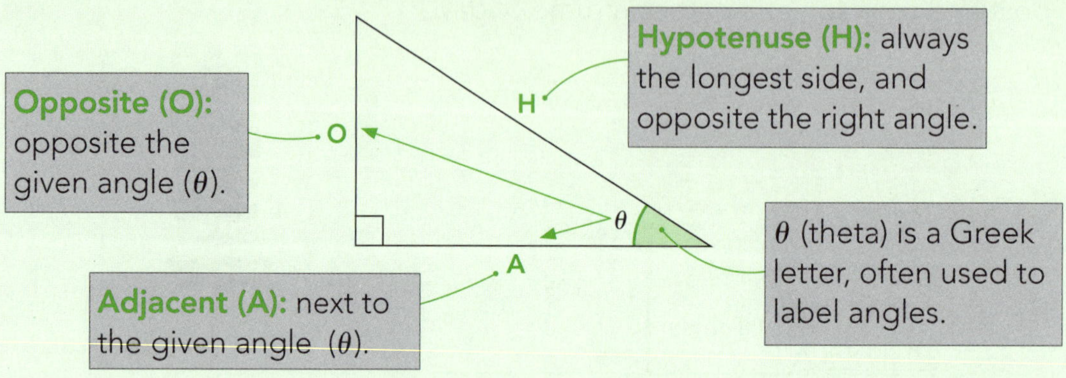


Label the sides of the following triangles with H, O and A.

**1**

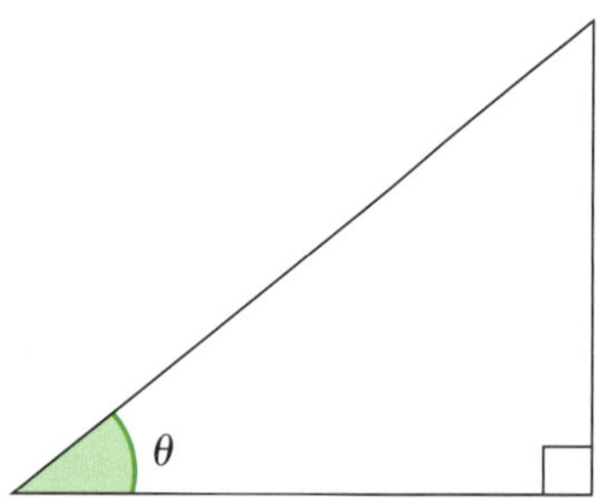


**2**

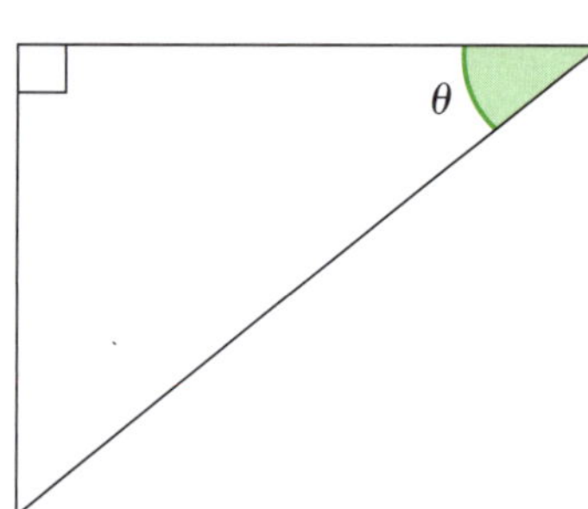


**3**

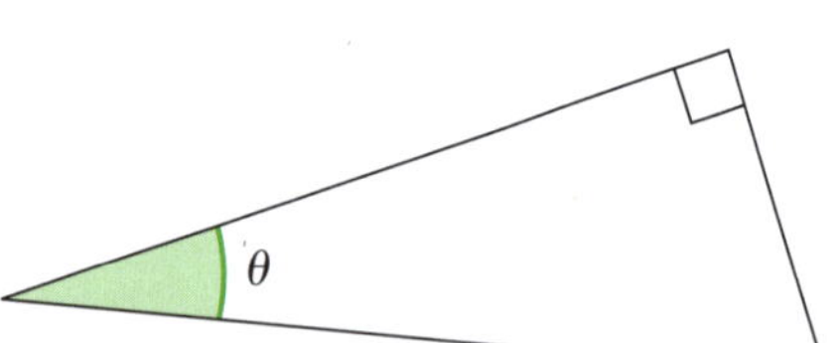


**4**

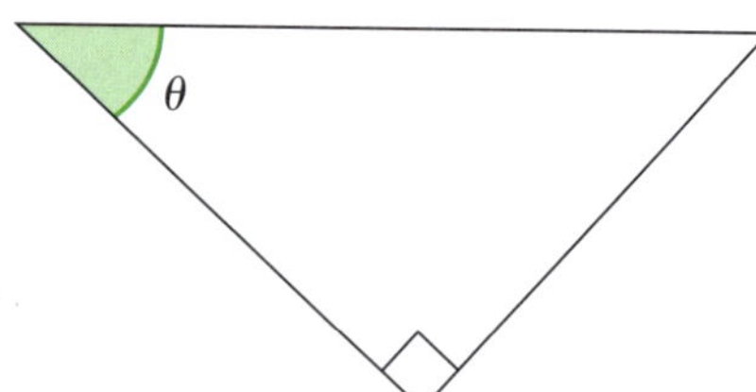


**5**

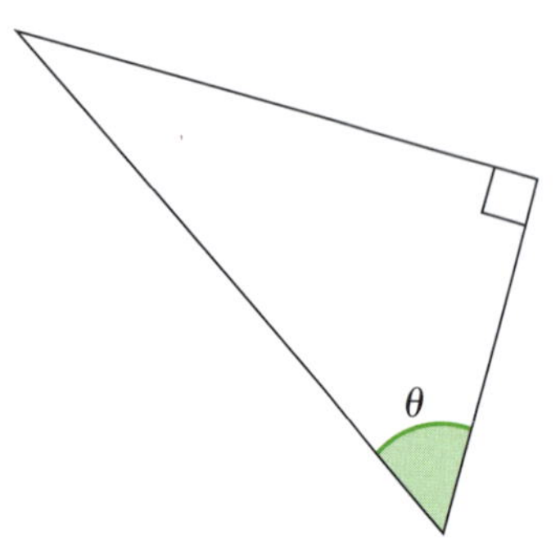


**6**

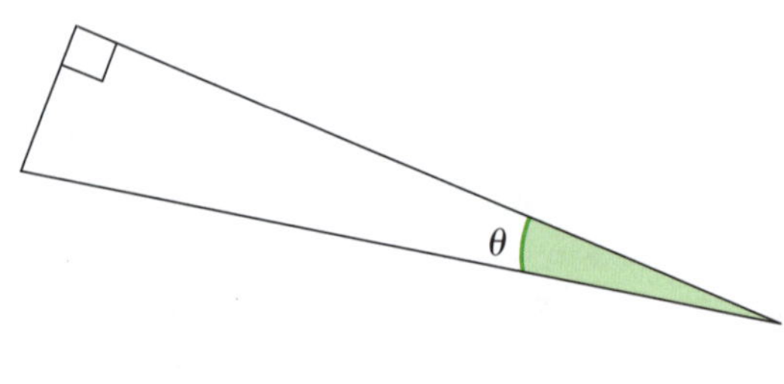




ISBN: 9780170451543

# SOHCAHTOA

- You need to know about three trigonometrical functions: **sin** $\theta$ (sine)
  **cos** $\theta$ (cosine)
  **tan** $\theta$ (tangent).
- These are the rules in trigonometry:

$$\sin\theta = \frac{O}{H} \qquad \cos\theta = \frac{A}{H} \qquad \tan\theta = \frac{O}{A}$$

- Organising SOHCAHTOA into triangles can help you remember how to use it:

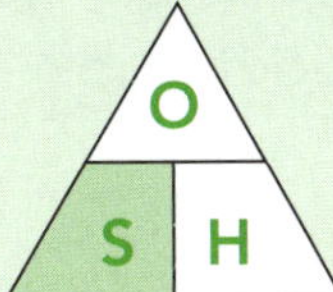

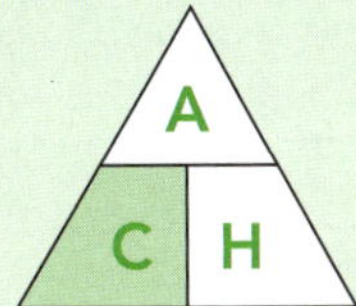

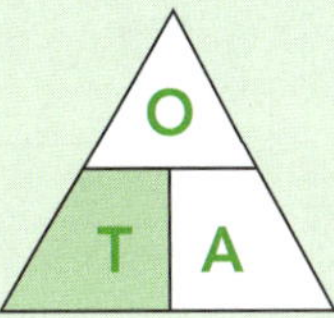


# Finding sides using sine

**Examples:**

**1** Calculate the length marked $y$.

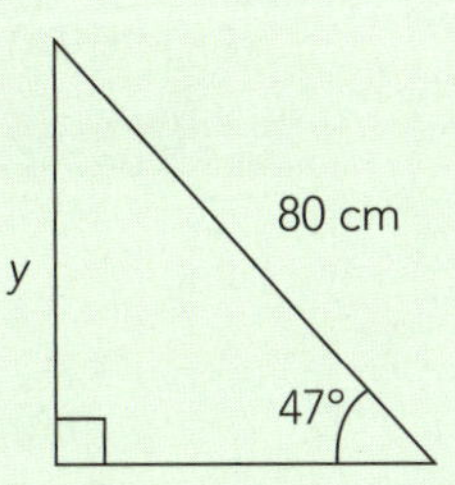


**Step 1:** Label the sides **that are involved** with A, O and H.

We don't know the length of this side. Nor do we need to know it.

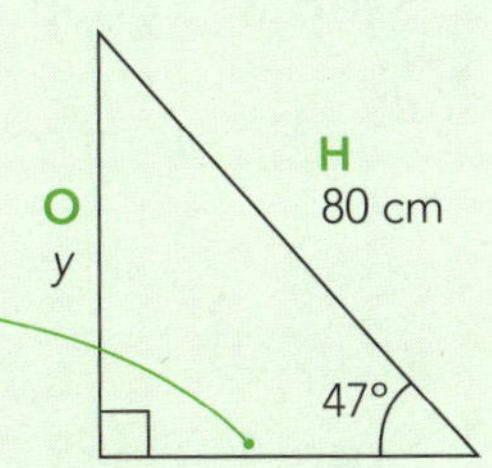


**Step 2:** The labelled sides are **O** and **H**, so write out the triangle involving these:

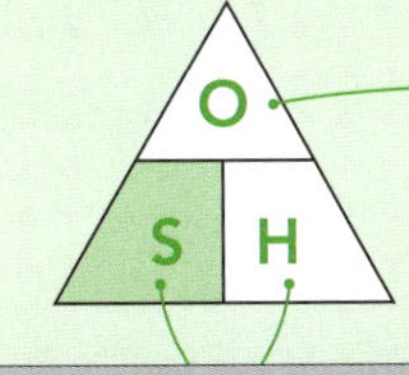


We need to find **y**, which is the **O**pposite side.

**O** = **s**in $\theta$ x **H**

**S** and **H** are on the same level in this triangle, so we **multiply** them.

**Step 3:** Substitute the numbers and calculate the answer.

O = sin 47° x 80
O = $y$ = 58.51 cm (2 dp)

Enter 'sin 47° **=** x 80', otherwise you will get 'sin(47° x 80)'.

You will find sin, cos and tan functions on your calculator. Before you use these, **check that your calculator is set to degrees (DRG or D)**.

**Step 4: Think** about your answer — does it seem about right? The hypotenuse is 80 cm, so 58.51 cm is reasonable for one of the shorter sides. ✓

ISBN: 9780170451543  

**2** Calculate the length marked *y*.

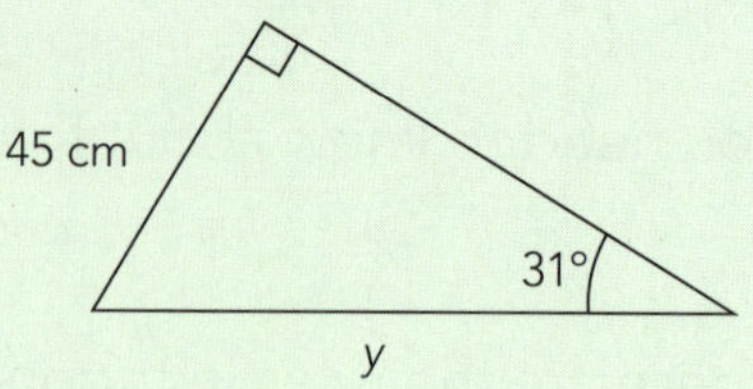


**Step 1:** Label the sides **that are involved** with A, O and H.

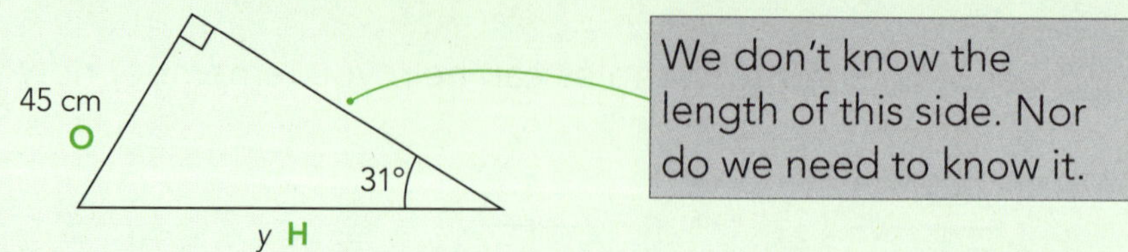


**Step 2:** The labelled sides are **O** and **H**, so write out the triangle involving these:

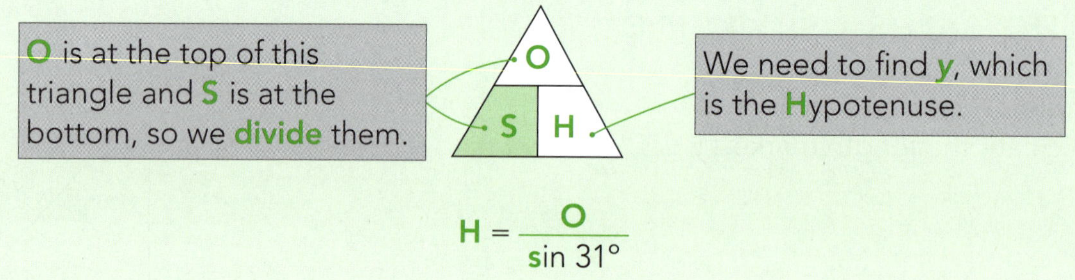


$$H = \frac{O}{\sin 31°}$$

**Step 3:** Substitute the numbers and calculate the answer.

$$H = \frac{45}{\sin 31°}$$

$$H = y = 87.37 \text{ cm (2 dp)}$$

**Step 4:** **Think** about your answer — does it seem about right?

*y* is the hypotenuse, so we would expect it to be longer than 45 cm. ✓

**Handy hint**

When checking your answers, remember that in any triangle:

- the **longest side** is always opposite the **biggest angle**
- the **shortest side** is always opposite the **smallest angle**.

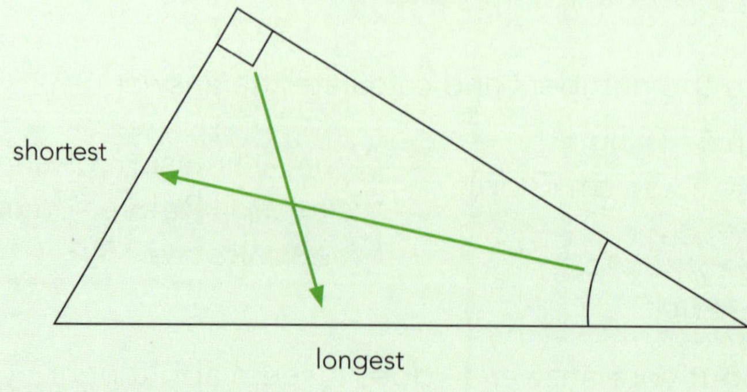




 ISBN: 9780170451543

Use trigonometry to calculate the unknown length of each triangle. Round your answers to 2 dp.

**1**

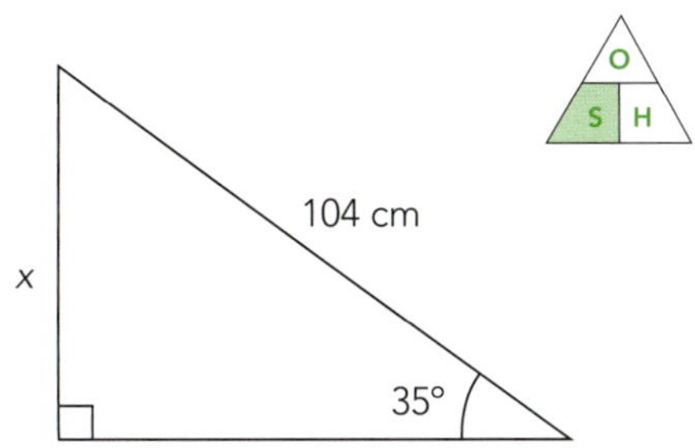


$O = \sin\theta \times H$

$x = \sin$ ________ x ________

= ________ cm (2 dp)

**2**

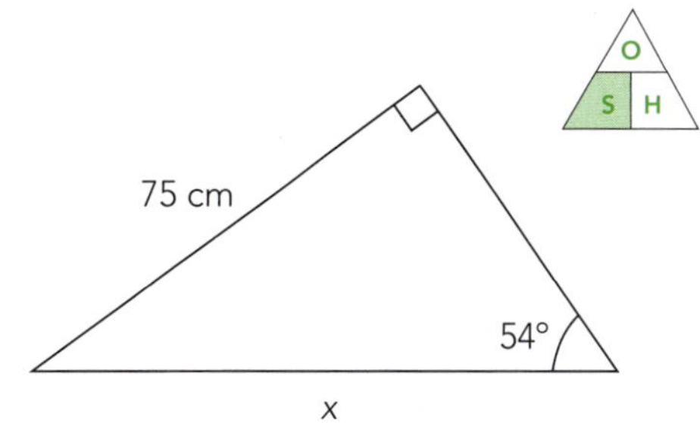


$H = \dfrac{O}{\sin\theta}$

$x =$ ________

= ________ cm (2 dp)

**3**

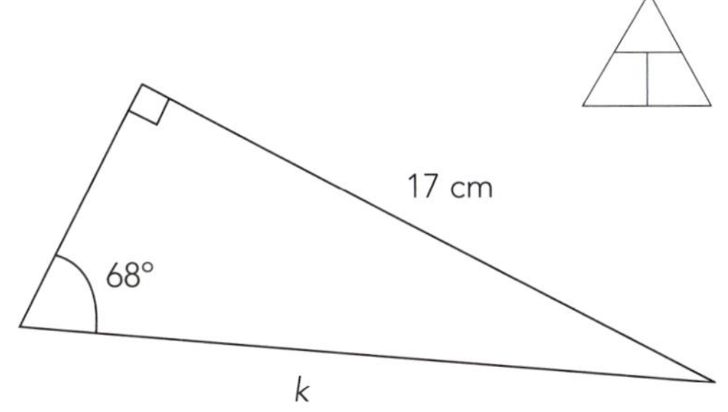


________

________

________

**4**

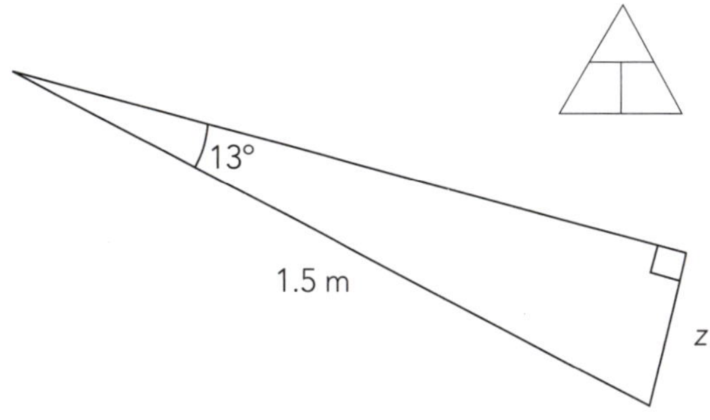


________

________

________

**5**

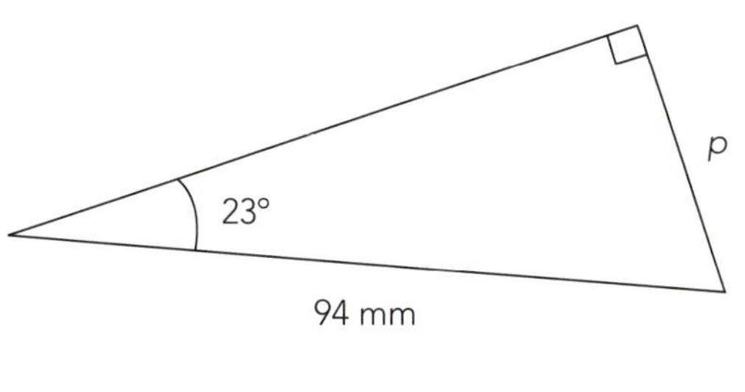


________

________

________

**6**

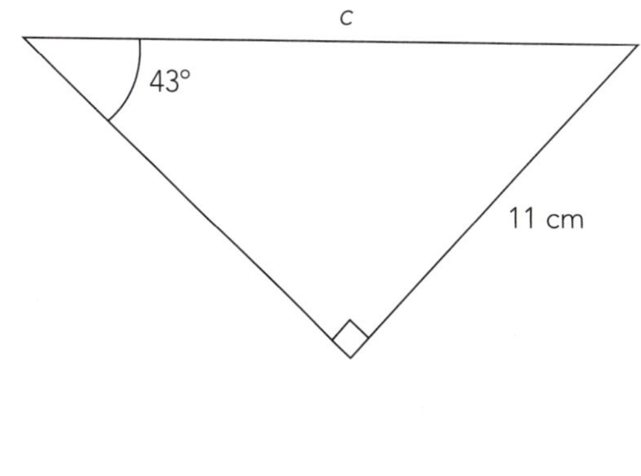


________

________

________

ISBN: 9780170451543  

**7**

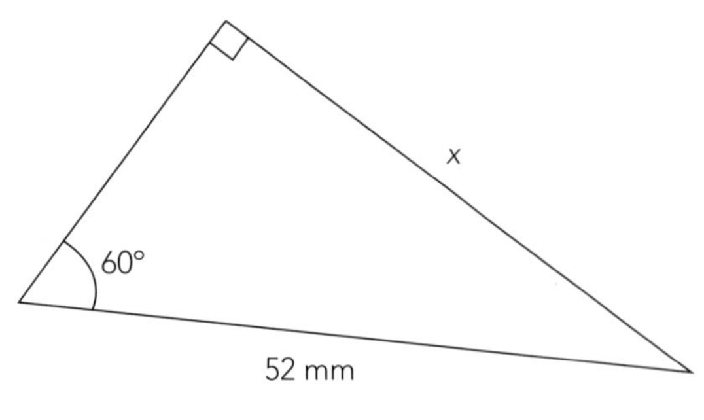


**8**

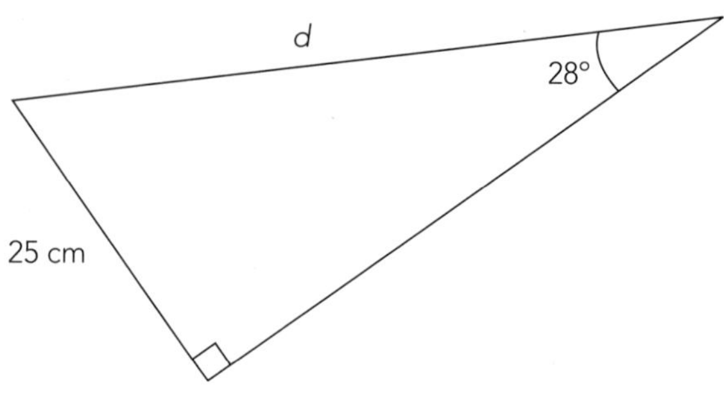


**9**

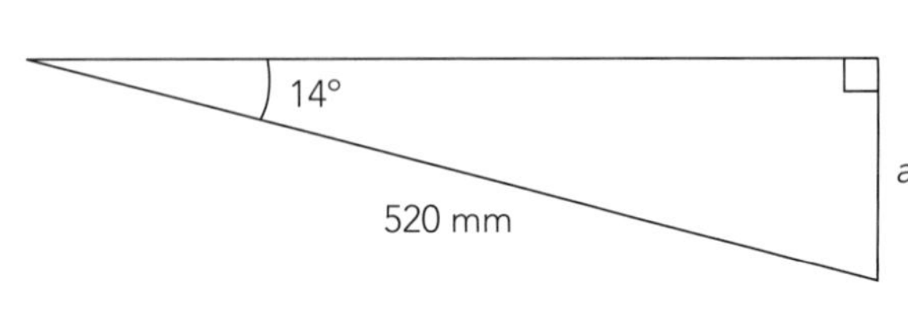


**10**

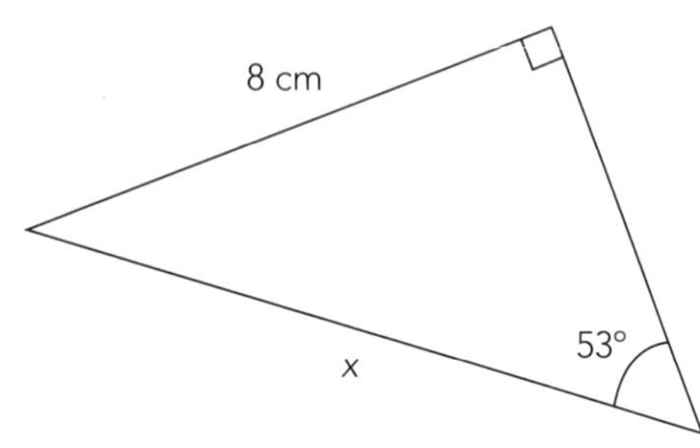


**11**

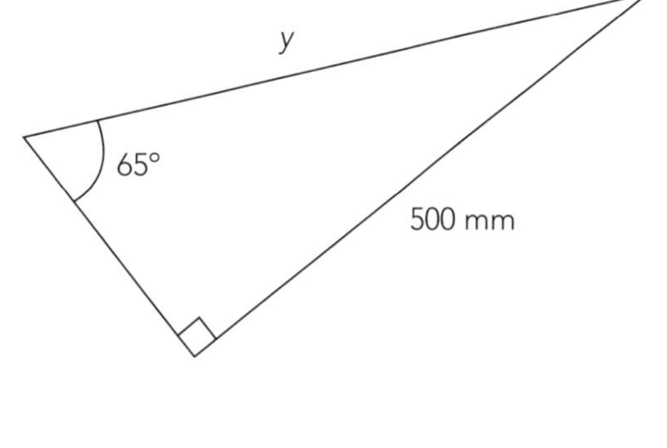


**12**

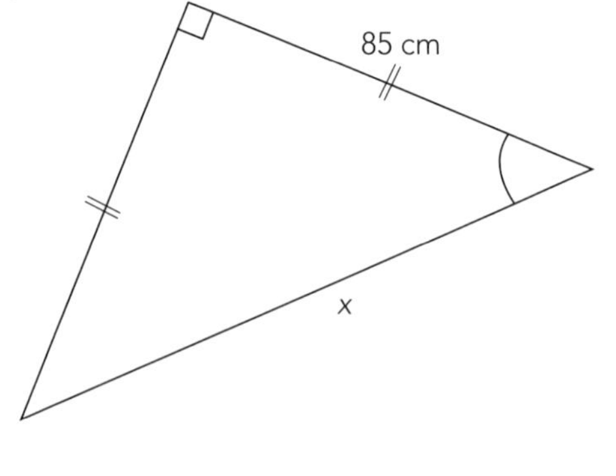




ISBN: 9780170451543

# Finding sides using cosine and tangent

- You can use the same steps along with these to find the lengths of right-angled triangle sides using cosines and tangents.

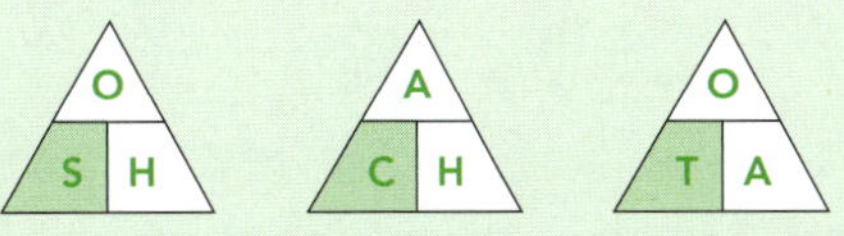


**Examples:**

**1** Calculate the length marked $y$.

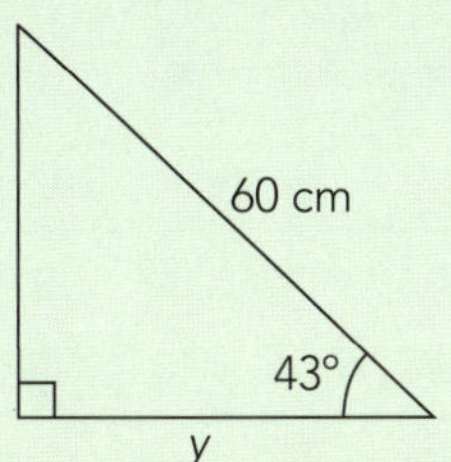


**Step 1:** Label the sides **that are involved** with A, O and H.

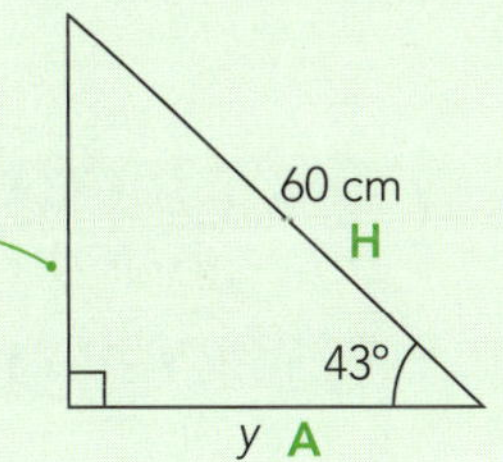


**Step 2:** The labelled sides are **A** and **H**, so write out the triangle involving these:

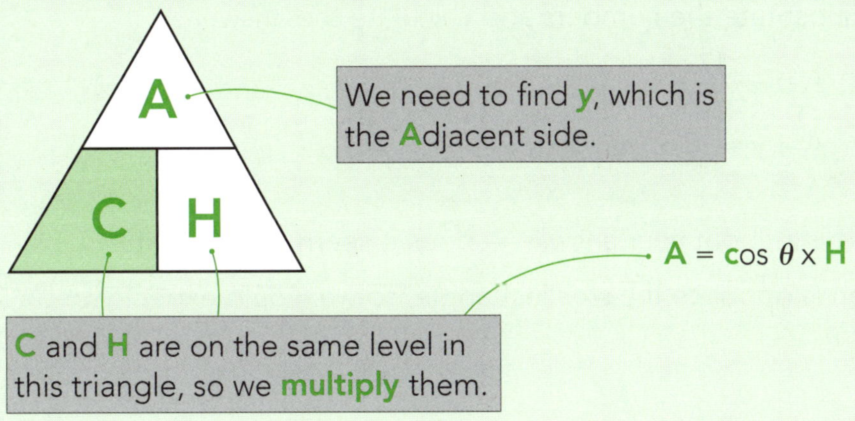


**Step 3:** Substitute the numbers and calculate the answer.

$A = \cos 43° \times 60$

$A = y = 43.88$ cm (2 dp)

**Step 4:** **Think** about your answer — does it seem about right?

The hypotenuse is 60 cm, so 43.88 cm is reasonable for one of the shorter sides. ✓

**2** Calculate the length marked *y*.

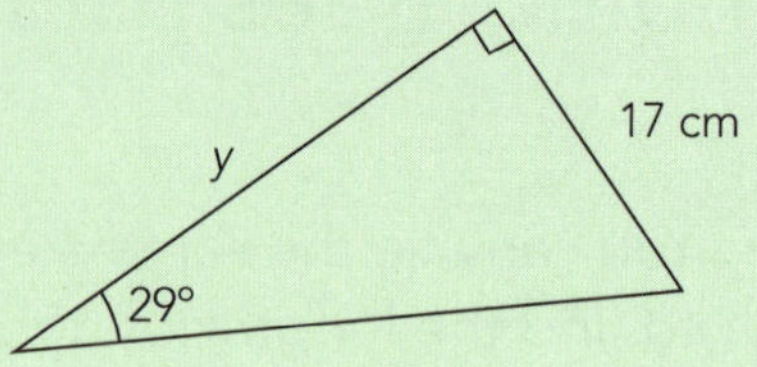


**Step 1:** Label the sides **that are involved** with A, O and H.

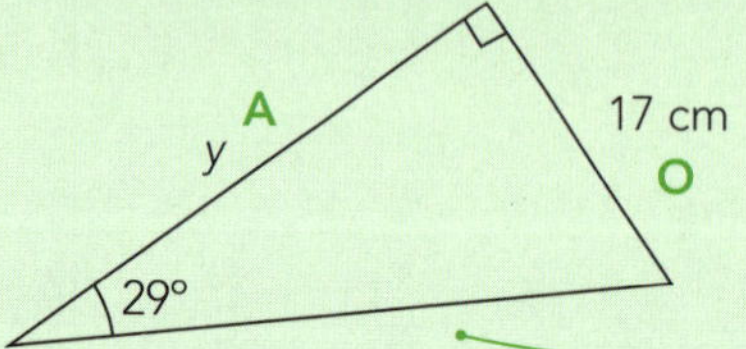


We don't know the length of this side. Nor do we need to know it.

**Step 2:** The labelled sides are **O** and **A**, so write out the triangle involving these:

**O** is at the top of this triangle and **T** is at the bottom, so we **divide** them.

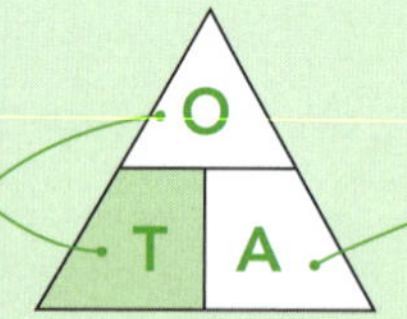


We need to find **y**, which is the **A**djacent side.

$$A = \frac{O}{\tan 29°}$$

**Step 3:** Substitute the numbers and calculate the answer.

$$A = \frac{17}{\tan 29°}$$

$A = y = 30.67$ cm (2 dp)

**Step 4:** **Think** about your answer — does it seem about right?

O = 17 cm is opposite the smallest angle, so we would expect *y* to be longer than 17 cm. ✓

Use trigonometry to calculate the unknown length of each triangle. Round your answers to 2 dp.

**1**

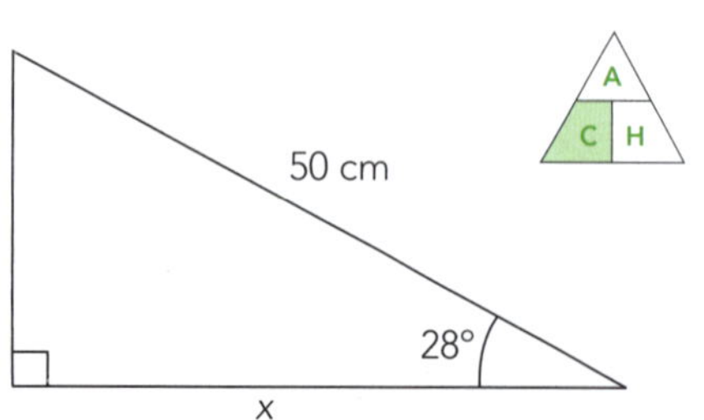


A = cos $\theta$ x H

$x$ = ___________

= ___________ cm (2 dp)

**2**

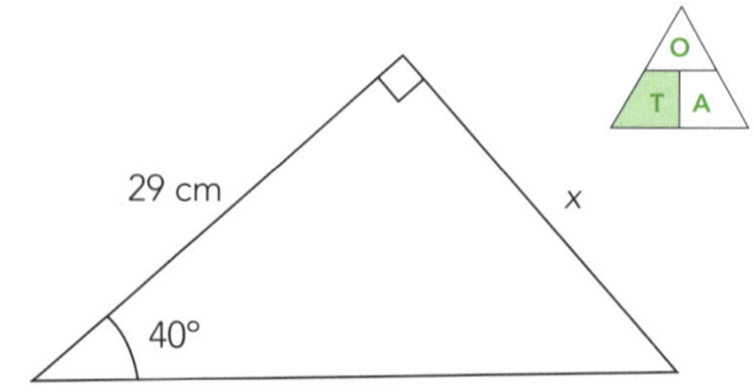


O = tan $\theta$ x H

$x$ = tan ___________ x ___________

= ___________ cm (2 dp)



 ISBN: 9780170451543

**3**

18°
37 cm
b
A
C H
O
T A

**4**

106 mm
34°
p
A
C H
O
T A

**5**

47°
y
146 mm

**6**

h
43°
7.2 m

**7**

20°
d
31 cm

**8**

24 cm
28°
a

**9**

89 mm
76°
b

**10**

21 m
z
37°

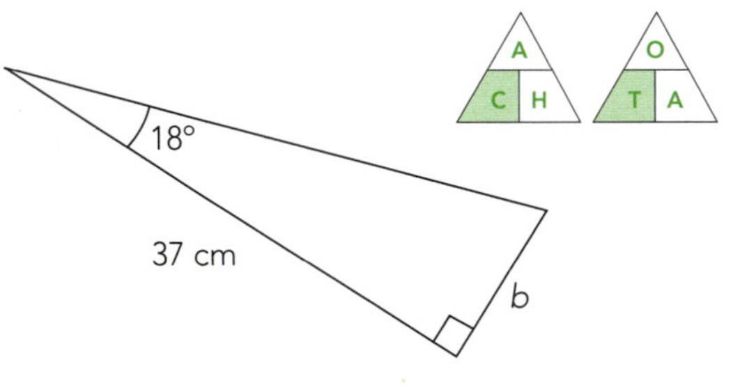

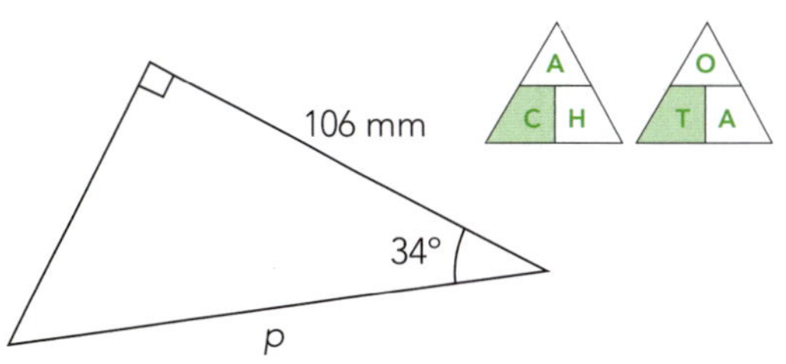

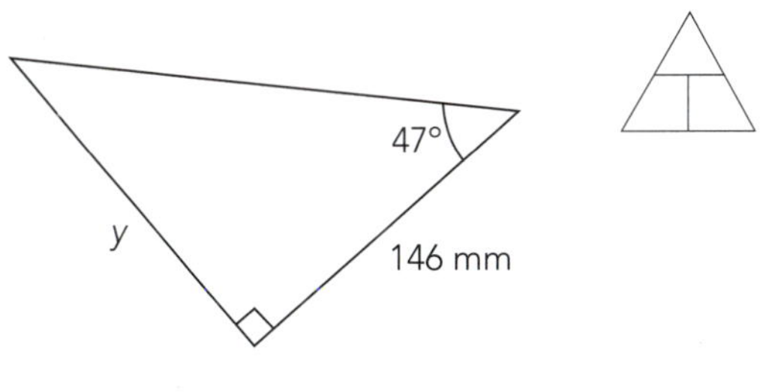

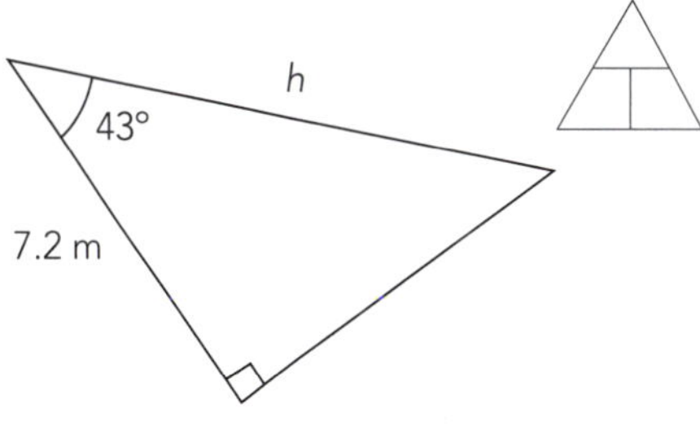

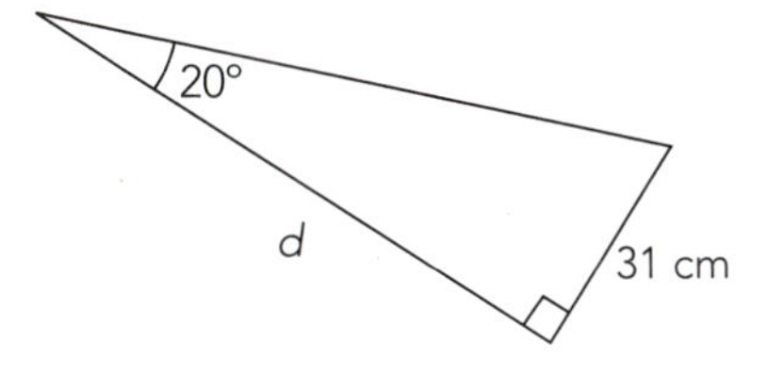

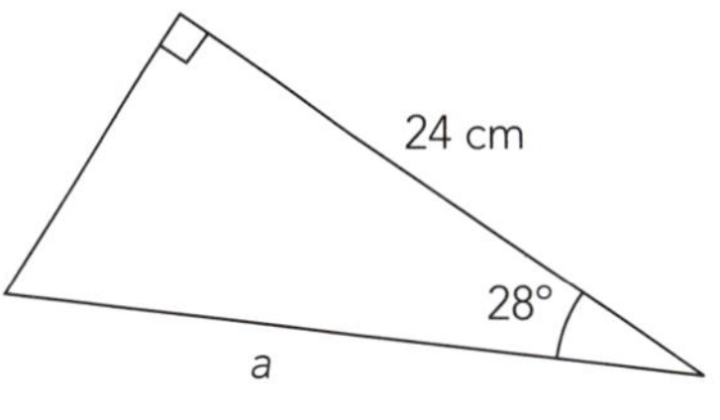

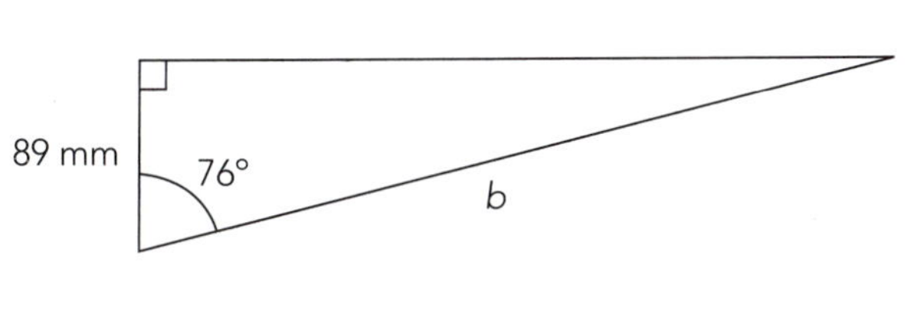

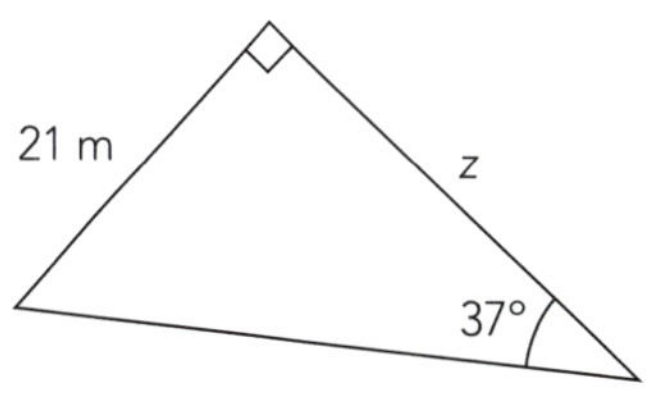

# Mixing it up

Use trigonometry to calculate the unknown length of each triangle. Round your answers to 2 dp.

**1**

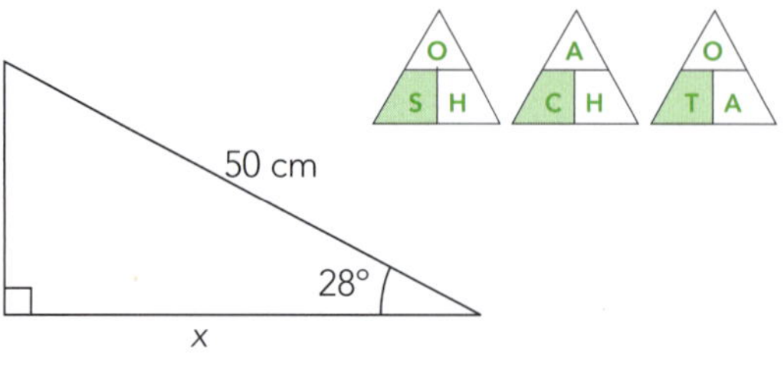


**2**

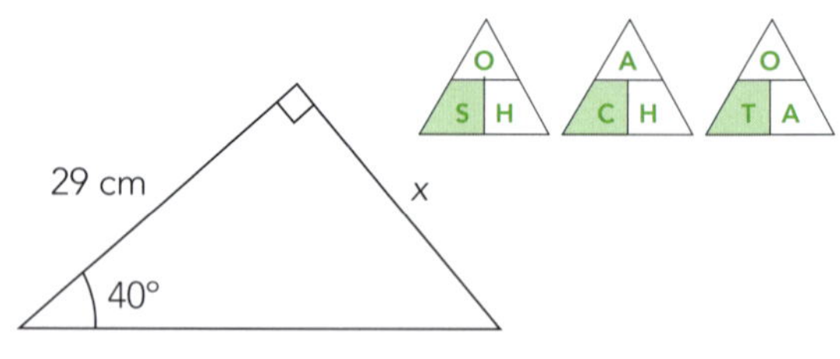


**3**

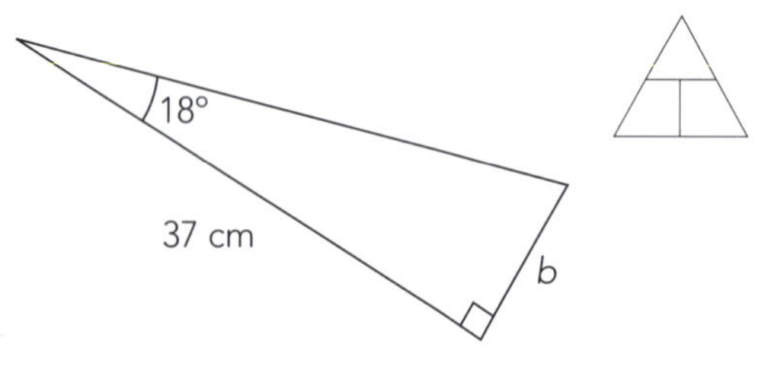


**4**

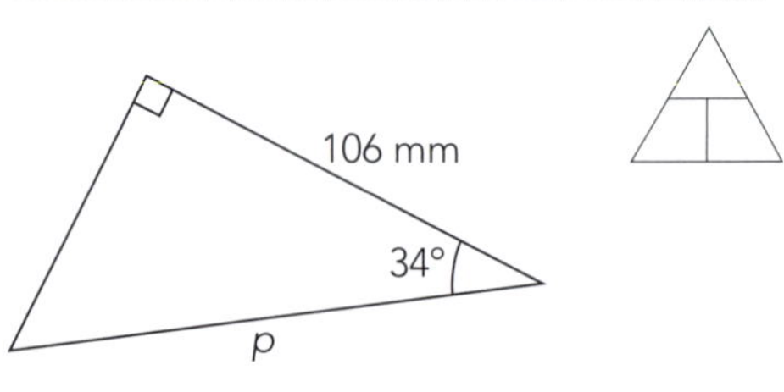


**5**

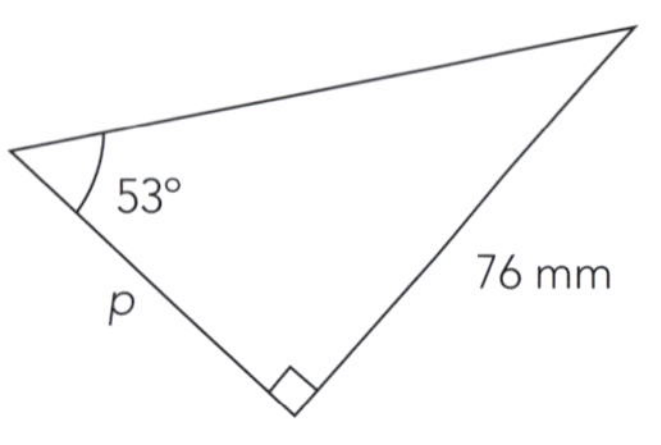


**6**

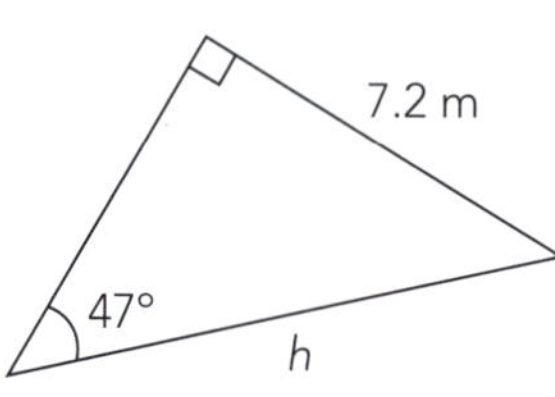


**7**

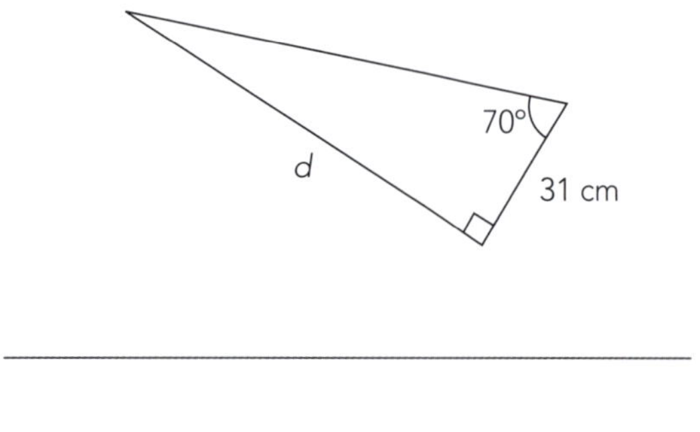


**8**

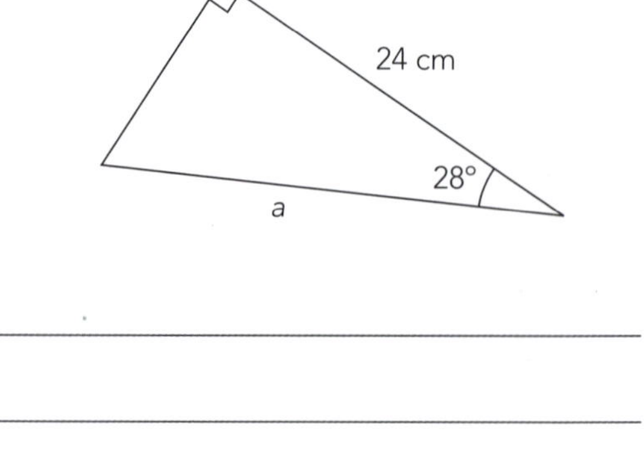




ISBN: 9780170451543

**9**

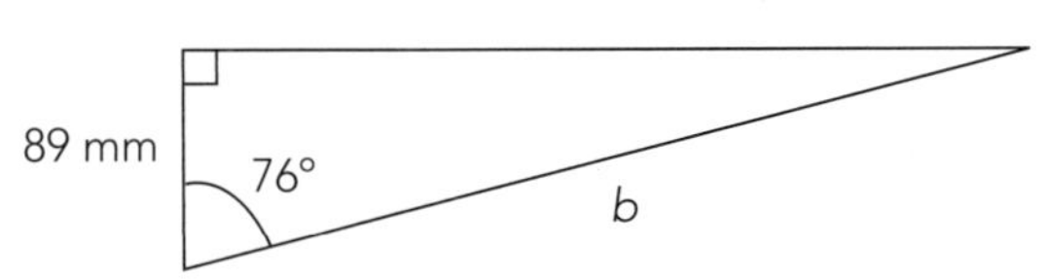


**10**

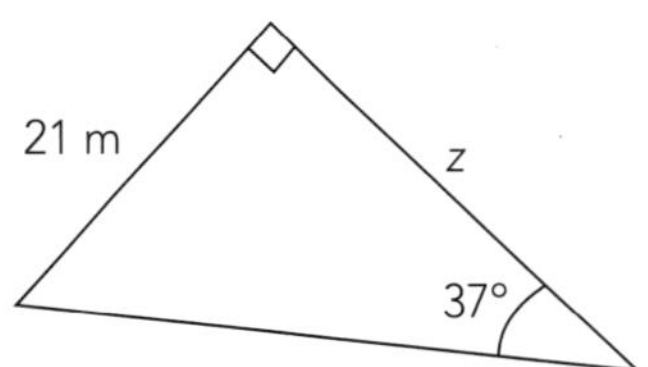


**11**

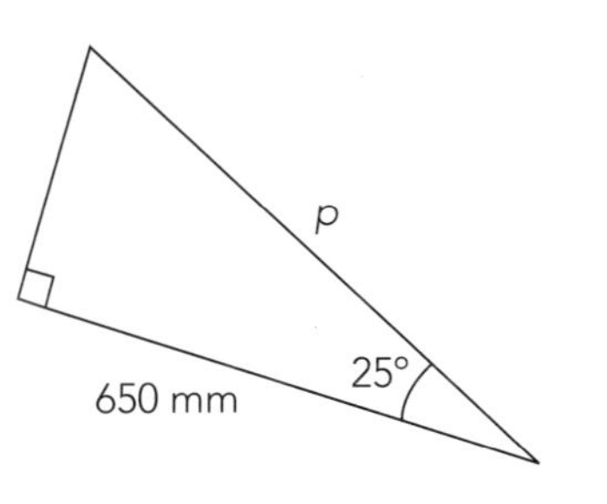


**12**

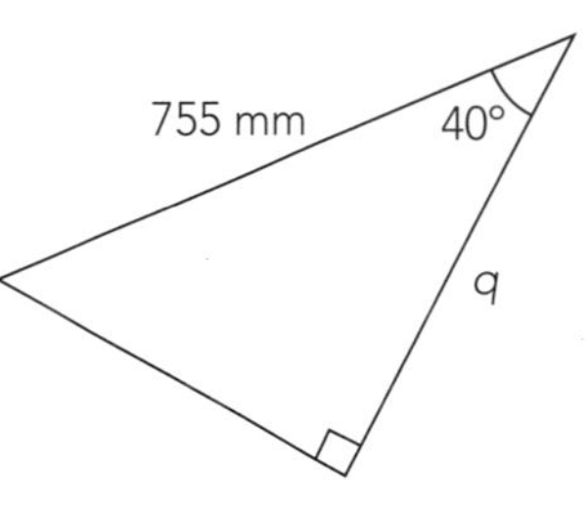


**13**

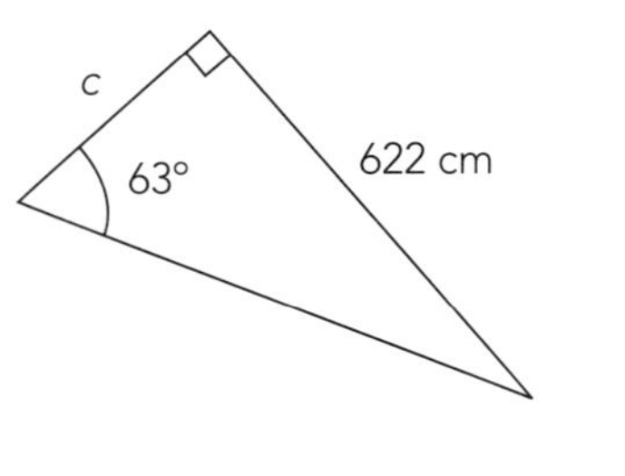


**14**

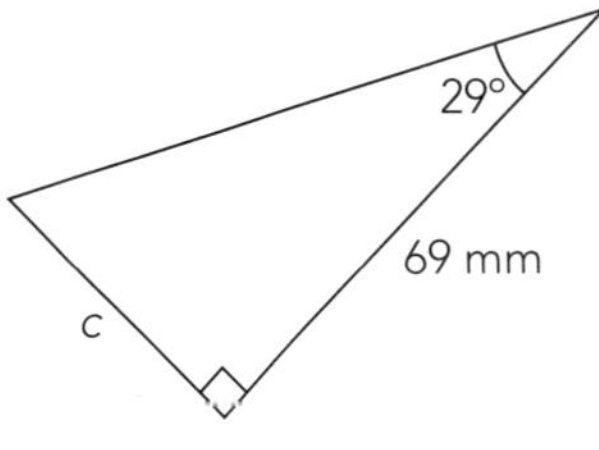


**15**

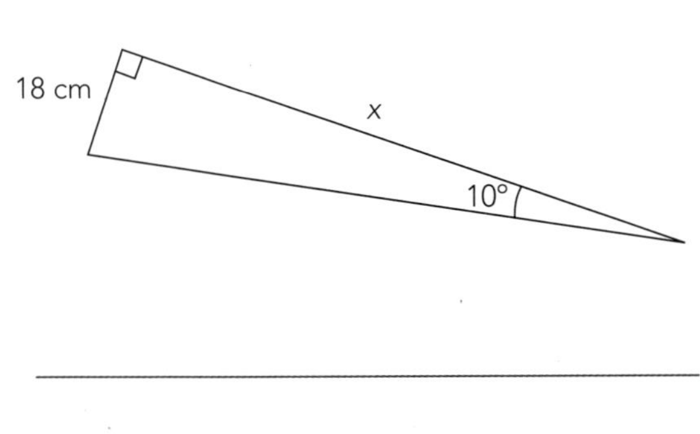


**16**

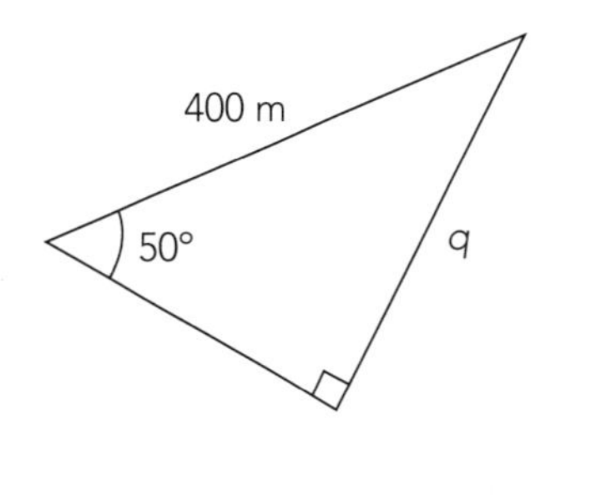


ISBN: 9780170451543 

# Finding sides using trigonometry and geometry

- Some problems require you to do several trigonometric calculations. It is best to do your calculations **all together** and **round only at the end** in order to avoid rounding errors.
- Sometimes this is difficult, in which case round the intermediate answers to **at least one more significant figure** than that required in the answer.

**Example:** Calculate the total height (CE) for the figure on the right.

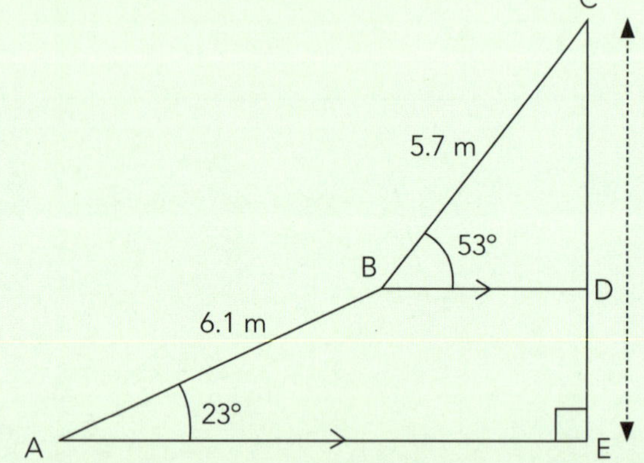


**Separate calculations:**

$CD = 5.7 \sin 53°$
$= 4.55$ m (2 dp)

$DE = 6.1 \sin 23°$
$= 2.38$ m (2 dp)

$\therefore CE = 4.55 + 2.38$
$= 6.93$ m (2 dp)

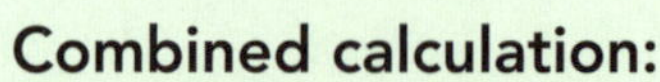

**Combined calculation:**

$CE = 5.7 \sin 53° + 6.1 \sin 23°$
$= 6.94$ m (2 dp)

This is a **more accurate** answer because the rounding was done **only once**, and at the **end** of the calculation.

Answer the following questions. In each case, show your reasoning.

**1** ABCD form the corners of a right trapezium. Angle ADC is 56°, AD is 5.4 m and AB is 6 m. Calculate the perimeter.

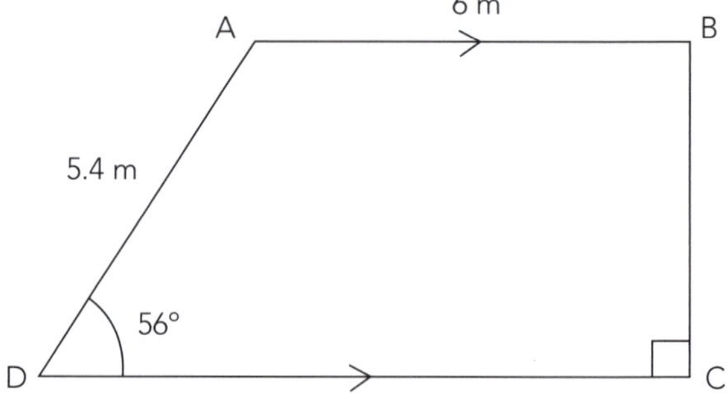


______________________________

______________________________

______________________________

______________________________

**2** ABCD is a rectangle whose diagonal is 100 mm. Angle ABD = 27°. Calculate the perimeter.

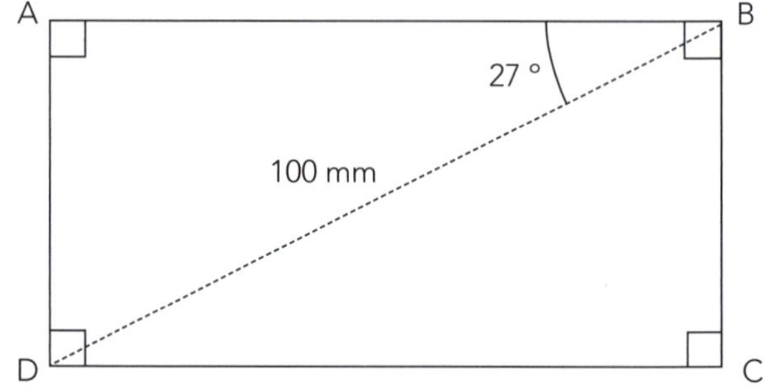


______________________________

______________________________

______________________________

______________________________



ISBN: 9780170451543

**3** ABC is an isosceles triangle, whose vertical height is 24 cm. Angle DBC = 43°. Calculate the perimeter.

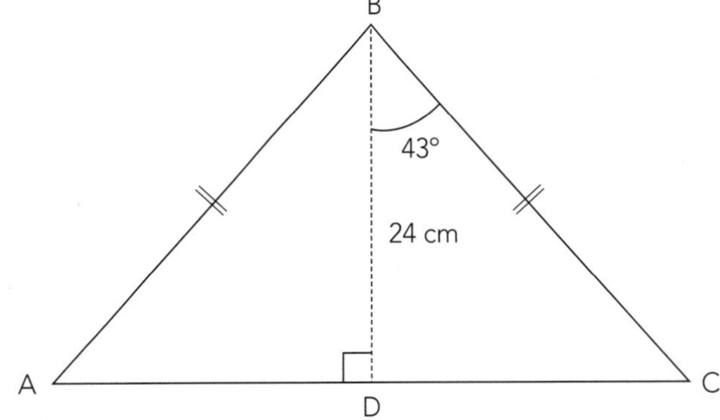


**4** ABCD is a rhombus. The length of its shorter diagonal (BD) is 45 cm. Angle ACD = 28°. Calculate the lengths of the sides.

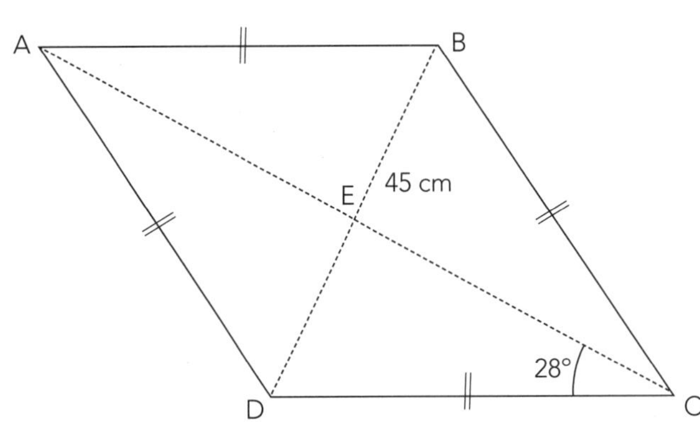


**5** ABCDEFGH is a regular octagon. The midpoint of EF is K. Each diagonal is 100 mm long. Calculate the perimeter of the octagon.

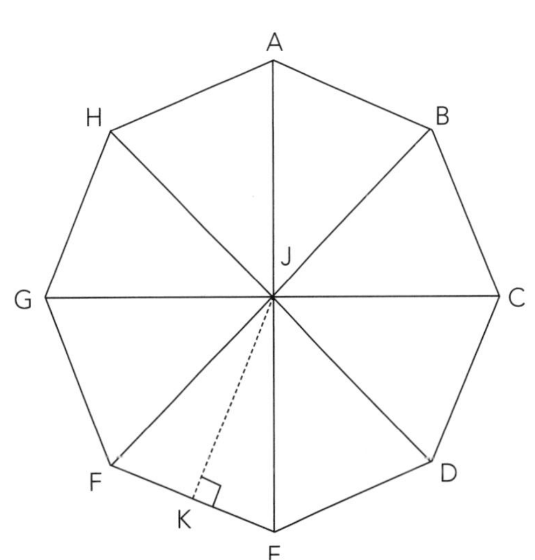


ISBN: 9780170451543 

# Finding angles using sine

- You can also use similar steps along with these to find the **angles** in right-angle triangles.

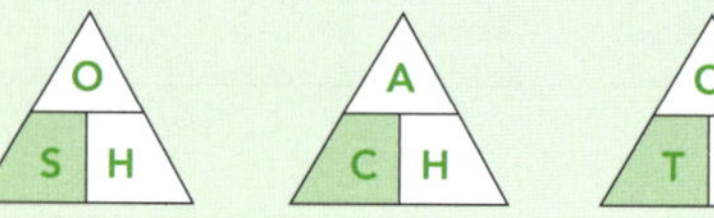


**Examples:**

**1** Calculate the size of angle $b$.

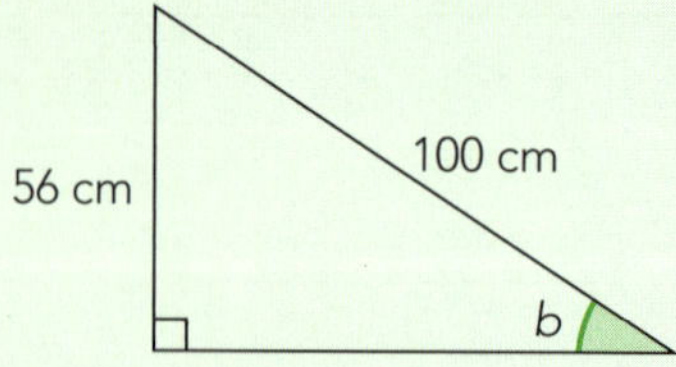


**Step 1:** Label the sides **that are involved** with A, O and H.

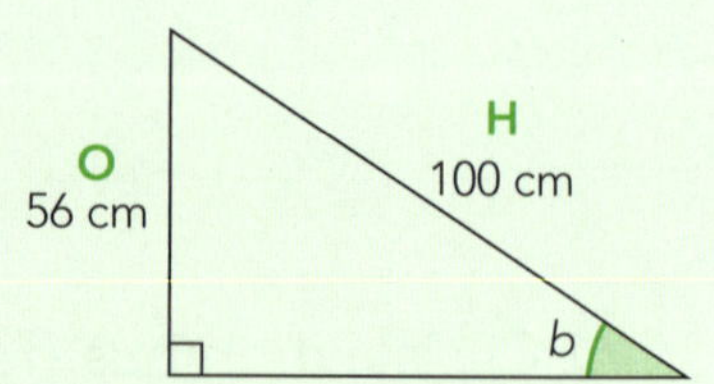


**Step 2:** The labelled sides are **O** and **H**, so write out the triangle involving these:

We need to find **angle $b$**, so we write an expression for **sin b**.

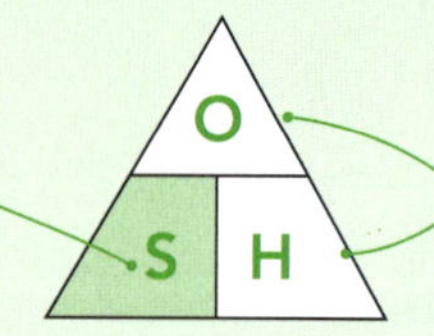


**O** is at the top of this triangle and **H** is at the bottom, so we **divide** them.

$$\sin b = \frac{O}{H}$$

**Step 3:** Substitute the numbers and calculate the answer.

'undo' sin

$$\sin b = \frac{56}{100}$$

$$b = \sin^{-1}\left(\frac{56}{100}\right)$$

'undo' sin

$$b = 34.1° \text{ (1 dp)}$$

In order to find $b$, we need to '**undo**' the sine of $b$.

As with any equation, we must do the **same to both sides**.

To '**undo**' a sine, cosine or tangent, you use the 'shift' (SHIFT) or the '2nd F' (2ndF) buttons before you press the sine, cosine or tangent buttons. Don't forget the brackets.
Note: if you get an 'error' message, check that your fraction is the right way up.

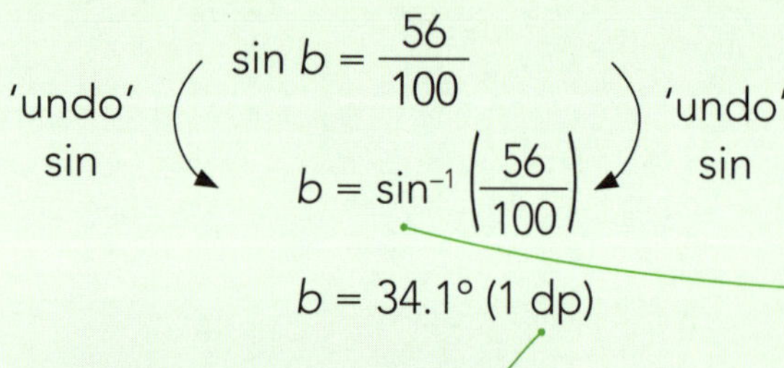

Angles are such small units of measure, that usually it is sensible to round them to just **1 dp**.

**Step 4:** **Think** about your answer — does it seem about right?

$b = 34.1°$ is opposite the shortest side, so we would expect $b$ to be less than 45° ✓



 ISBN: 9780170451543

Use your 'inverse sin' button ($\sin^{-1}$) to find the answers to the following. Round the answers to 1 dp.

**1** If $\sin \theta = 0.5$, then $\theta =$ ______________

**2** If $\sin \theta = 0.45$, then $\theta =$ ______________

**3** If $\sin \theta = 0.99$, then $\theta =$ ______________

**4** If $\sin \theta = \frac{1}{5}$, then $\theta =$ ______________

**5** If $\sin \theta = \frac{51}{63}$, then $\theta =$ ______________

**6** If $\sin \theta = \frac{8}{55}$, then $\theta =$ ______________

Use trigonometry to calculate the unknown angle in each triangle. Round your answers to 1 dp.

**7**

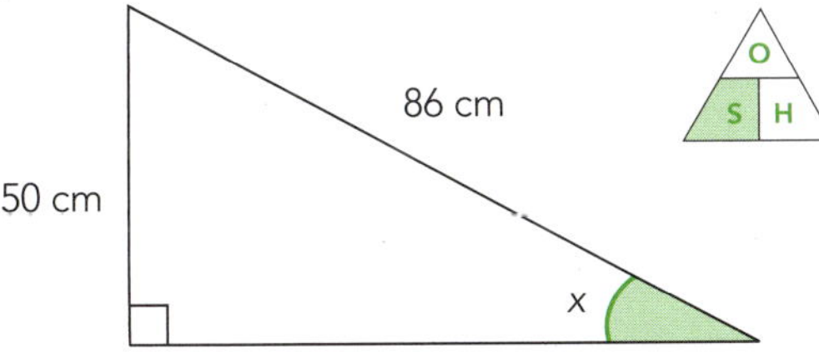


'undo' sin

$\sin x = \frac{50}{86}$

$x = \sin^{-1}\left(\frac{\quad}{\quad}\right)$

'undo' sin

= ______________ (1 dp)

**8**

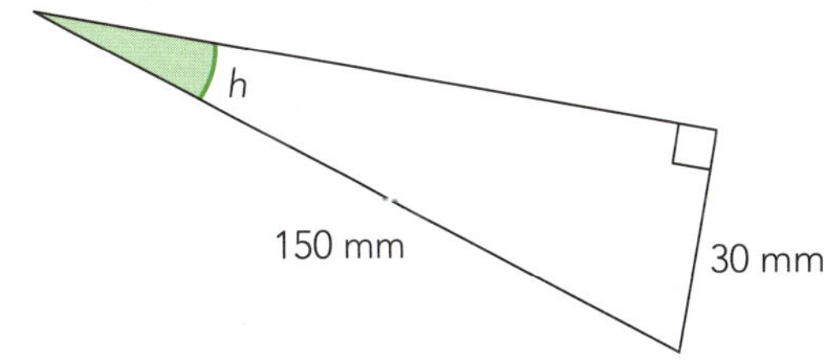


______________

______________

______________

**9**

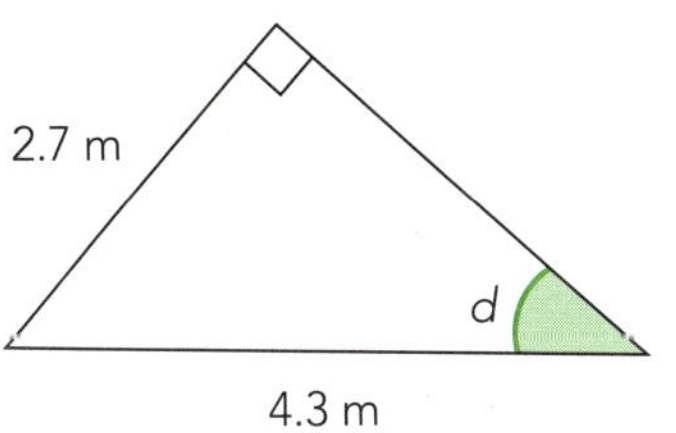


______________

______________

______________

**10**

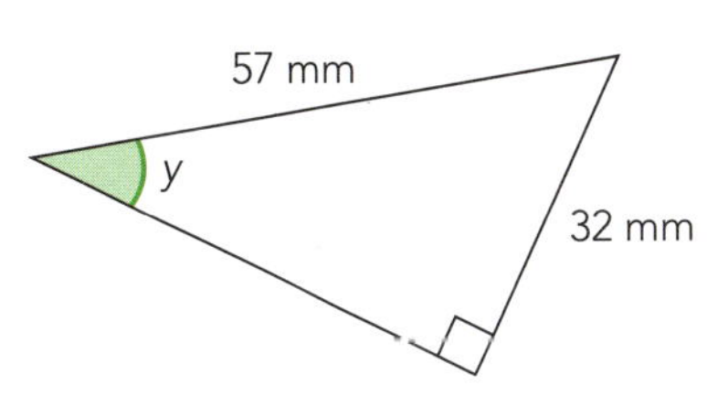


______________

______________

______________

**11**

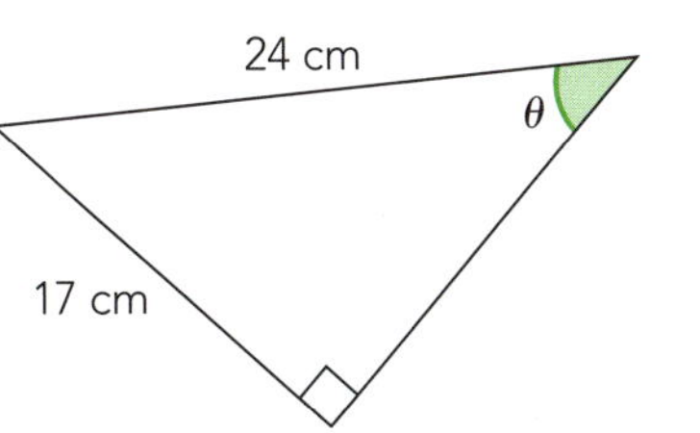


______________

______________

______________

**12**

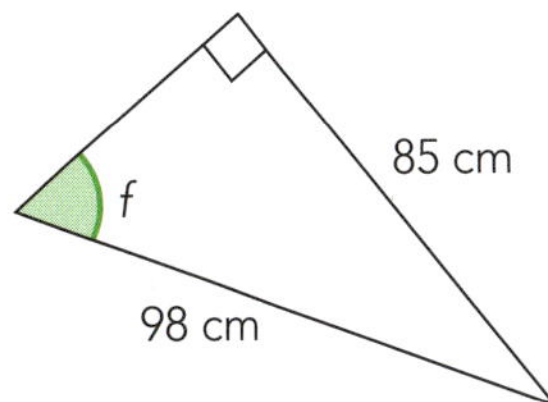


______________

______________

______________

ISBN: 9780170451543 

# Finding angles using cosine and tangent

- You can use the same steps to find angles in right-angled triangles using cosine and tangent.

**Examples:**

1 Calculate the size of angle $\theta$.

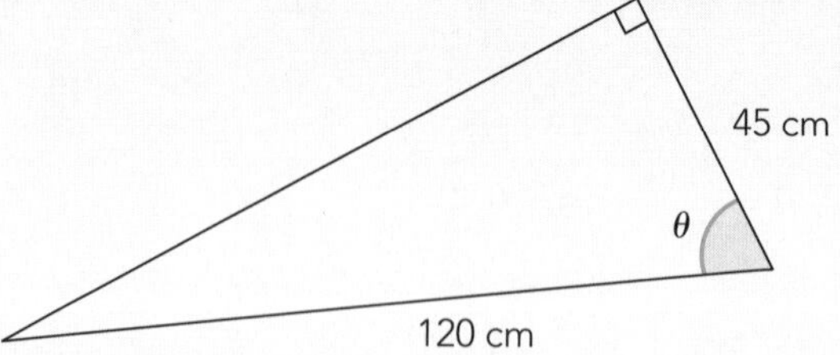


**Step 1:** Label the sides **that are involved** with A, O and H.

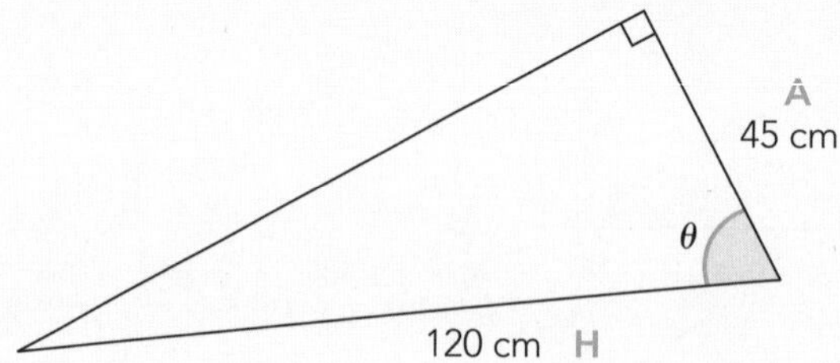


**Step 2:** The labelled sides are A and H, so write out the triangle involving these:

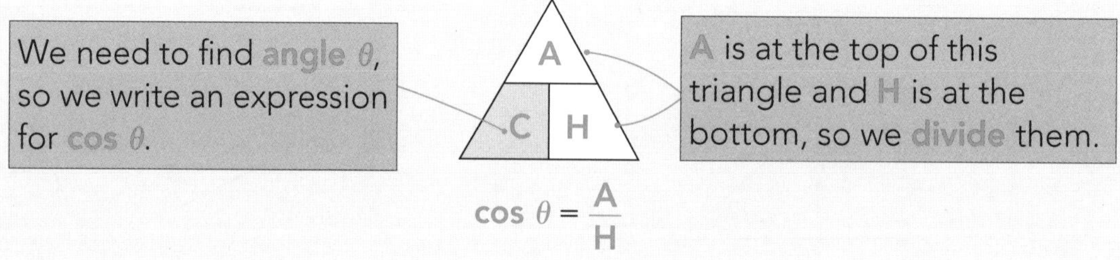


$$\cos\theta = \frac{A}{H}$$

**Step 3:** Substitute the numbers and calculate the answer.

$$\cos\theta = \frac{45}{120}$$

'undo' cos      'undo' cos

$$\theta = \cos^{-1}\left(\frac{45}{120}\right)$$

$$\theta = 68.0^\circ \text{ (1 dp)}$$

**Step 4:** Think about your answer — does it seem about right?

$\theta = 68.0^\circ$ is opposite the longer side (not counting the hypotenuse), so we would expect $\theta$ to be more than $45^\circ$ ✓



 ISBN: 9780170451543

**2** Calculate the size of angle $y$.

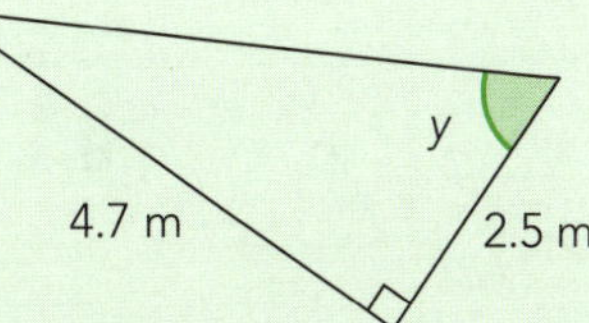


**Step 1:** Label the sides **that are involved** with A, O and H.

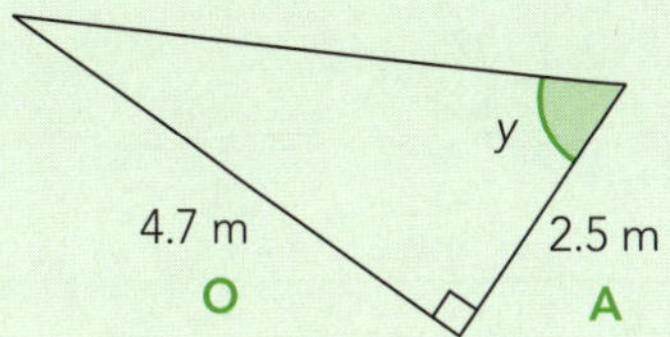


**Step 2:** The labelled sides are **O** and **A**, so write out the triangle involving these:

We need to find **angle $y$**, so we write an expression for **tan $y$**.

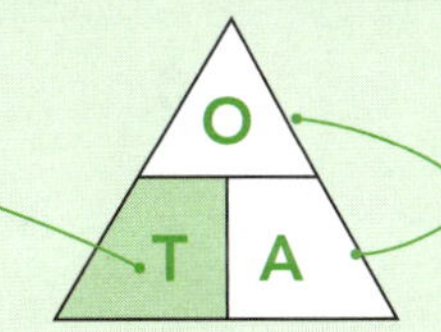


**O** is at the top of this triangle and **A** is at the bottom, so we **divide** them.

$$\tan y = \frac{O}{A}$$

**Step 3:** Substitute the numbers and calculate the answer.

$$\tan y = \frac{4.7}{2.5}$$

'undo' tan  'undo' tan

$$y = \tan^{-1}\left(\frac{4.7}{2.5}\right)$$

$$y = 62.0° \text{ (1 dp)}$$

**Step 4:** **Think** about your answer — does it seem about right?

$y = 62.0°$ is opposite the longer side (not counting the hypotenuse), so we would expect $y$ to be more than 45° ✓

Use your 'inverse cos' button ($\cos^{-1}$) or 'inverse tan' button ($\tan^{-1}$) to find the answers to the following. Round the answers to 1 dp.

**1** If $\cos \theta = 0.5$, then $\theta =$ ____________

**2** If $\tan \theta = 4.5$, then $\theta =$ ____________

**3** If $\tan \theta = 1$, then $\theta =$ ____________

**4** If $\cos \theta = \frac{2}{9}$, then $\theta =$ ____________

**5** If $\tan \theta = \frac{87}{33}$, then $\theta =$ ____________

**6** If $\cos \theta = \frac{128}{155}$, then $\theta =$ ____________

ISBN: 9780170451543 

Use trigonometry to calculate the unknown angle in each triangle. Round your answers to 1 dp.

**7**

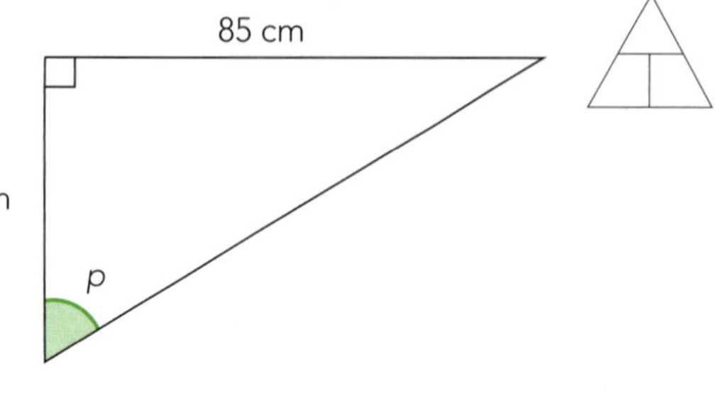


**8**

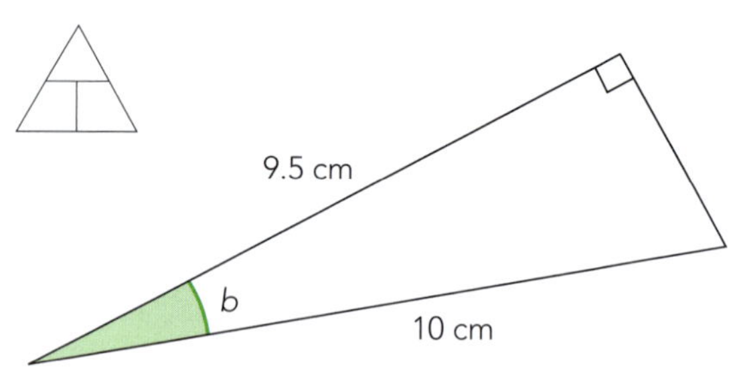


**9**

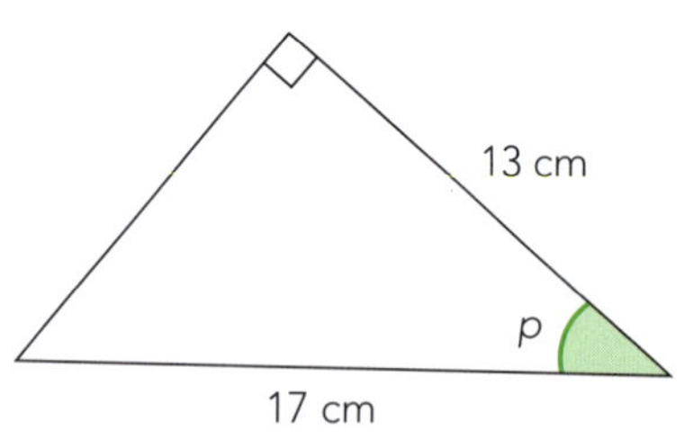


**10**

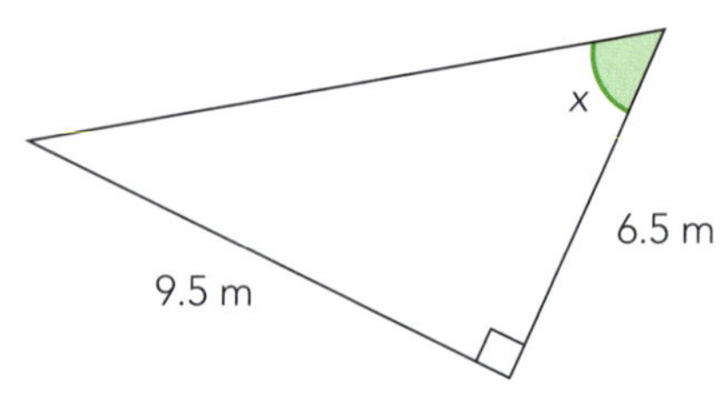


**11**

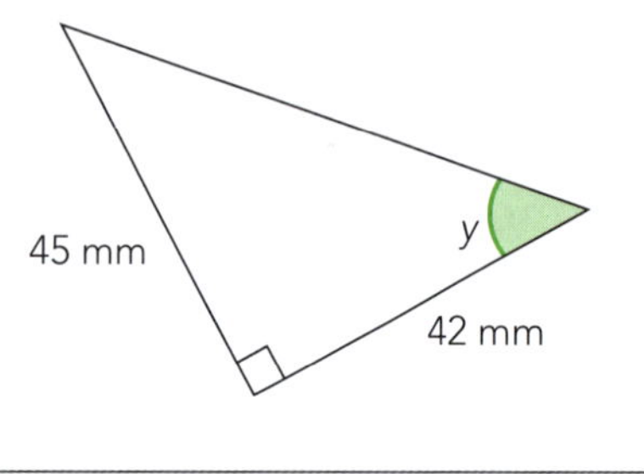


**12**

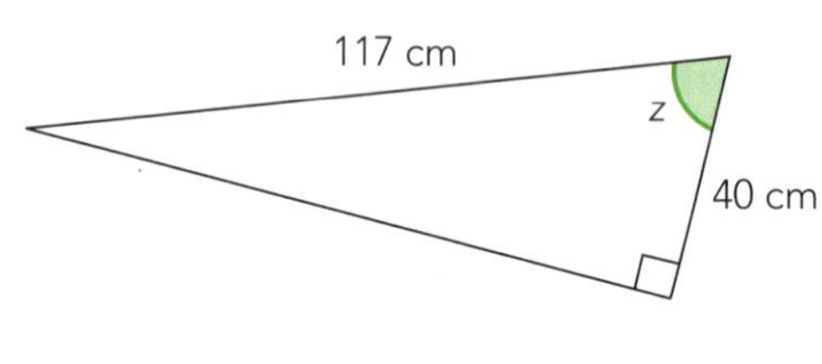


**13**

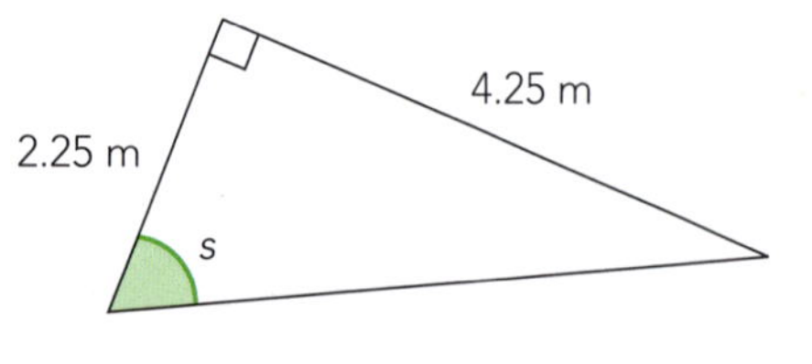


**14**

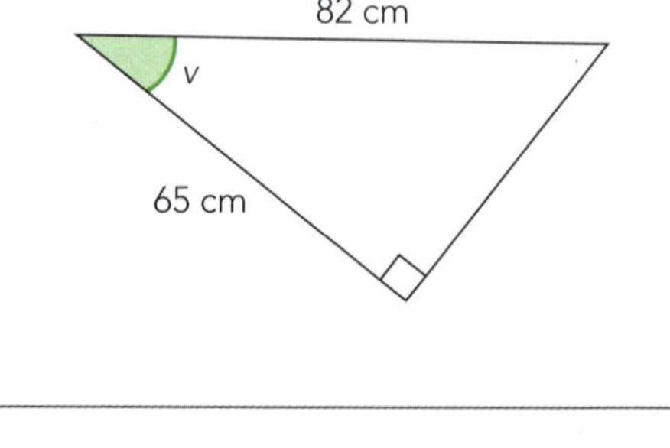




 ISBN: 9780170451543

# Mixing it up

Use trigonometry to calculate the unknown side or angle in each triangle. Round your answers to 1 dp.

**1**

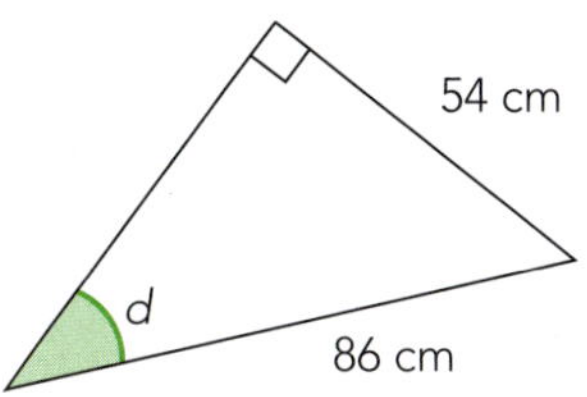


**2**

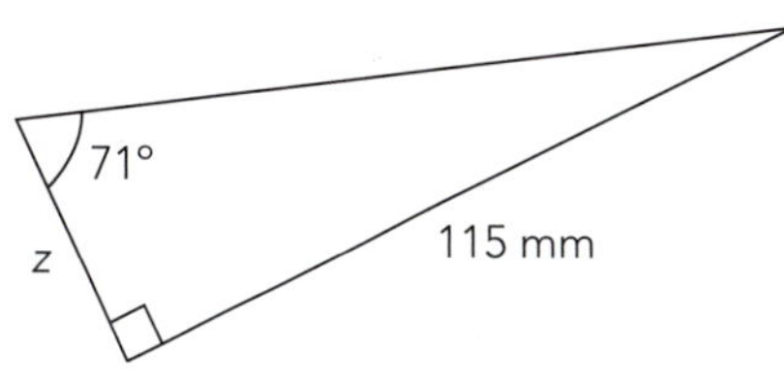


**3**

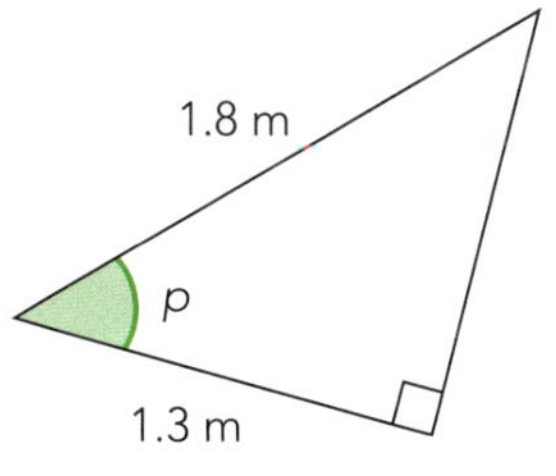


**4**

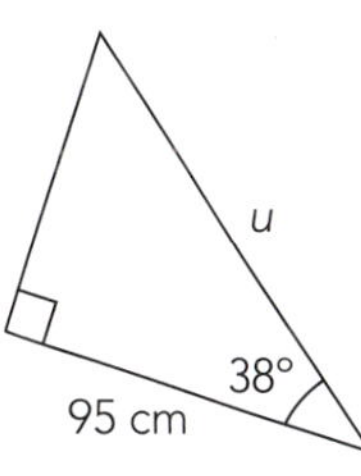


**5**

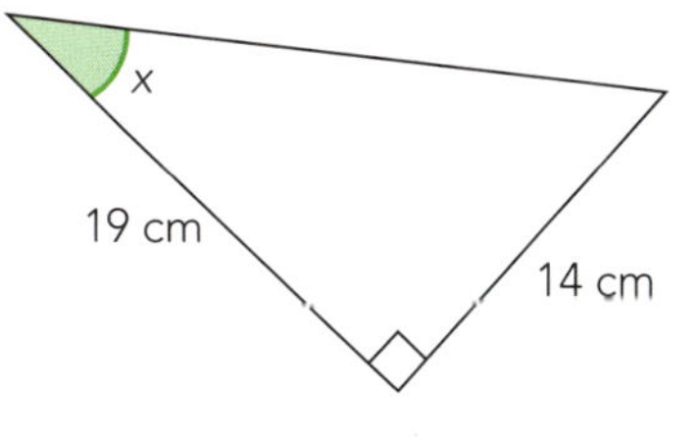


**6**

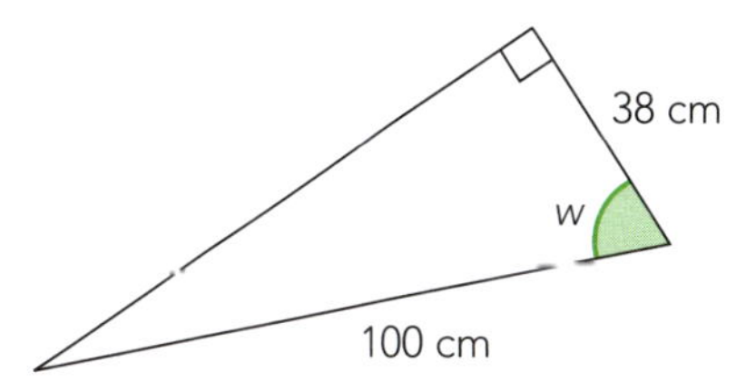


**7**

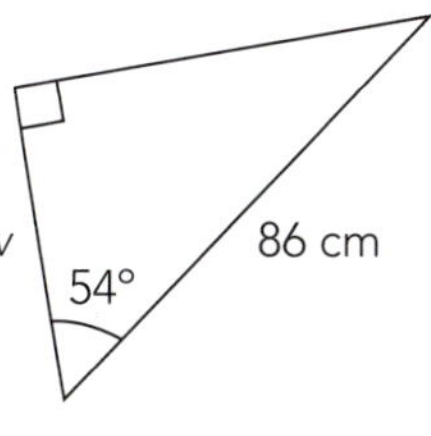


**8**

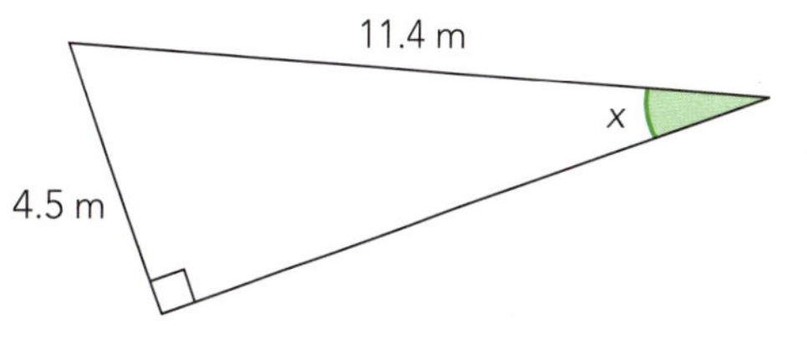


ISBN: 9780170451543  

# Finding angles using trigonometry and geometry

Answer the following questions using trigonometry and geometry. In each case, show your reasoning.

**1** ABCD is a rhombus. The length of its shorter diagonal (BD) is 8.3 cm, and that of its longer diagonal (AC) is 13.5 cm. Calculate the size of angle DAB.

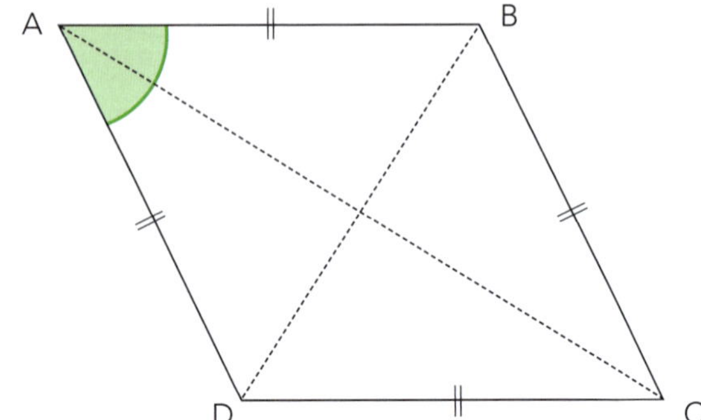


**2** ABC form the corners of a triangle. Angle BCA is 47°, AD is 35 cm and BC is 40.5 cm. Calculate the size of angle BAD.

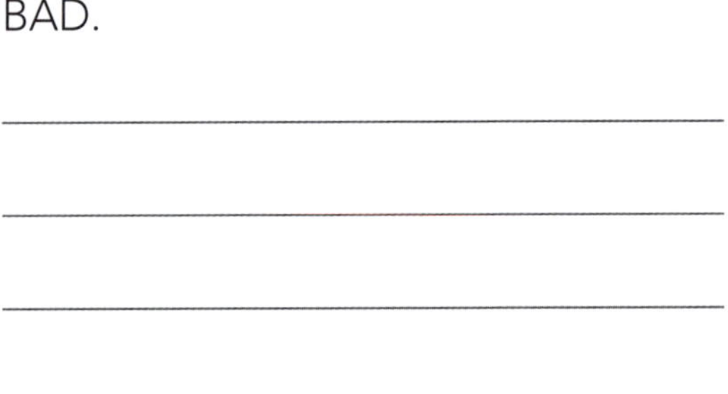

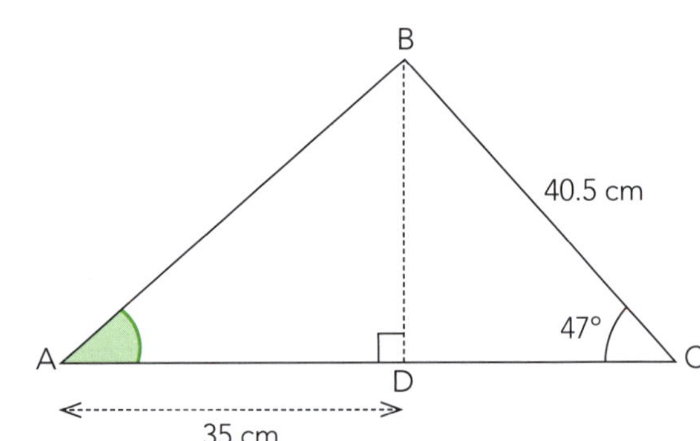


**3** ABC form the corners of a triangle. Angle BDC = 47°, its vertical height is 59 cm, and AD is 35 cm. Calculate the size of angle BAD.

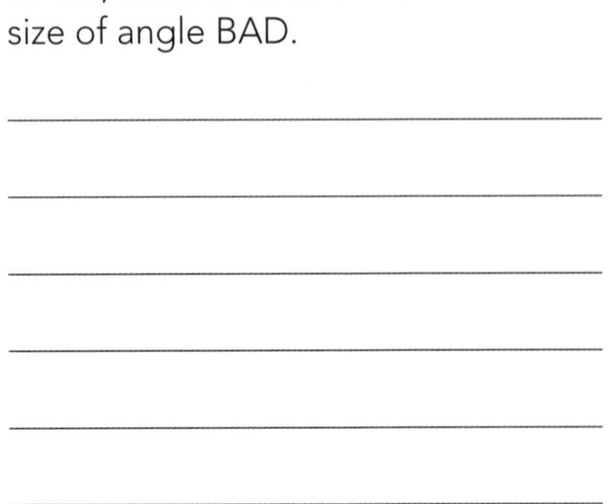

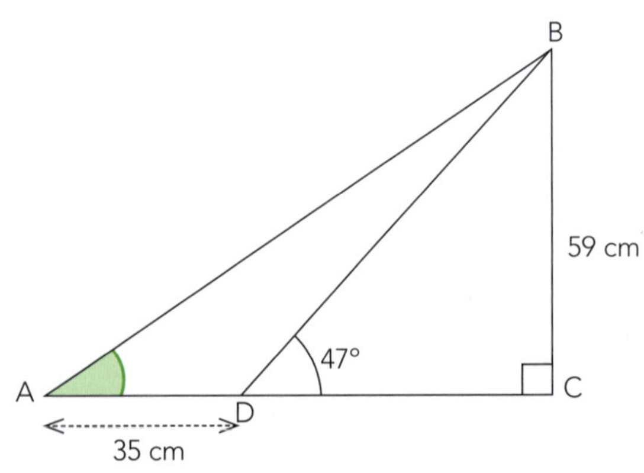




 ISBN: 9780170451543

**4** ABCD is a quadrilateral. AB is 72 cm, CD is 53 cm, and the vertical height of ABC is 56 cm. Calculate the sizes of angles BCE and CAD.

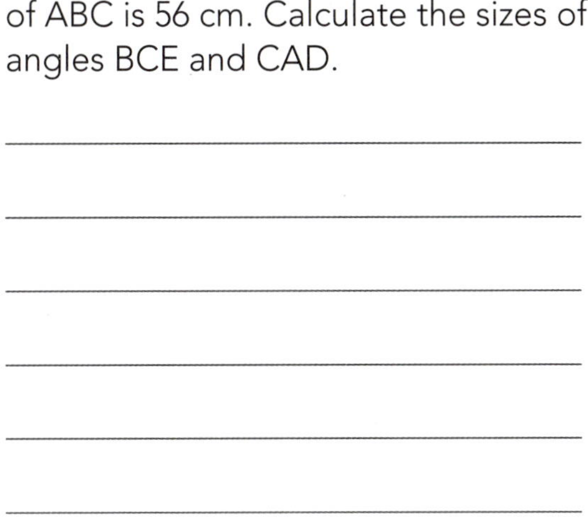

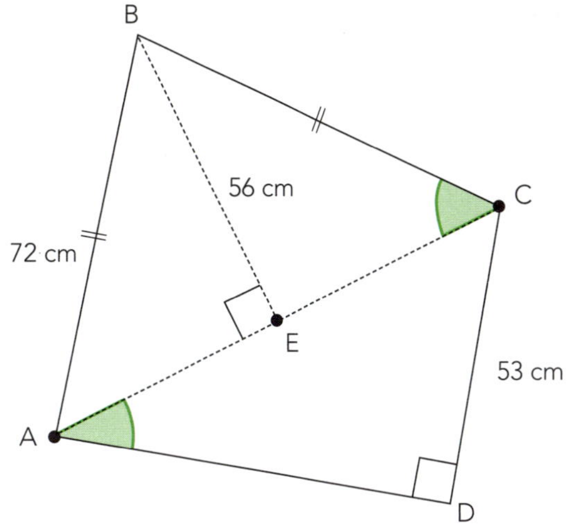


**5** ABCD is a quadrilateral. AE is parallel to DC. Angle ABC is 63°, BC is 6 m, AE is 7 m and DC is 2.5 m. Calculate the size of angle EAD.

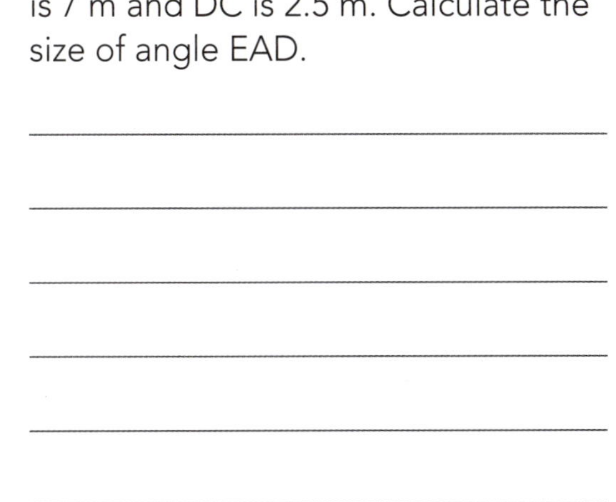

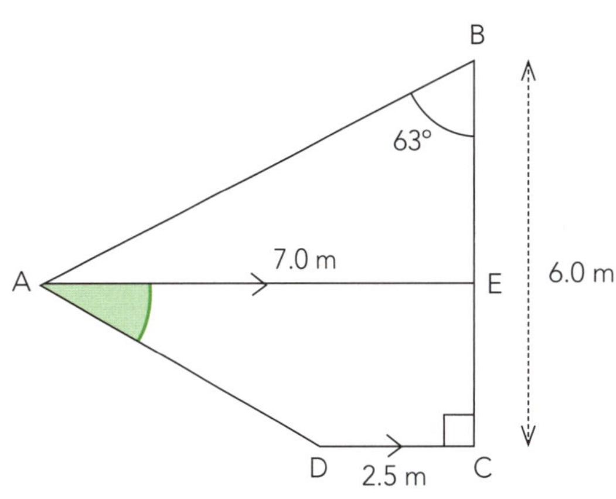


**6** ABCD is a kite. AB is 92 mm, CD is 73 mm and DE is 20 mm. Calculate the sizes of angles DAC and BAD.

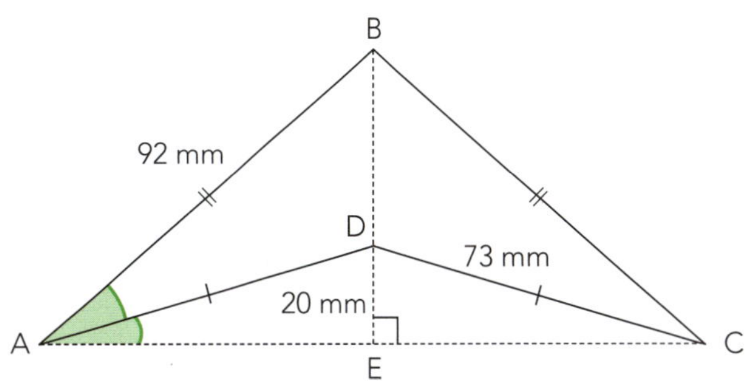


ISBN: 9780170451543  

# Challenge 2

## 1 Area mystery

The triangles below have each been divided into a rectangle and two smaller triangles. Calculate the area of each.

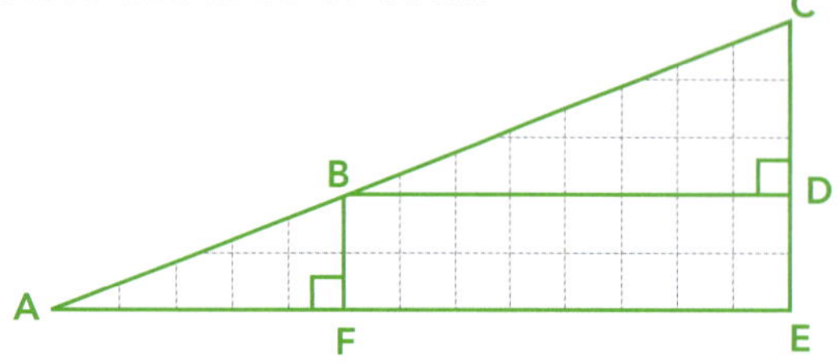


Area = ______________________

= ______________ units²

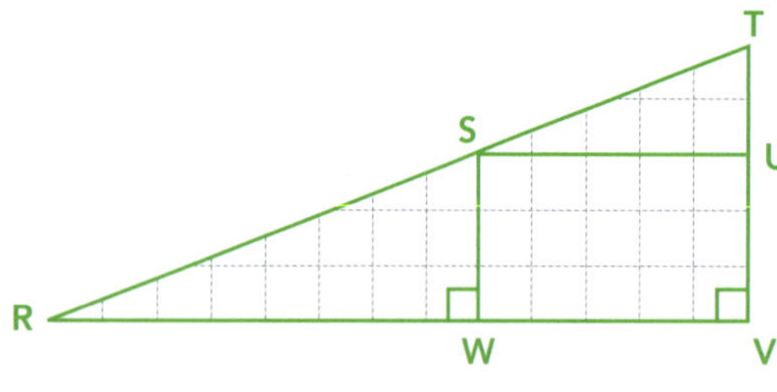


Area = ______________________

= ______________ units²

What do you notice about these areas? ______________________

Investigate and explain the difference. Hint: trigonometry may be helpful.

______________________

______________________

______________________

## 2 Pythagorean triples

- It is possible to draw a right-angled triangle which has sides of exactly 3, 4 and 5 units long.
- (3, 4, 5) is known as a **Pythagorean triple** — groups of three integers for which $a^2 + b^2 = c^2$.
- There are many others, e.g. (5, 12, 13), (8, 15, 17), (7, 24, 25).

Fill in the gaps with Pythagorean triples. Your answers must be integers, and you will be able to calculate some using $x^2 = a^2 + b^2$, but others will require $x^2 = a^2 - b^2$.

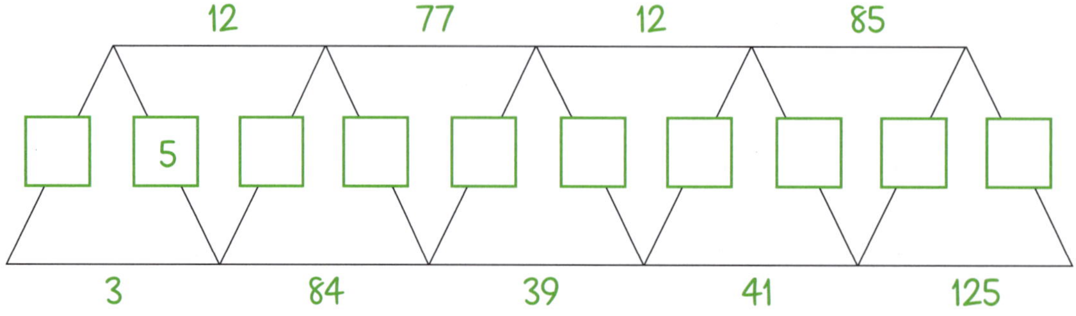




 ISBN: 9780170451543

# Revision 1

**1** Select the **best** term to describe the coloured angles or line in each of the following figures.

| Opposite side | Adjacent side | Corresponding angles | Supplementary angles |
|---|---|---|---|
| Alternate angles | Complementary angles | Hypotenuse | Parallel lines |

**a**

**b**

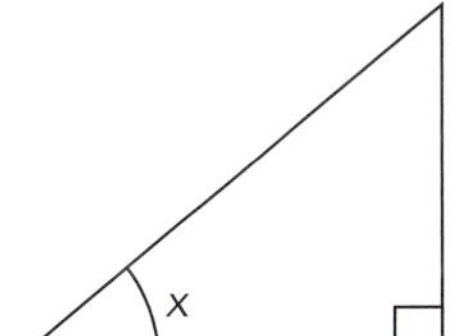


**c**

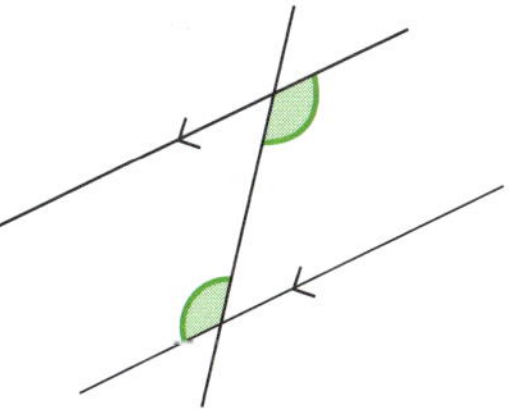

**2** Calculate the size of the marked angles.

**a**

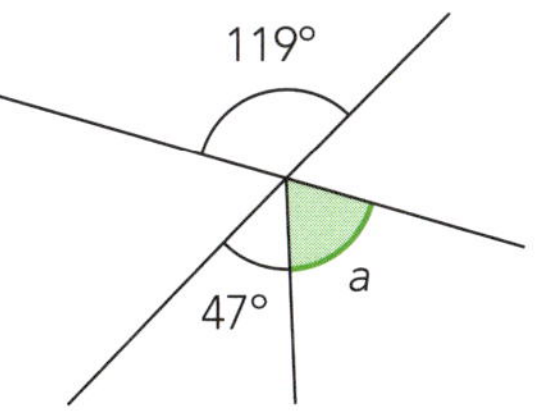


**b**

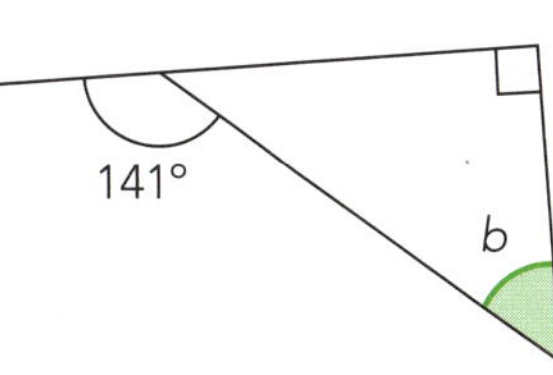


**c**

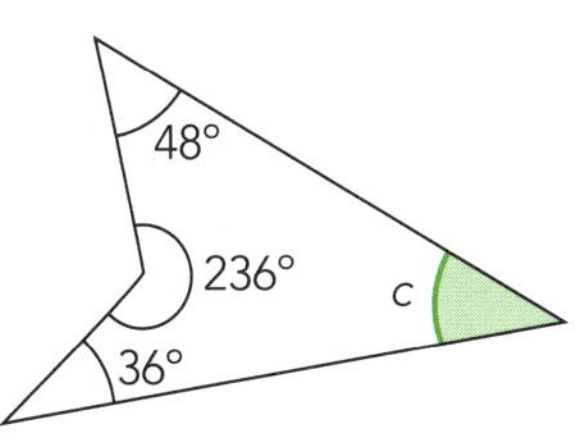


**d**

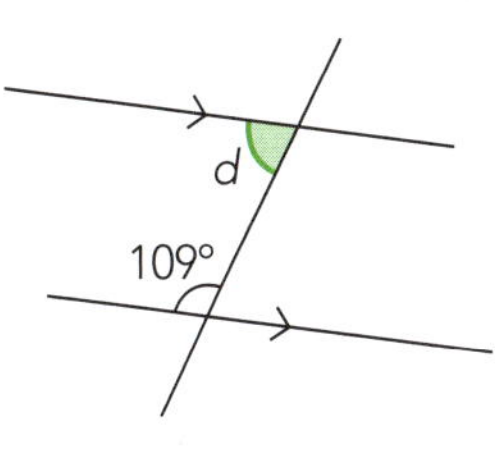


**e**

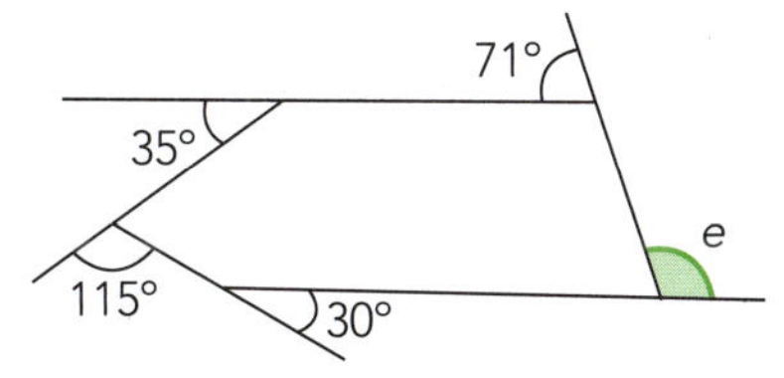


**f**

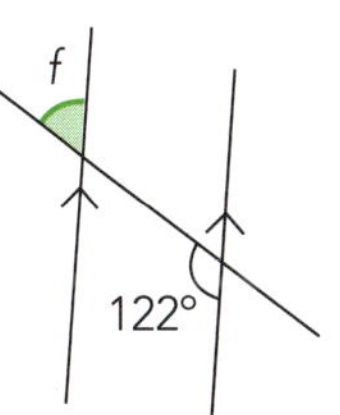


ISBN: 9780170451543 

3 Use this map to answer the following questions. The distance between the grid lines is 10 km.

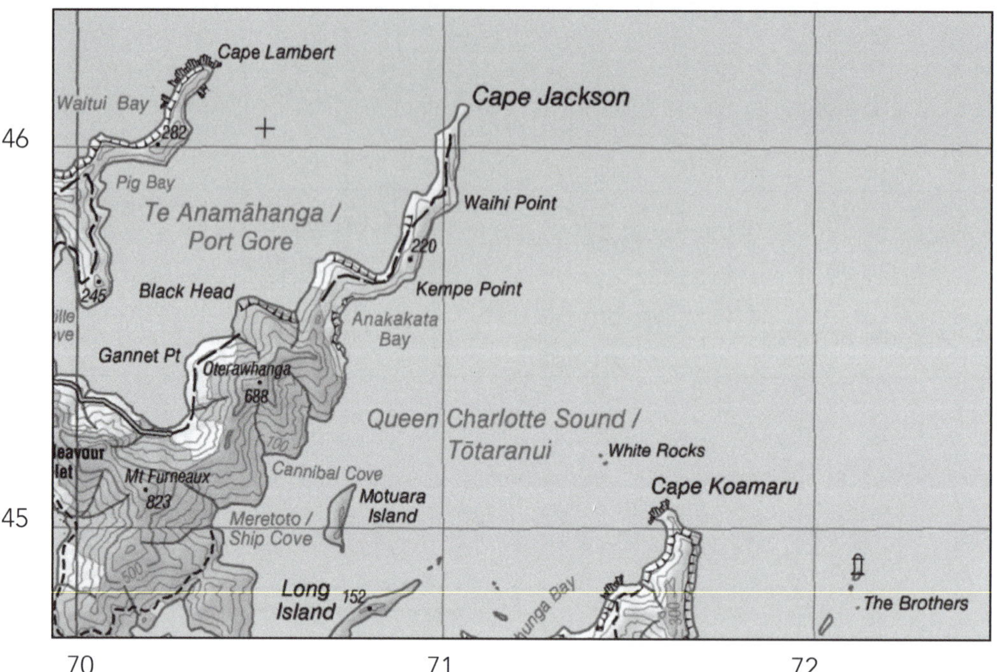


**a** Circle the direction and bearing for a line from Cape Lambert to Kempe Point.

SE SW NE NW

045° 225° 315° 135°

**b** What would you find at at 705452? ____________________

**c** Write the grid reference for Waihi Point. ____________________

**d** Estimate the distance between Cape Jackson and Cape Koamaru. ____________________

**e** A boat is at sea and located an equal distance from Cape Jackson and Cape Koamaru. Sketch the locus for the possible positions of the boat.

4 Write the scale factor for this enlargement.

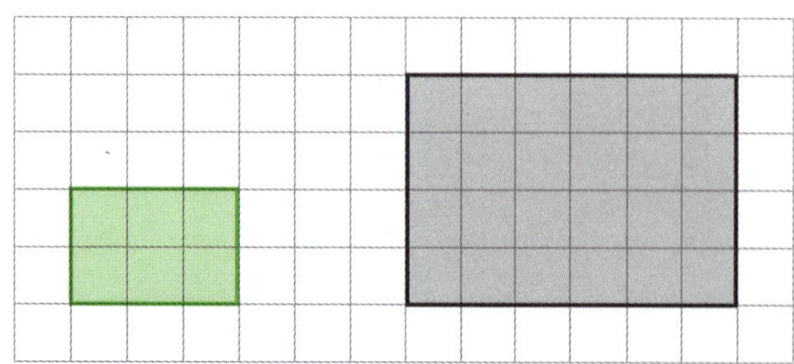

Scale factor

= __________

5 Write the order of rotational symmetry for this image.

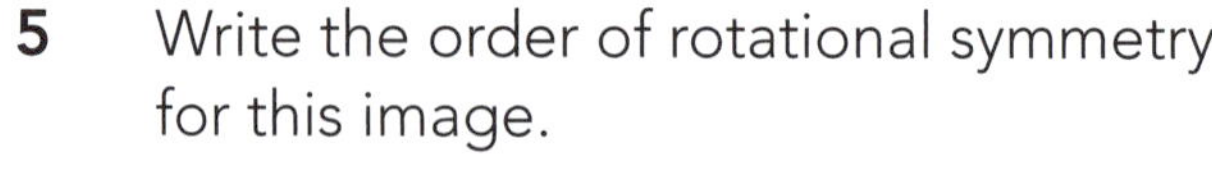

Order of rotational symmetry

= __________



 ISBN: 9780170451543

**6** Find the centre of enlargement for these images.

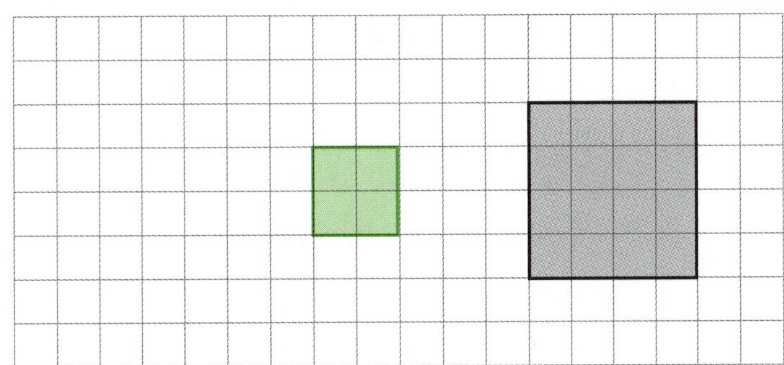

**7** Use Pythagoras to calculate the unknown side in each triangle. Round your answers to 1 dp.

**a**

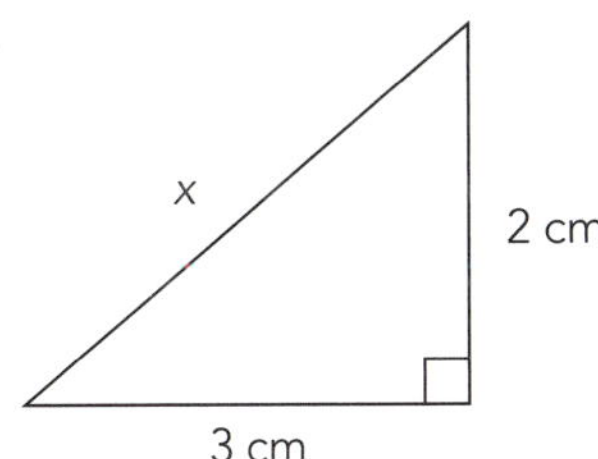


**b**

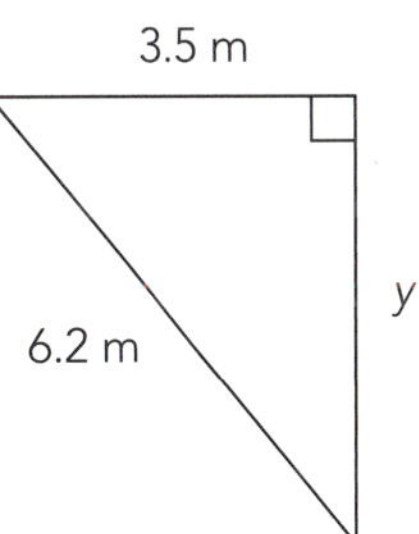


**8** Use trigonometry to calculate the unknown side or angle in each triangle. Round your answers to 1 dp.

**a**

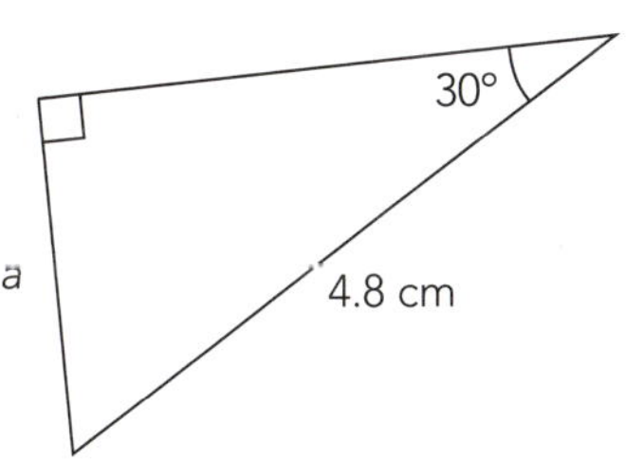


**b**

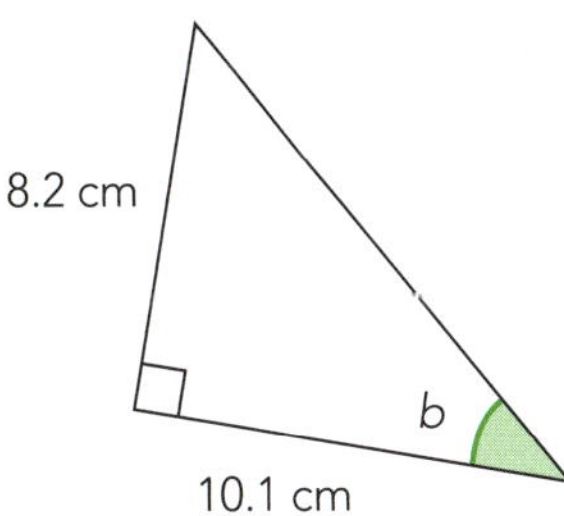


**c**

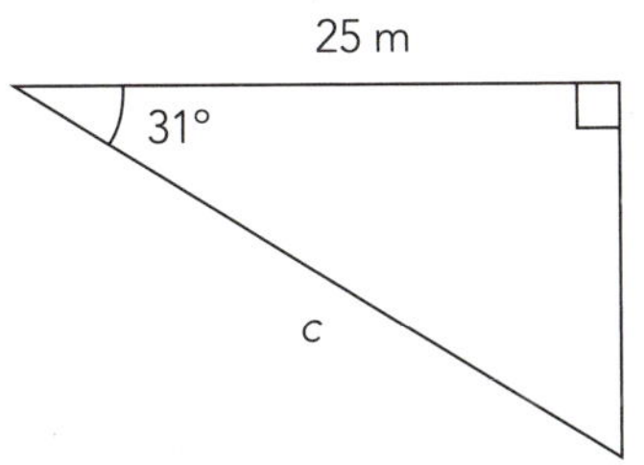


**d**

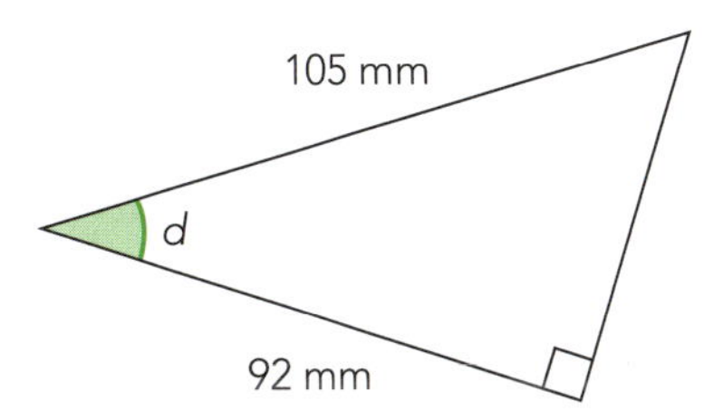


ISBN: 9780170451543  

# Revision 2

**1** Select the **best** term to describe the coloured angles or line in each of the following figures.

| Opposite side | Adjacent side | Corresponding angle | Supplementary angle |
|---|---|---|---|
| Alternate angles | Complementary angles | Hypotenuse | Parallel lines |

**a**

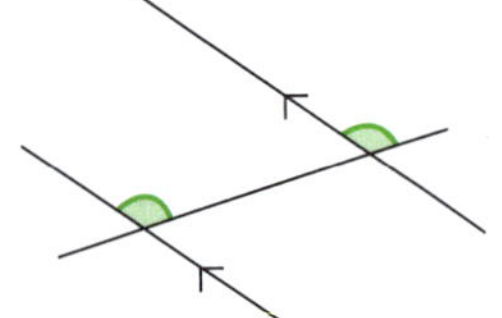

**b**

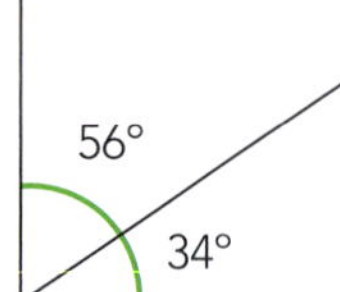


**c**

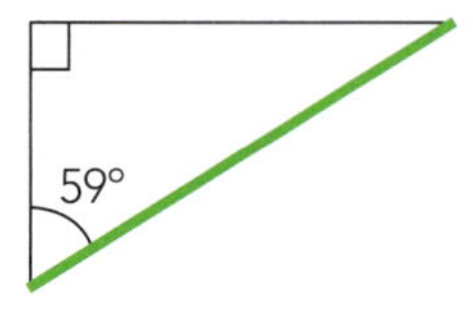


**2** Calculate the size of the marked angles.

**a**

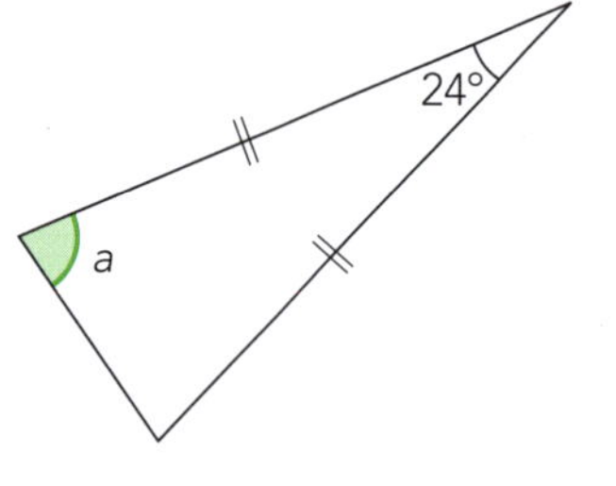


**b**

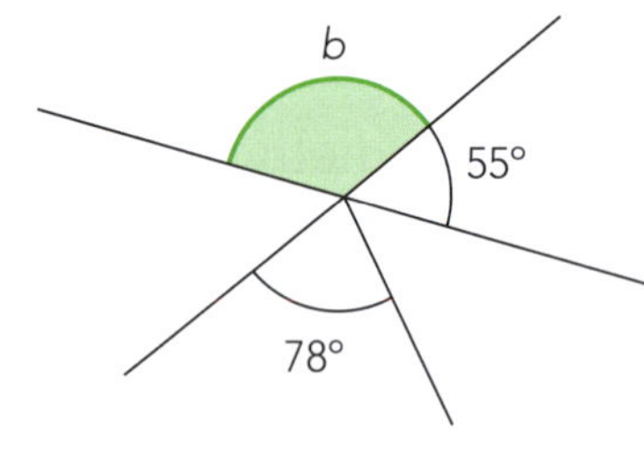


**c**

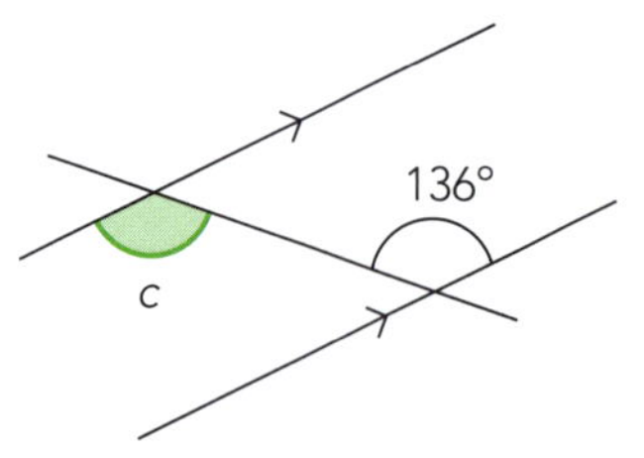


**d**

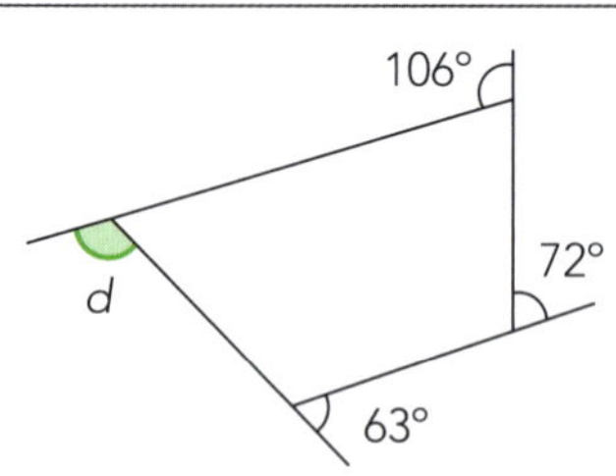


**e**

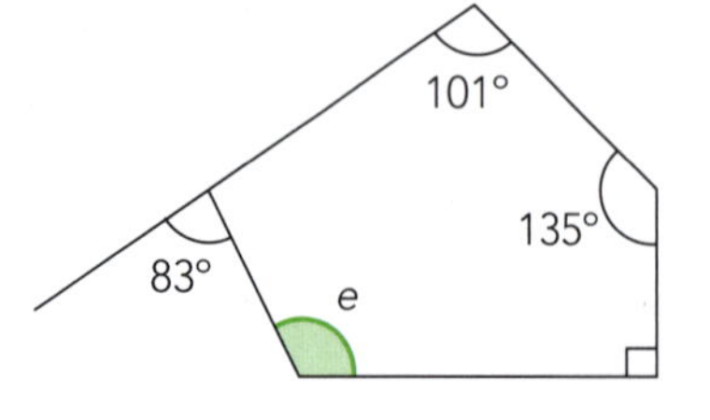


**f**

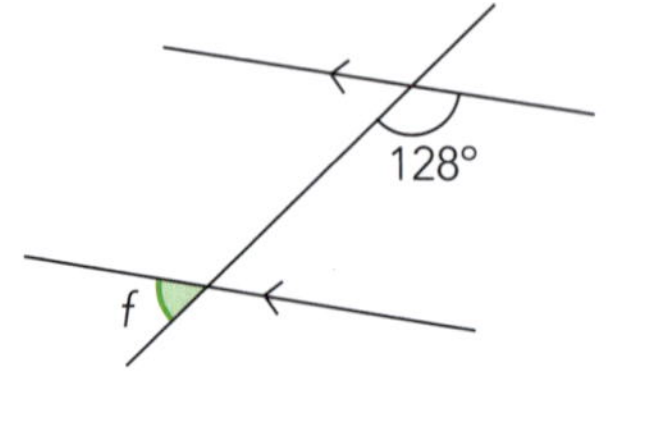




 ISBN: 9780170451543

**3** Use this map to answer the following questions. The distance between the grid lines is 10 km.

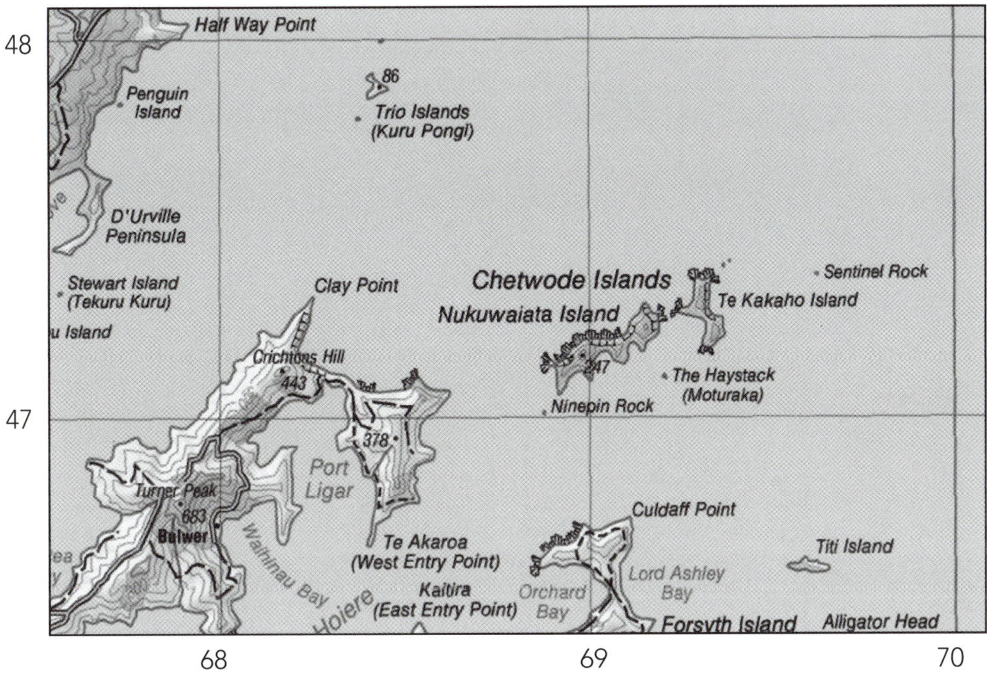


**a** Circle the direction and bearing for a line from Ninepin Rock to Half Way Point.

SE SW NE NW

045° 225° 315° 135°

**b** What would you find at at 696474? ____________________

**c** Write the grid reference for The Haystack. ____________________

**d** Estimate the distance between the peak on Trio Islands (Kuru Pongi) and Sentinel Rock. ____________________

**e** Suppose fishing is prohibited within 2 km of Sentinel Rock. Sketch and shade the area where fishing is prohibited.

**4** Write the scale factor for this enlargement.

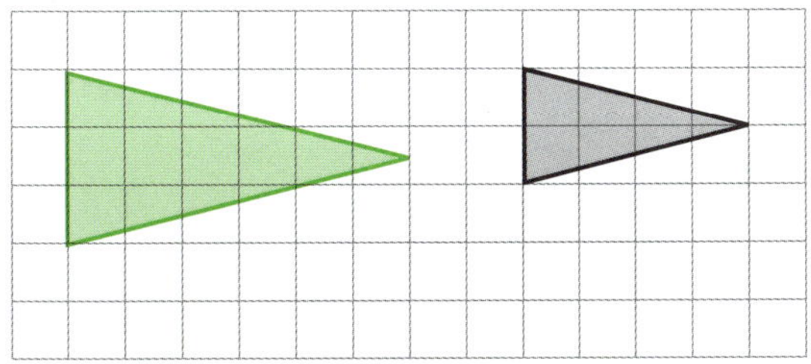

Scale factor

= ____________

**5** Write the order of rotational symmetry for this image.

Order of rotational symmetry

= ____________

ISBN: 9780170451543 

**6** Enlarge this triangle by a scale factor of 3.

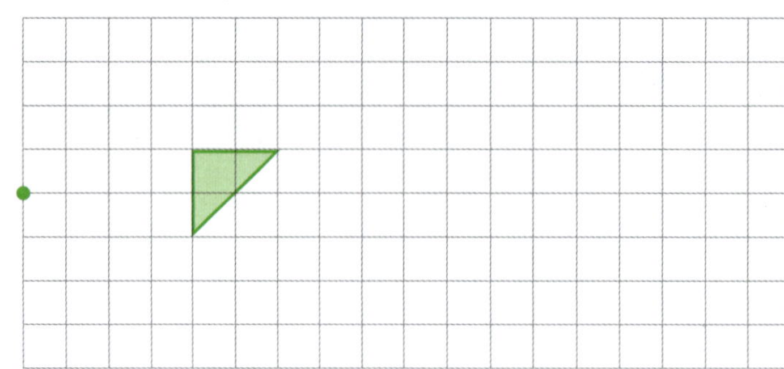

**7** Use Pythagoras to calculate the unknown side in each triangle. Round your answers to 1 dp.

**a**

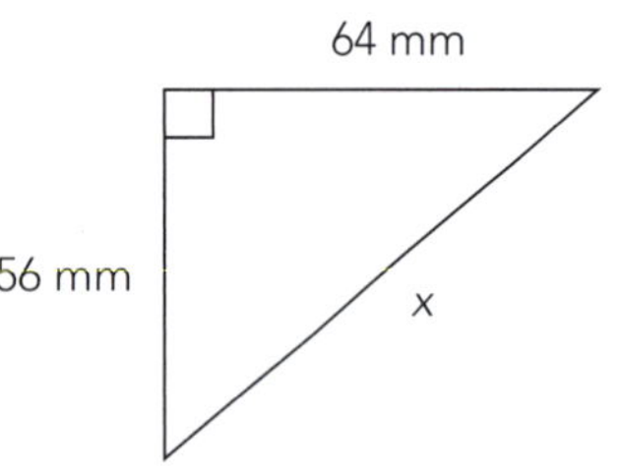


**b**

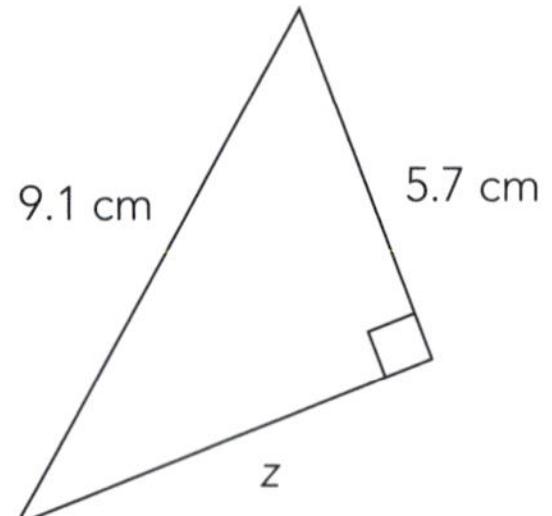


**8** Use trigonometry to calculate the unknown side or angle in each triangle. Round your answers to 1 dp.

**a**

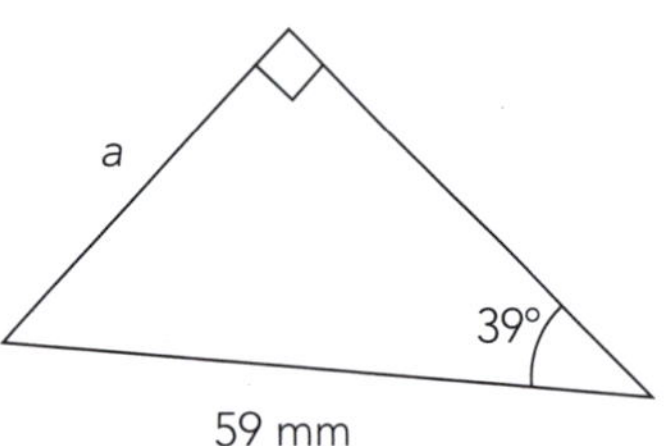


**b**

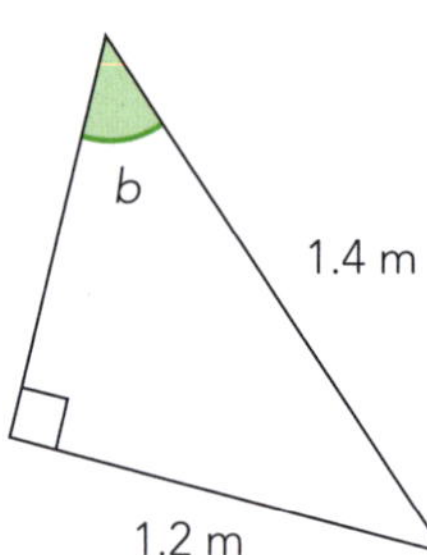


**c**

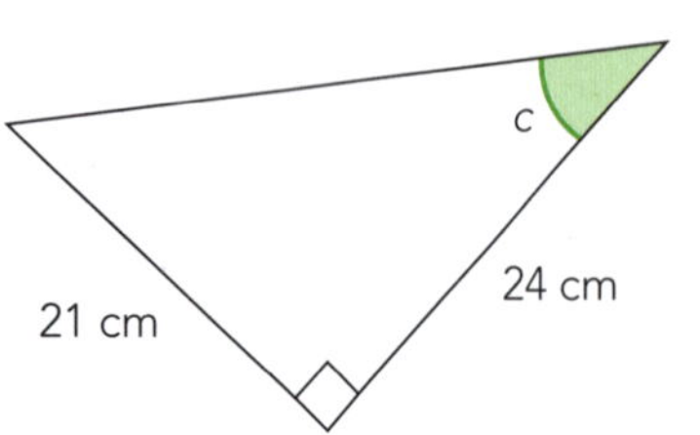


**d**

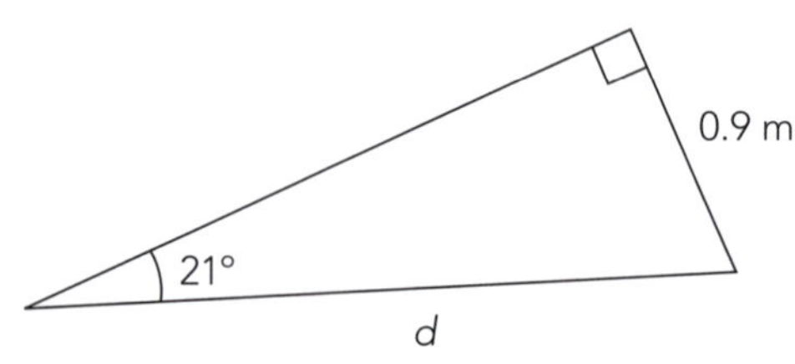




 ISBN: 9780170451543

# Answers

## Language of geometry (p. 6)

1 Supplementary
2 Regular
3 Right angle
4 Obtuse angle
5 Reflex angle
6 Quadrilateral
7 Irregular
8 Parallel lines
9 Complementary
10 Hexagon
11 Trapezium
12 Acute angle

## Angles (pp. 7–22)

### Angle revision (pp.7–9)

1 $b = 29°$
$\angle$s on a line = 180°.
2 $k = 131°$
$\angle$s at a point = 360°.
3 $y = 73°$
Vert opp $\angle$s are equal.
4 $a = 69°$
$\angle$s on a line = 180°.
5 $e = 119°$
$\angle$s on a line = 180°.
6 $x = 91°$
$\angle$s at a point = 360°.
7 $d = 22°$
$\angle$s on a line = 180°.
8 $f = 119°$
Vert opp $\angle$s are equal.
9 $k = 64°$
$\angle$s on a line = 180°.
10 $b = 207°$
$\angle$s at a point = 360°.
11 $s = 53°$
Vert opp $\angle$s are equal.
12 $p = 52°$
Vert opp $\angle$s are equal and $\angle$s at a point = 360° or $\angle$s on a line = 180°.
13 $t = 42°$
Vert opp $\angle$s are equal and $\angle$s at a point = 360° or $\angle$s on a line = 180°.
14 $g = 43°$
$\angle$s on a line = 180° or vert opp $\angle$s are equal.

### Angles in a triangle (pp. 10–11)

1 $x = 75°$
$\angle$s in a $\Delta$ = 180°.
2 $y = 94°$
ext $\angle$ of $\Delta$ = sum of int opp $\angle$s.
3 $z = 67°$
$\angle$s in a $\Delta$ = 180°.
4 $x = 37°$
ext $\angle$ of $\Delta$ = sum of int opp $\angle$s.
5 $p = 60°$
ext $\angle$ of $\Delta$ = sum of int opp $\angle$s.
6 $b = 124°$
$\angle$s in a $\Delta$ = 180°.
7 $m = 66°$
ext $\angle$ of $\Delta$ = sum of int opp $\angle$s.
8 $d = 44°$
$\angle$s in a $\Delta$ = 180° and ext $\angle$ of $\Delta$ = sum of int opp $\angle$s.

### Angles in a quadrilateral (pp. 12–13)

1 $y = 35°$
$\angle$s in a quad = 360°.
2 $z = 119°$
$\angle$s in a quad = 360°.
3 $x = 40°$
$\angle$s at a point = 360°.
4 $b = 141°$
$\angle$s in a quad = 360°.
5 $z = 120°$
$\angle$s in a quad = 360° and $\angle$s at a point = 360°.
6 $d = 78°$
$\angle$s in a quad = 360°.
7 $c = 37°$
$\angle$s on a line = 180° and $\angle$s in a quad = 360°.
8 $f = 112°$
$\angle$s on a line = 180°, $\angle$s at a point = 360° and $\angle$s in a quad = 360°.

### Polygons (pp. 14–17)

**Exterior angles**

1 $y = 123°$
2 $c = 122°$
3 $x = 95°$
4 $z = 105°$
5 $f = 72°$
6 $a = 109°$
7 $g = 110°$
8 $p = 138°$

**Interior angles**

1 $b = 116°$
2 $y = 109°$
3 $x = 103°$
4 $z = 166°$
5 $s = 128.57°$ (2 dp)
6 $w = 62°$

### Parallel lines (pp. 18–20)

1 alternate
2 co-interior
3 corresponding
4 alternate
5 corresponding
6 alternate
7 co-interior
8 corresponding
9 $a = 124°$
Corr $\angle$s =, $\parallel$ lines.
10 $d = 51°$
Alt $\angle$s =, $\parallel$ lines.

**11** $y = 51°$
Co-int ∠s add to 180°, ∥ lines.
**12** $x = 137°$
Corr ∠s =, ∥ lines.
**13** $e = 62°$
Co-int ∠s add to 180°, ∥ lines.
**14** $f = 62°$
Alt ∠s =, ∥ lines.

**Mixing it up (pp. 21–22)**

**1** $y = 55°$
∠s in a Δ = 180°.
**2** $a = 30°$
vert opp ∠s =.
**3** $z = 78°$
∠s on a line = 180°.
**4** $b = 136°$
∠s at a point = 360°.
**5** $f = 102°$
∠s in a quad = 360° and ∠s on a line = 180°.
**6** $y = 118°$
alt ∠s =, ∥ lines.
**7** $g = 36°$
Ext ∠ of a Δ = sum of int opp ∠s.
**8** $x = 72°$
∠s in a quad = 360° and ∠s on a line = 180°.
**9** $p = 39°$
co-int ∠s =, ∥ lines.
**10** $d = 108°$
alt ∠s =, ∥ lines.
**11** $n = 108°$
Ext ∠s of a polygon = 360° and ∠s on a line = 180° or int ∠s of a pentagon = 540°.
**12** $f = 124°$
corr ∠s =, ∥ lines.
**13** $t = 103°$
∠s in a Δ = 180°, corr ∠s =, ∥ lines and ∠s on a line = 180°.
**14** $t = 114°$
Co-int ∠s =, ∥ lines = 180° and ∠s at a point = 360°.

## Isometrics revision (pp. 24)

**1**

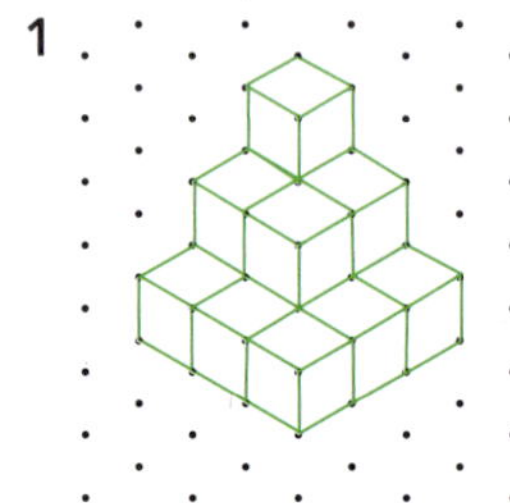

**2**

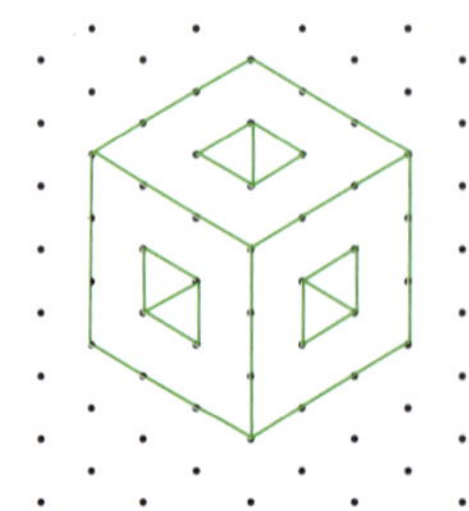

**3**

| 3 | 4 | 2 |
|---|---|---|
| 1 | 2 | 2 |
| 1 | 1 | 2 |

**4**

**5** B
**6** C
**7** A

## Challenge 1 (p. 25)

## Position and orientation (pp. 26–41)

**Direction: bearings (pp. 26–27)**

**1** 329°
**2** 114°
**3** 239°
**4** 068°
**5** 202°
**6** 017°
**7** 81°
**8** 155°
**9**

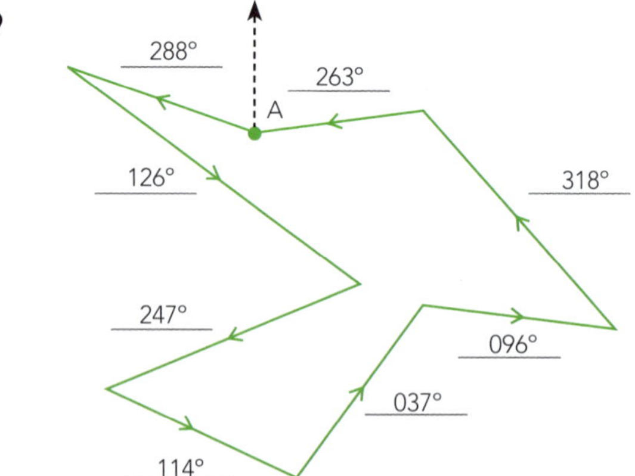


**Using a protractor to find bearings (pp. 28–29)**

**1** Loading buoy
**2** Sunday Rock
**3** Graveyard Point
**4** Eel Rock
**5** Western disused mine
**6** Cowes Bay
**7** Quarry



ISBN: 9780170451543

### Location: loci (pp. 30–33)

1 a

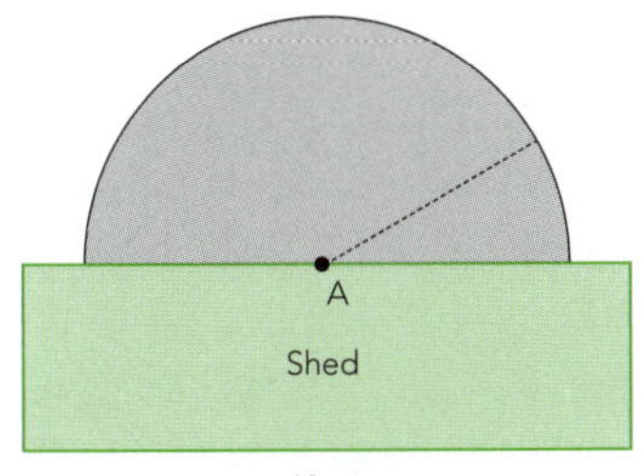


b

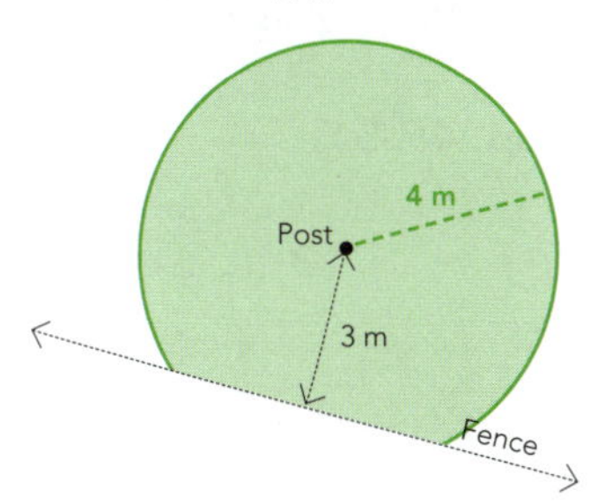


c

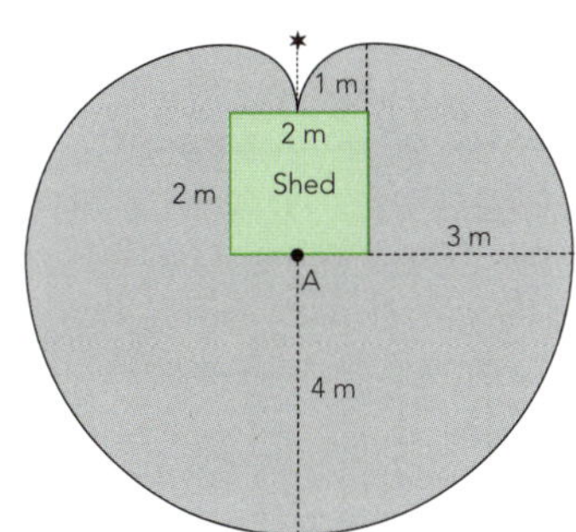


d No. She cannot reach the thistle.

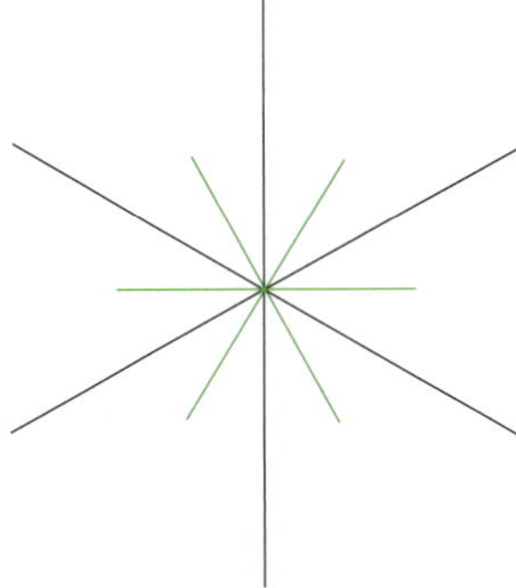


2

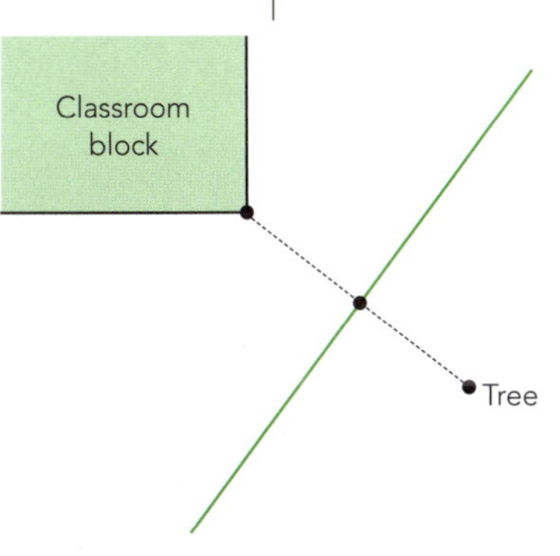

3



### Distance: scales on maps and diagrams (pp. 34–39)

1 1 cm ≡ 1 m

2 1 cm ≡ 10 km

3 1 cm ≡ 50 m

4 1 cm ≡ 25 m

5 1 cm ≡ 0.5 mm

6 1 cm ≡ 2 mm or 0.2 m

7 260 km

8 4.1 or 4.2 km

9 11.5 km

10 25.5 km

Accept answers that are ± 0.5 km.

11 a 36.5 km b 24.5 km
c 48.5 km d 18.5 km

Accept answers that are ± 0.1 m.

12 a 9 m x 9 m b 6.3 m
c 2.3 m x 2.7 m

Accept answers that are ± 0.1 mm.

13 a 6.4 mm b 5.0 mm
c 2.6 or 2.7 mm

### Mixing it up (pp. 40–41)

Accept answers that are ± 10 km.

1 Bearing: 225°
Distance: 100 km

2 Bearing: 225°
Distance: 560 km

3 Bearing: 090°
Distance: 230 km

4 Bearing: 315°
Distance: 170 km

5 Bearing: 045°
Distance: 330 km

6 Bearing: 315°
Distance: 340 km

7 Bearing: 000° or 360°
Distance: 660 km

8 Bearing: 135°
Distance: 130 km

9 Bearing: 045°
Distance: 410 km

10 Bearing: 135°
Distance: 470 km

11 Bearing: 270°
Distance: 220 km

12 Bearing: 045°
Distance: 140 km

## Transformation geometry (pp. 42–51)

### Rotation

| | Invariant |
|---|---|
| **Size** | ✓ |
| **Shape** | ✓ |
| **Orientation** | ✓ |

### Enlargement

| | Invariant |
|---|---|
| **Size** | × |
| **Shape** | ✓ |
| **Orientation** | ✓ |

1 Enlargement

2 None

3 Reflection

ISBN: 9780170451543 

## Revision of translation, reflection and rotation (pp. 44–45)

1 a $\begin{pmatrix} 4 \\ -3 \end{pmatrix}$ b $\begin{pmatrix} -2 \\ 1 \end{pmatrix}$

2 $\begin{pmatrix} -5 \\ 4 \end{pmatrix}$

3

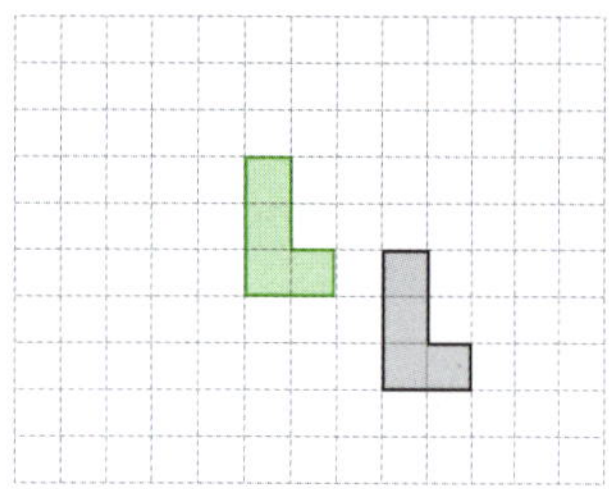

4 a

b

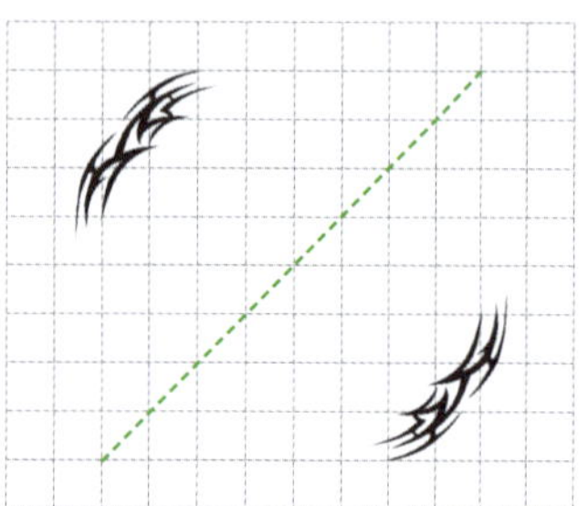

5

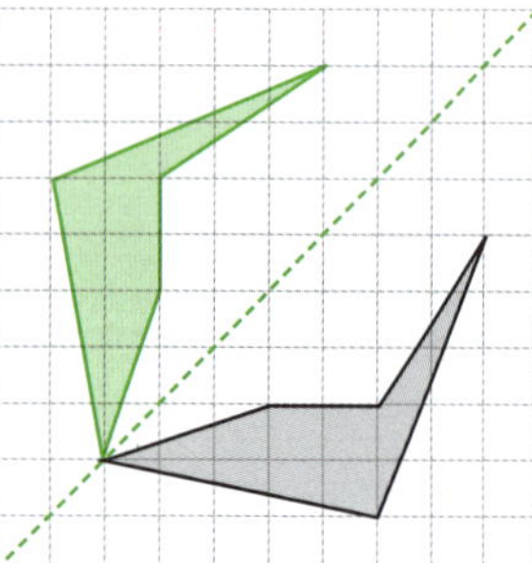

6

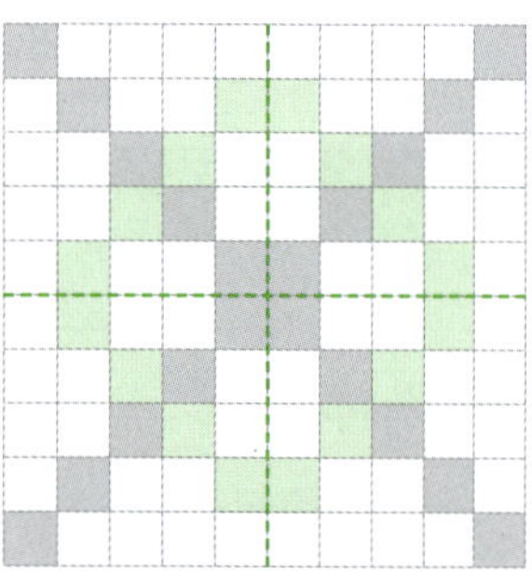

7 a Order of line symmetry = 1
b Order of line symmetry = 8

8 a Angle of rotation = 270°
b Angle of rotation = 90°

9 a

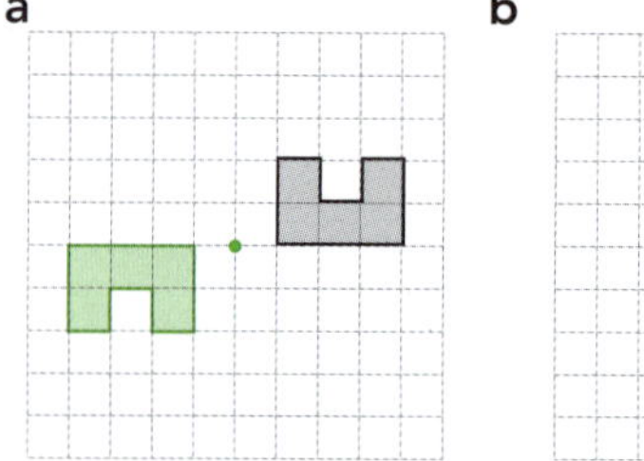

b

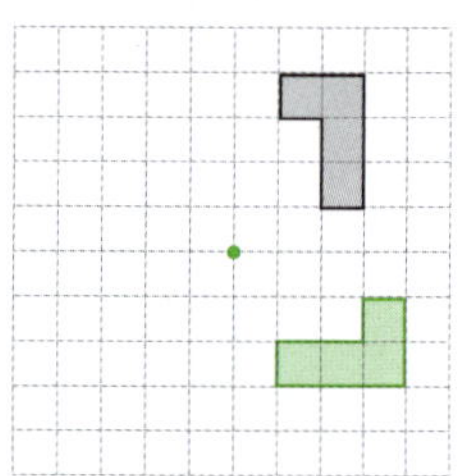

10 a Order of rotational symmetry = 5
b Order of rotational symmetry = 2

## Enlargement (pp. 46–51)

### Scale factor

1 scale factor = 2

scale factor = $\frac{1}{2}$

scale factor = $\frac{3}{2}$

2 scale factor = 2

scale factor = $\frac{2}{3}$

scale factor = $\frac{5}{3}$

3 scale factor = $\frac{3}{4}$

scale factor = $\frac{3}{2}$

scale factor = $\frac{1}{2}$

scale factor = $\frac{1}{4}$

### Finding the centre of enlargement

1

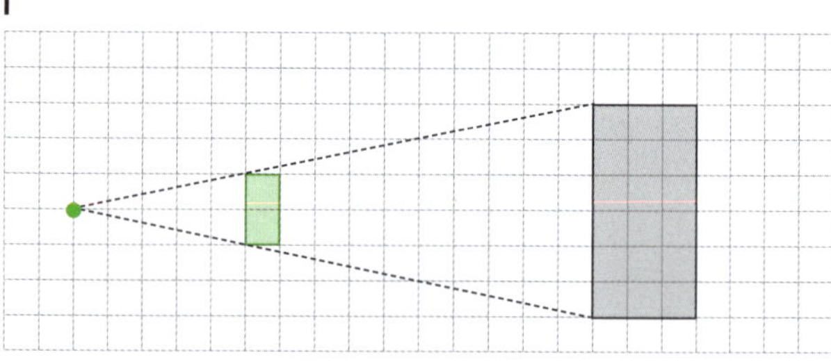

scale factor = 2

2

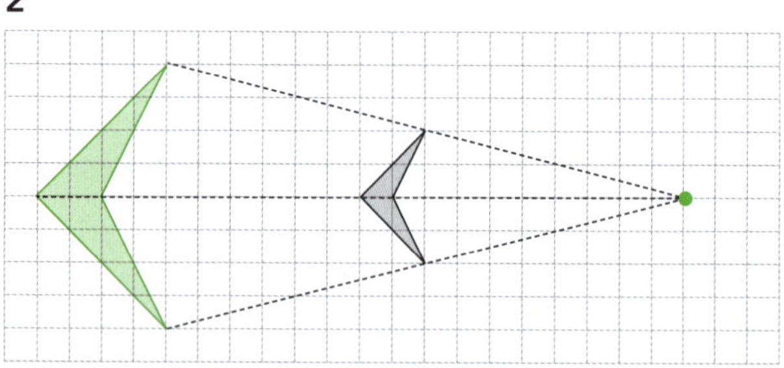

scale factor = $\frac{1}{2}$

3

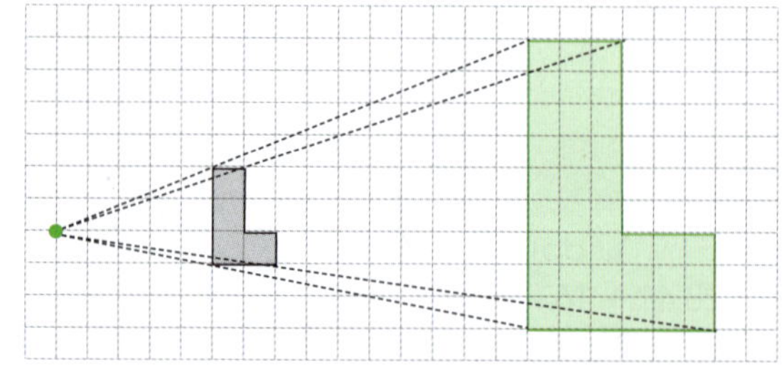

scale factor = $\frac{1}{3}$



 ISBN: 9780170451543

### Drawing enlargements

1

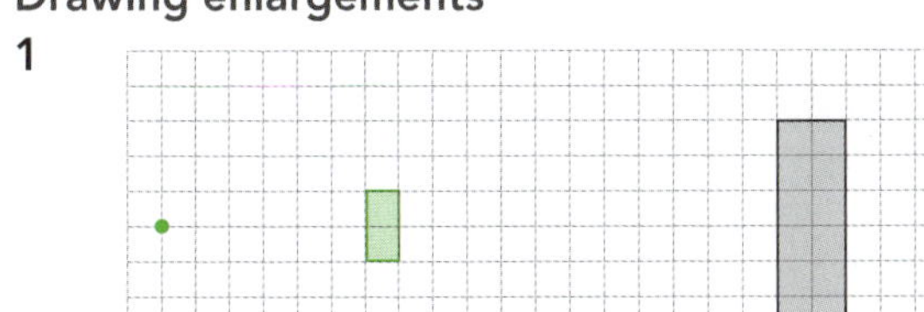

2

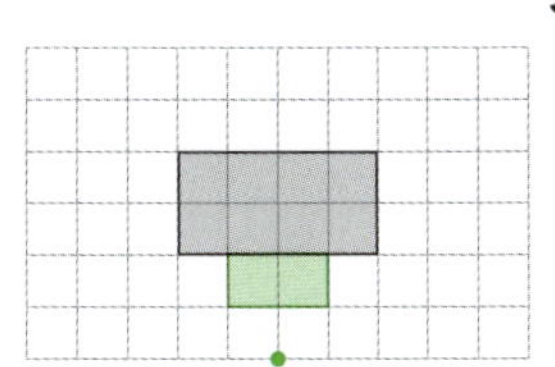

3

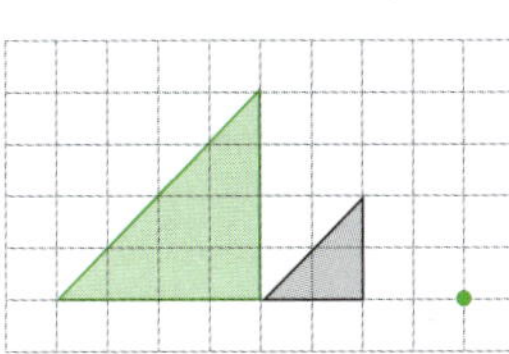

4

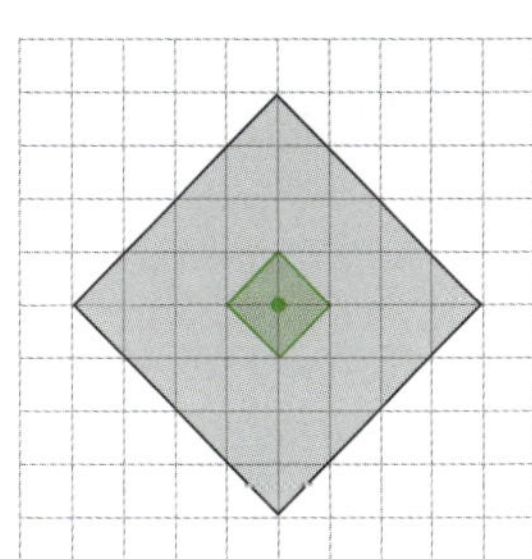

5

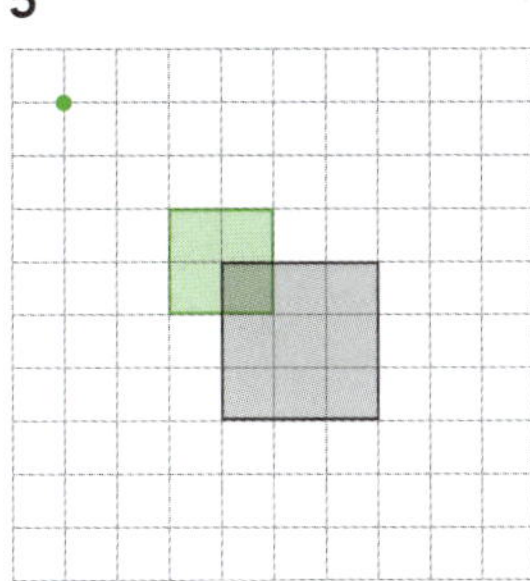

## The theorem of Pythagoras (pp. 52–60)

### Finding the length of the hypotenuse (pp. 53–55)

1 7.62 cm (2 dp)
2 12.73 cm (2 dp)
3 13.60 cm (2 dp)
4 7.11 cm (2 dp)
5 16.64 cm (2 dp)
6 1.70 m (2 dp)
7 13.00 km (2 dp)
8 77.78 m (2 dp)
9 89.02 mm (2 dp)
10 85.00 cm (2 dp)
11 3.75 m (2 dp)
12 77.62 cm (2 dp)

### Finding the lengths of short sides (pp. 56–57)

1 54.99 cm (2 dp)
2 8.00 cm (2 dp)
3 49.96 mm (2 dp)
4 9.00 cm (2 dp)
5 0.75 m (2 dp)
6 84.00 mm (2 dp)
7 40.14 cm (2 dp)
8 2.80 km (2 dp)
9 45.83 cm (2 dp)
10 0.38 m (2 dp)
11 4.98 m (2 dp)
12 7.48 cm (2 dp)

### Mixing it up (p. 58)

1 121.76 cm (2 dp)
2 66.51 cm (2 dp)
3 74.67 cm (2 dp)
4 77.78 cm (2 dp)
5 178.90 mm (2 dp)
6 11.27 m (2 dp)
7 534.13 cm (2 dp)
8 219.85 mm (2 dp)

### Mixing the theorem of Pythagoras with geometry (pp. 59–60)

1 19.80 cm (2 dp)
2 89.98 cm (2 dp)
3 86.02 cm (2 dp)
4 3.25 m (2 dp)
5 2 x 23.41 + 16 = 62.82 cm (2 dp)
6 6.71 cm (2 dp)
7 34.64 + 80 = 114.64 cm (2 dp)
8 7.07 cm (2 dp)

## Trigonometry (pp. 61–82)

### What is trigonometry? (pp. 61–62)

For the tree: $\text{Ratio} = \frac{\text{height of tree}}{\text{length of shadow}} = \frac{7}{17.5} = 0.40 \text{ (2 dp)}$

For the goal post: $\text{Ratio} = \frac{\text{height of goal post}}{\text{length of shadow}} = \frac{3.05}{7.6} = 0.40 \text{ (2 dp)}$

For the person: $\text{Ratio} = \frac{\text{height of person}}{\text{length of shadow}} = \frac{1.8}{4.5} = 0.40 \text{ (2 dp)}$

- Notice that the ratios are **the same** (or **equal**).

1

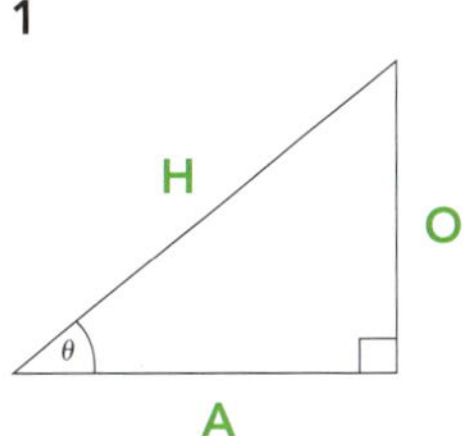


2

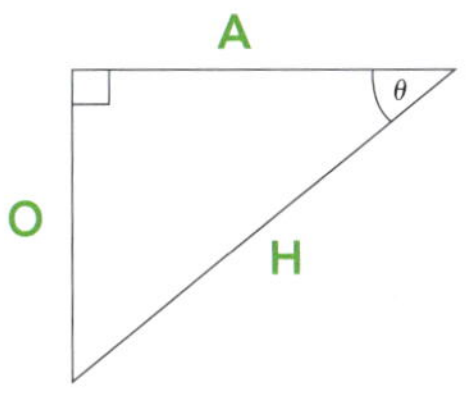


3

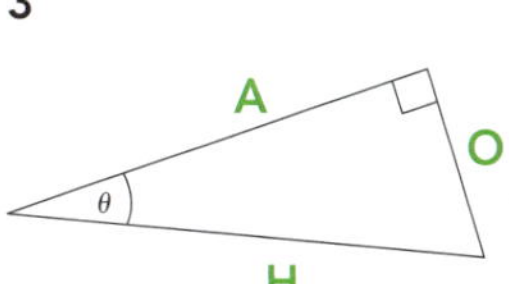


4

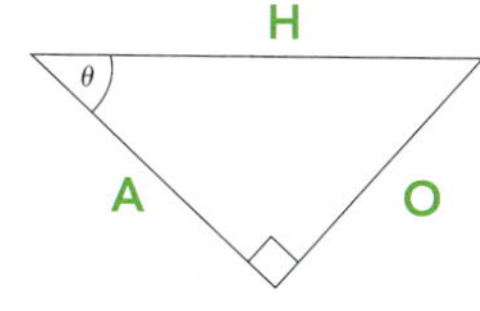


5

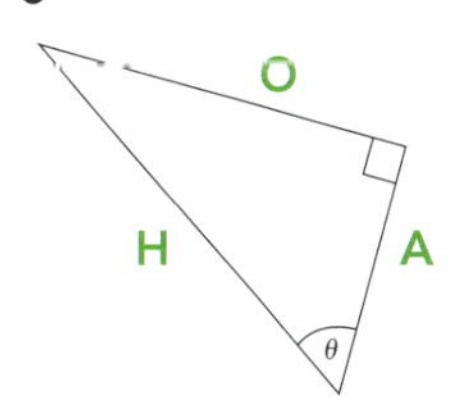


6

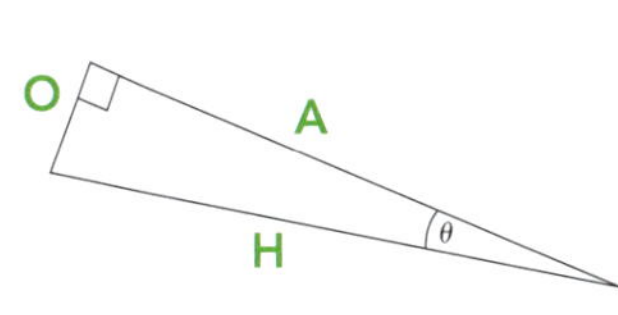


### Finding sides using sine (pp. 63–66)

1 59.65 cm (2 dp)
2 92.71 cm (2 dp)
3 18.34 cm (2 dp)
4 0.34 m (2 dp)
5 36.73 mm (2 dp)
6 16.13 cm (2 dp)
7 45.03 cm (2 dp)
8 53.25 cm (2 dp)
9 125.80 mm (2 dp)
10 10.02 cm (2 dp)
11 551.69 mm (2 dp)
12 120.21 cm (2 dp)

### Finding sides using cosine and tangent (pp. 67–69)

1 44.15 cm (2 dp)
2 24.33 cm (2 dp)
3 12.02 cm (2 dp)
4 127.86 mm (2 dp)
5 156.57 mm (2 dp)
6 9.84 m (2 dp)
7 85.17 cm (2 dp)
8 27.18 cm (2 dp)
9 367.89 mm (2 dp)
10 27.87 m (2 dp)

ISBN: 9780170451543 

### Mixing it up (pp. 70–71)

| | | | |
|---|---|---|---|
| **1** | 44.15 cm (2 dp) | **2** | 24.33 cm (2 dp) |
| **3** | 12.02 cm (2 dp) | **4** | 127.86 mm (2 dp) |
| **5** | 57.27 mm (2 dp) | **6** | 9.84 m (2 dp) |
| **7** | 85.17 cm (2 dp) | **8** | 27.18 cm (2 dp) |
| **9** | 367.89 mm (2 dp) | **10** | 27.87 m (2 dp) |
| **11** | 717.20 mm (2 dp) | **12** | 578.36 mm (2 dp) |
| **13** | 316.92 mm (2 dp) | **14** | 38.25 mm (2 dp) |
| **15** | 102.08 cm (2 dp) | **16** | 306.42 mm (2 dp) |

### Finding sides using trigonometry and geometry (pp. 72–73)

**1** Perimeter $= 2(6) + 5.4 + 5.4\cos 56° + 5.4\sin 56°$
$= 24.90$ cm (2 dp)

**2** Perimeter $= 2(100\cos 27°) + 2(100\sin 27°)$
$= 269.00$ cm (2 dp)

**3** Perimeter $= 2\left(\frac{24}{\cos 43°}\right) + 2(24\tan 43°)$
$= 110.39$ cm

**4** Diagonals intersect at right angles and bisect each other.
$DC = \frac{22.5}{\sin 28°}$
$= 47.93$ cm (2 dp)

**5** $\angle KJE = 22.5°$ ($360° \div 16$, internal angles of an octagon).
Perimeter $= 16 \times 50\sin 22.5°$
$= 306.15$ mm (2 dp)

### Finding angles using sine (pp. 74–75)

| | | | |
|---|---|---|---|
| **1** | 30.0° | **2** | 26.7° |
| **3** | 81.9° | **4** | 11.5° |
| **5** | 54.0° | **6** | 8.4° |
| **7** | 35.5° (1 dp) | **9** | 11.5° (1 dp) |
| **9** | 38.9° (1 dp) | **10** | 34.2° (1 dp) |
| **11** | 45.1° (1 dp) | **12** | 60.2° (1 dp) |

### Finding angles using cosine and tangent (pp. 76–78)

| | | | |
|---|---|---|---|
| **1** | 30.0° | **2** | 77.5° |
| **3** | 45.0° | **4** | 77.2° |
| **5** | 69.2° | **6** | 34.3° |
| **7** | 59.5° (1 dp) | **8** | 18.2° (1 dp) |
| **9** | 40.1° (1 dp) | **10** | 55.6° (1 dp) |
| **11** | 47.0° (1 dp) | **12** | 70.0° (1 dp) |
| **13** | 62.1° (1 dp) | **14** | 37.6° (1 dp) |

### Mixing it up (p. 79)

| | | | |
|---|---|---|---|
| **1** | 38.9° | **2** | 39.6 mm |
| **3** | 43.8° | **4** | 120.6 cm |
| **5** | 36.4° | **6** | 67.7° |
| **7** | 50.6 cm | **8** | 23.2° |

### Finding angles using trigonometry and geometry (pp. 80–81)

**1** Diagonals intersect at right angles and bisect each other.
$\angle DAB = 2 \times \tan^{-1}\left(\frac{4.15}{6.75}\right)$
$= 63.2°$ (1 dp)

**2** $\angle BAD = \tan^{-1}\left(\frac{BD}{AD}\right)$
$= \tan^{-1}\left(\frac{40.5 \times \sin 47°}{35}\right)$
$= 40.2°$ (1 dp)

**3** $\angle BAD = \tan^{-1}\left(\frac{BC}{35 + DC}\right)$
$= \tan^{-1}\left(\frac{59}{35 + (59 \div \tan 47°)}\right)$
$= 33.2°$ (1 dp)

**4** $\triangle ABC$ is isosceles, so BC = 72 cm.
$\angle BCE = \sin^{-1}\left(\frac{56}{72}\right)$
$= 51.1°$ (1 dp)
$\angle CAD = \sin^{-1}\left(\frac{53}{2\sqrt{72^2 - 56^2}}\right)$
$= 35.8°$ (1 dp)

**5** $\angle EAD = \tan^{-1}\left(\frac{BC}{35 + DC}\right)$
$= \tan^{-1}\left(\frac{6.0 - (7.0 \div \tan 63°)}{7.0 - 2.5}\right)$
$= 28.4°$ (1 dp)

**6** $\angle DAC = \sin^{-1}\left(\frac{20}{73}\right)$
$= 15.90°$ (2 dp)
$\angle BAE = \cos^{-1}\left(\frac{\sqrt{73^2 - 20^2}}{92}\right)$
$= 40.26°$ (2 dp)
$\angle BAD = 40.26° - 15.90°$
$= 24.4$ (1 dp)

## Challenge 2 (p. 82)

**1 Area mystery**

Area = 16 + 12 + 5
= 33 units$^2$

Area = 15 + 5 + 12
= 32 units$^2$

Your explanation may differ from either of the ones below. If so, ask your teacher.

1 Find base angles of the triangles:

Triangle ABF: $\angle = \tan^{-1}\left(\frac{2}{5}\right) = 21.80°$ (2 dp)

Triangle BCD: $\angle = \tan^{-1}\left(\frac{3}{8}\right) = 20.56°$ (2 dp)

∴ line AC is not straight, and it 'bulges' out a little resulting in a bigger area.



 ISBN: 9780170451543

Triangle RSW: $\angle = \tan^{-1}\left(\frac{3}{8}\right) = 20.56°$ (2 dp)

Triangle STU: $\angle = \tan^{-1}\left(\frac{2}{5}\right) = 21.80°$ (2 dp)

| ∴ line RT is not straight, and it 'bulges' in a little resulting in a smaller area. |
|---|

2 Find the gradient of the hypotenuse of each triangle:

Triangle ABF: $m = \frac{2}{5} = 0.4$

Triangle BCD: $m = \frac{3}{8} = 0.375$

| ∴ line AC is not straight, and it 'bulges' out a little resulting in a bigger area. |
|---|

Triangle RSW: $m = \frac{3}{8} = 0.375$

Triangle STU: $m = \frac{2}{5} = 0.4$

| ∴ line RT is not straight, and it 'bulges' in a little resulting in a smaller area. |
|---|

**2 Pythagorean triples**

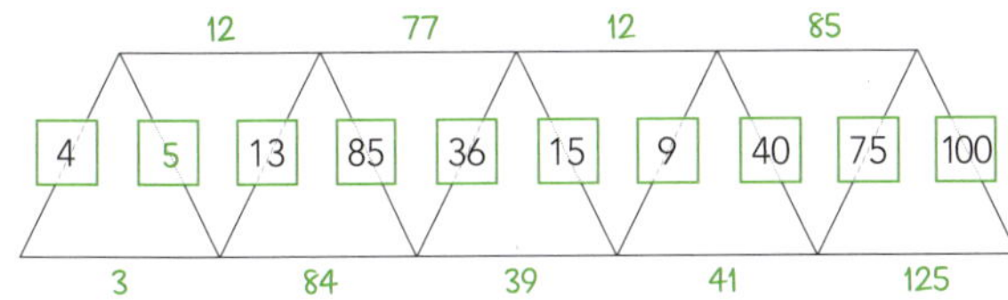


## Revision 1 (pp. 83–85)

1 **a** Supplementary **b** Adjacent
**c** Alternate

2 **a** $a = 72°$ **b** $b = 51°$
**c** $c = 40°$ **d** $d = 71°$
**e** $e = 109°$ **f** $f = 58°$

3 **a** SE 135°
**b** Cannibal Cove
**c** 711458
**d** 12 km
**e**

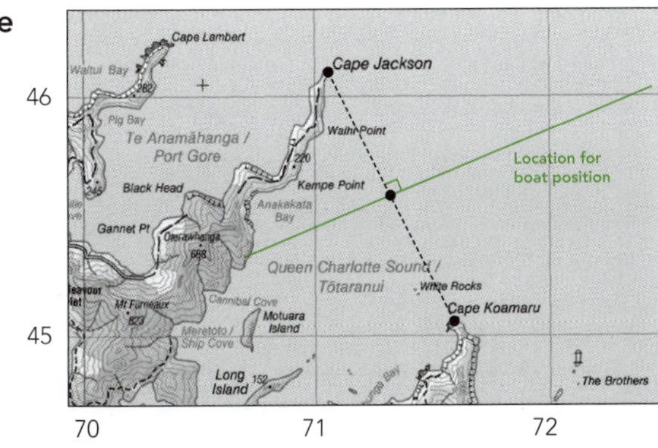


4 Scale factor = 2

5 Order of rotational symmetry = 8

6

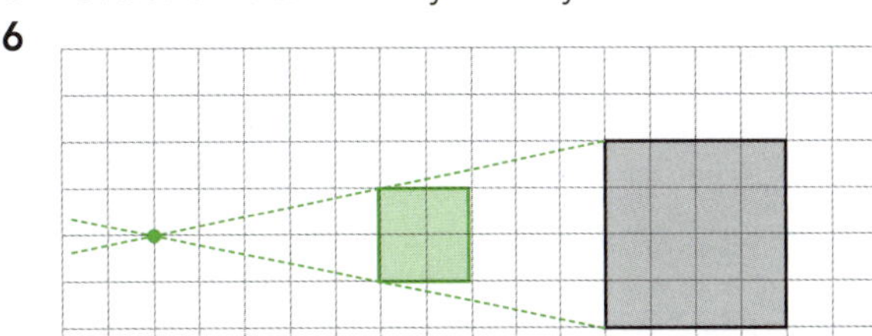

7 **a** $x = 3.6$ cm **b** $y = 5.1$ m

8 **a** $a = 2.4$ cm **b** $b = 39.1°$
**c** $c = 29.2$ m **d** $d = 28.8°$

## Revision 2 (pp. 86–88)

1 **a** Corresponding **b** Complementary
**c** Hypotenuse

2 **a** $a = 78°$ **b** $b = 125°$
**c** $c = 136°$ **d** $d = 119°$
**e** $e = 117°$ **f** $f = 52°$

3 **a** NW 315°
**b** Sentinal Rock
**c** 693472
**d** 13 km
**e**

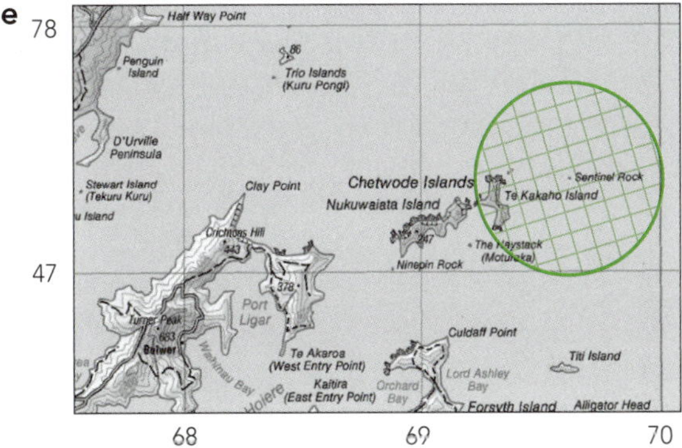


4 Scale factor = $\frac{2}{3}$

5 Order of rotational symmetry = 8

6

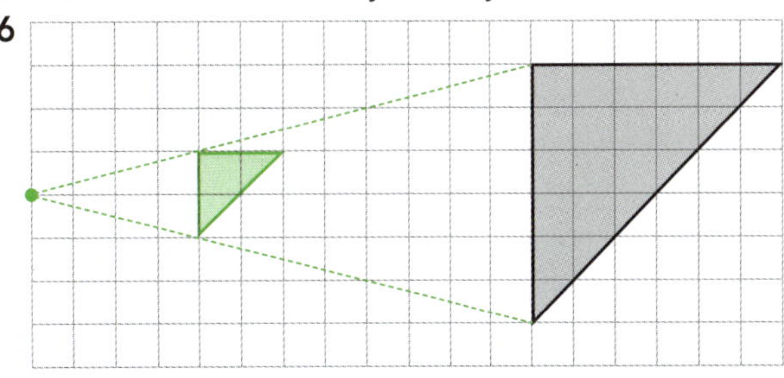

7 **a** $x = 85.0$ cm **b** $z = 7.1$ cm

8 **a** $a = 37.1$ mm **b** $b = 59.0°$
**c** $c = 41.2°$ **d** $d = 2.5$ m

ISBN: 9780170451543